Communications
in Computer and Information Science

1627

More information about this series at https://link.springer.com/bookseries/7899

Ozan Önder Özener · Salih Ofluoglu ·
Umit Isikdag (Eds.)

Advances in Building Information Modeling

Second Eurasian BIM Forum, EBF 2021
Istanbul, Turkey, November 11–12, 2021
Revised Selected Papers

Springer

Editors
Ozan Önder Özener 🆔
Istanbul Technical University
Sisli, Istanbul, Turkey

Salih Ofluoglu 🆔
Mimar Sinan Fine Arts University
Sisli, Istanbul, Turkey

Umit Isikdag 🆔
Mimar Sinan Fine Arts University
Sisli, Istanbul, Turkey

ISSN 1865-0929   ISSN 1865-0937 (electronic)
Communications in Computer and Information Science
ISBN 978-3-031-16894-9   ISBN 978-3-031-16895-6 (eBook)
https://doi.org/10.1007/978-3-031-16895-6

This Springer imprint is published by the registered company Springer Nature Switzerland AG
The registered company address is: Gewerbestrasse 11, 6330 Cham, Switzerland

Preface

Welcome to the proceedings of the 2nd Eurasian BIM Forum (EBF 2021), held virtually during November 11–12, 2021. Building information modeling (BIM) is rapidly changing the architecture, engineering and construction (AEC) industry as the catalyst for more integrated, sustainable, and efficient processes. This paradigm change leads to knowledge-based economies in AEC which open new trajectories for industry-wide transformation. BIM is a process, method, and technology but, more importantly, it is now the new common language of the AEC industry across all disciplines. Keeping pace with these developments, the BIM paradigm also evolves with new possibilities and novel approaches.

Grounded on these premises, this book focuses on providing a comprehensive view of BIM by concentrating on the current theoretical and practical aspects of the subject matter with four thematically organized parts. The chapters in the first part elaborate on the adoption of BIM in the AEC industry. Chapters include well-articulated survey studies, BIM use in specific phases in architectural design, and novel BIM uses coupled with machine learning methods. The second part of the book emphasizes the role of BIM in project management. It covers subjects such as BIM-enabled supply chain management, value engineering, risk management, and automated code checking through customized BIM frameworks. The third part is about BIM and current educational practices, where issues related to the role of BIM in architectural and engineering education are discussed. The fourth part of the book covers novel viewpoints on specific implementations of BIM methods such as heritage BIM (HBIM), kinetic architecture, building energy modeling, and smart city applications.

EBF 2021 received a total of 27 submissions. Each paper was reviewed by at least 3 members of the Scientific Program Committee in a single-blind review process, resulting in the selection of 17 submissions for presentation and 12 of which for publication in this proceedings (an acceptance rate of 44%). We hope that readers will find this book useful for exchanging theoretical and practical knowledge and experience on the novel developments in BIM methods and technologies, as well as BIM-based information and project management approaches.

We conclude this preface by thanking the many people who contributed their time and efforts to EBF 2021 and made this publication possible. We also thank all the organizations that supported the event. We thank Istanbul Technical University and Mimar Sinan Fine Arts University which co-organized EBF 2021. We extend our sincere gratitude to the members of the Scientific Program Committee and Steering Committee, all the special session chairs, and the reviewers who invested their time generously to ensure the timely review of the submitted manuscripts. Finally, we would like to thank our family members for their support during the editing process and for the positive energy they have brought into our lives.

June 2022

Ozan Önder Özener
Salih Ofluoglu
Umit Isikdag

Organization

Program Committee Chairs

Salih Ofluoğlu   Mimar Sinan Fine Arts University, Turkey
Ozan Önder Özener   Istanbul Technical University, Turkey
Ümit Işıkdağ   Mimar Sinan Fine Arts University, Turkey

Scientific Program Committee

F. Henry Abanda	Oxford Brookes University, UK
Alias Abdul-Rahman	Univesiti Tekonologi Malaysia, Malaysia
Cemil Akcay	Istanbul University, Turkey
Yenal Akgün	Yasar University, Turkey
Sema Alaçam	Istanbul Technical University, Turkey
Yusuf Arayici	Northumbria University, UK
Gebrail Bekdaş	Istanbul University-Cerrahpasa, Turkey
Marzia Bolpagni	Mace, UK
Tanyel Bülbül	Virginia Tech, USA
Olcay Çetiner	Yildiz Technical University, Turkey
Attila Dikbas	Istanbul Medipol University, Turkey
Lucía Díaz Vilariño	Universidad de Vigo, Spain
Omer Giran	Istanbul University-Cerrahpasa, Turkey
Jack Goulding	University of Wolverhampton, UK
Eric Guilbert	Laval University, Canada
Leman Figen Gul	Istanbul Technical University, Turkey
James Haliburton	Texas A&M University, USA
Mustafa Emre Ilal	Izmir Institute of Technology, Turkey
Ümit Işıkdağ	Mimar Sinan Fine Arts University, Turkey
Abdul Samad Kazi	VTT Technical Research Centre of Finland, Finland
Carlos Alejandro Nome	Universidade Federal de Paraiba, Brazil
Salih Ofluoğlu	Mimar Sinan Fine Arts University, Turkey
Ken Arroyo Ohori	TU Delft, The Netherlands
Ozan Önder Özener	Istanbul Technical University, Turkey
Mine Ozkar	Istanbul Technical University, Turkey
Sule Taşlı Pektaş	Bilkent University, Turkey
Rudi Stouffs	National University of Singapore, Singapore
Ali Murat Tanyer	Middle East Technical University, Turkey

Jason Underwood	University of Salford, UK
Sevil Yazici	Istanbul Technical University, Turkey
Sisi Zlatanova	University of New South Wales, Australia

Organizing Committee

Salih Ofluoğlu	Mimar Sinan Fine Arts University, Turkey
Ozan Önder Özener	Istanbul Technical University, Turkey
Ümit Işıkdağ	Mimar Sinan Fine Arts University, Turkey
Kemal Şahin	Mimar Sinan Fine Arts University, Turkey
Sertaç Karsan Erbaş	Mimar Sinan Fine Arts University, Turkey

Contents

Novel Viewpoints on BIM

BIM Adoption and Design Process

Identifying Factors Limiting the Prevalent Use of BIM Technology in the Turkish Construction Industry

Seda Tan[iD] and Gülden Gümüşburun Ayalp[✉][iD]

Department of Architecture, Hasan Kalyoncu University, Gaziantep, Turkey
seda.tan@std.hku.edu.tr, gulden.ayalp@hku.edu.tr

Abstract. BIM can be defined in many ways such as system, approach, method, process, and information model. BIM technology has been adopted and used worldwide in recent years and continues to become widespread with its multidimensional approach and implementation possibilities. Despite the well-documented advantages of BIM, the use and adoption levels stay at limited levels in Turkey compared to its counter partners. The objective of this study is to identify the factors currently affecting the pervasive use of BIM in the Turkish AEC industry. For this purpose, an extensive survey study was conducted among the architects and engineers working in the Turkish AEC Industry. Reliability analysis, the index of relative importance (IRI) and exploratory factor analysis were made with the collected data using SPSS v. 22.0 statistical software. Findings from the study indicate the existence of eight factors affecting the prevalent use of BIM technology in the Turkish AEC industry.

Keywords: Building Information Modeling (BIM) · BIM technology adoption · Turkish AEC industry

1 Introduction

The Architecture/Engineering and Construction (AEC) industry faces new challenges in the last decade and this requires continuous change and technological advancements to ensure efficient time and cost management. These developments in construction technology and digital design tools underlined the process of transformation and changed the business models from past to present. Initial development began with the development of Computer-Aided Design (CAD) programs. In line with the requirements and to meet the expectations of the AEC industry, the theoretical premises of Building Information Modeling (BIM) began to realize and became extremely popular among AEC industry stakeholders. From a conceptual standpoint, it is possible to define BIM in many ways such as system, approach, method, process and an electronic information model. Generally, BIM encompasses the entire life cycle of a building, from the design phase to the construction and management phase [1]; It can be defined as a comprehensive methodology that provides effective data management as well as sharing information with the

O. Ö. Özener et al. (Eds.): EBF 2021, CCIS 1627, pp. 3–18, 2022.
https://doi.org/10.1007/978-3-031-16895-6_1

use of three-dimensional digital models and connected database [2], and an adequate technology to create and process information during the whole building lifecycle.

There are various studies in the literature concerning the increasing adoption and use of BIM in the AEC [3], particularly in North America, Europe and developed construction markets since the early 2000s [4]. However, studies regarding the use of BIM technology in the Turkish construction industry are limited. Previous studies focusing on the Turkish construction industry have identified the stakeholders' awareness levels about BIM implementation [5], primary challenges of BIM implementation in mega construction projects [6], the relationship between facility management and BIM use [7], critical success factors of BIM implementation [8], lean interactions resulting from BIM processes [9]. When the former studies on BIM technology are investigated, the method along with the case study; it can be seen analyzes are made according to the percentage, frequency and average values of the data obtained only by the survey or discussion method [10–16]. In addition, there are available studies that variables affecting the success in the use of BIM were determined and factor analysis was applied to the variables [15] and identified the factors affecting of BIM effectiveness [17] and determined the factors of BIM challenges and preventatives in the Turkish transportation infrastructure industry [18]. Despite the significance of this issue, the number of previous studies regarding BIM in the Turkish AEC industry lags underlying the factors hindering the common use of BIM implementation in construction firms from a different aspect and also lags in ranking based on their importance. Therefore, there is a gap in the literature on BIM research that identifies the factors limiting the BIM implementation from several perspectives.

To fill this gap in the literature, the main objectives of the current study are fourfold: (1) to determine causes/obstacles affecting the BIM implementation from several perspectives (practice, organization, awareness, and education), (2) to identify the most important and the least important causes affecting the use of BIM technology (3) underlying the factors limiting the common use of BIM in the Turkish AEC industry, and (4) ranking the determined factors according to this importance.

2 Identifying the Potential Causes of Factors that Affect the Extensive Use of BIM Technology

Before the identification of underlying factors affecting the extensive use of BIM technology in the Turkish AEC industry, it is important to define the key sources of reasons that may cause this negative effect. Within this framework, a set of topics were selected to organize the literature survey and interpretation as (1) BIM practices in the transition to BIM use, (2) BIM awareness in the adoption and use of BIM, (3) organizational-based and (4) BIM education-related obstacles/causes. The conducted literature review yielded 46 possible causes that have been identified for BIM use. The identified causes and the summary of the relevant literature are given in Table 1 with references.

Table 1. Causes/obstacles affecting the extensive use of BIM technology.

Causes/obstacles	Code of causes	Causes	Sources
Obstacles related to BIM practices	P1	Thought of increasing design duration and cost	[19–22]
	P2	The thought that workflow, productivity, and efficiency will be affected in the transition to BIM technology	[20, 23–25]
	P3	Reluctancy of abandoning the traditional project delivery system	[26–29]
	P4	Lack of government support for BIM technology/lack of obligations with current legal legislation	[25, 30–35]
	P5	Lack of government-led initiatives to promote BIM technology	[31–34, 36–39]
	P6	Stakeholders/companies and subcontractors with have little or no use of BIM	[21, 27, 36, 38]
	P7	Poor knowledge sharing among stakeholders	[20, 25, 29, 36, 38, 40, 41]
	P8	Requires the participation, coordination, and control of the project stakeholders in the project at the design stage	[3, 20, 21, 25, 27, 29, 35, 38, 39, 42, 43, 50]
	P9	Difficulty of learning BIM-software	[38, 39]
	P10	License problem of BIM-software tools	[40, 44, 45]
	P11	Possibility of data loss during file transfer between different BIM-based programs	[25, 35, 42]
	P12	Increased workload due to BIM library preparation at the beginning of the project	[25, 36, 39]
	P13	Possibility of difficulties in version control due to model updates	[20, 25, 35, 39, 42, 45, 46]
Obstacles related to BIM awareness	A1	Unknowns of design, schedule, and budget data during the design stage with the BIM	[20–22, 29, 38, 42]
	A2	Unknowns of quality, schedule, and cost data during the construction stage with BIM	[20–22, 29, 38]

(*continued*)

Table 1. (*continued*)

Causes/obstacles	Code of causes	Causes	Sources
	A3	Unknown accessibility of performance, usability, and financial data during the management stage with BIM	[20, 29, 38, 44]
	A4	Unknown that alternative design options can be analyzed, and the most suitable project can be selected with BIM	[21, 38, 39, 47–50]
	A5	Lack of knowledge about effective scheduling and cost estimation	[19, 20, 38, 39, 49]
	A6	Lack of knowledge about clash detection	[20, 22, 38, 39]
	A7	Not being aware of possibility for quick and easy intervention	[20, 29, 38, 42]
	A8	Lack of knowledge about file format sufficiency	[25, 29, 40, 44]
	A9	Lack of knowledge about simulation possibility	[21, 51, 52]
Obstacles related to organization	O1	Lack of support for the use of BIM at top and mid management levels	[25, 35, 36, 38, 39, 41, 49, 53–55]
	O2	Not to be included in competitive construction environment	[21, 38, 56, 57]
	O3	Lack of BIM-capable workforce	[21, 25, 28, 33, 35, 38, 39, 41, 46, 58, 59]
	O4	Additional expenditures of consultancy required for the use of BIM	[3, 35, 40–42, 44, 58–60]
	O5	Seeing/considering the need for BIM training for personnel within organization as an extra expenditure and waste of time	[25, 36, 38, 39]
	O6	Increased initial investments (software, hardware, training) and inadequate financial resources of the organization for the transition to BIM	[25, 27, 38, 39, 42]
	O7	Probability that the investment made for the transition to BIM technology cannot respond the expected economic impact (return of investment)	[23, 36, 61]

(*continued*)

Table 1. (*continued*)

Causes/obstacles	Code of causes	Causes	Sources
	O8	Requirement of individual and group motivation from top management to the lowest level employee for BIM adoption	[23, 38, 55]
	O9	Difficulty of personnel adoption	[29, 62]
	O10	Lack of Client's/user's knowledge on BIM and demand	[28, 34, 36–38, 54, 57–61]
	O11	Need for significant organizational structure change (size of the organization type, structure, culture, etc.)	[21, 27, 38, 42]
	O12	BIM use/new business model causing a change in the decision mechanisms and workload distribution	[27, 46, 62]
	O13	Lack of time for learning due to the nature of the industry	[29]
	O14	Fail to implement immediately after BIM trainings	[20, 27, 29, 37, 43, 54]
	O15	Legal disputes, software updates and require additional funds for other expenses	[25, 34, 35, 38, 42]
	O16	Rising the workload with data transfer after the transition to BIM technology	[25, 35, 42]
	O17	Lack of organization's BIM project experience and the possibility of negative consequences	[2, 25, 35, 36, 38, 39, 42, 50]
	O18	Desire to switch to BIM technology, however, the lack of/low number of units to provide consultancy or training on this subject	[22, 27, 32, 33, 50, 61]
Obstacles related to BIM education	E1	Lack of BIM related courses at higher education	[2, 63]
	E2	Lack of faculty members who have knowledge of BIM applications/technology in universities	[22, 40, 46]
	E3	Lack of professional chambers' informative activities presenting the differentiation between traditional and BIM project delivery systems	[64]

(*continued*)

Table 1. (*continued*)

Causes/obstacles	Code of causes	Causes	Sources
	E4	Lack of informative documents for BIM implementation provided by government and professional chambers	[22, 27, 40]
	E5	Lack of resources in Turkish	[13]
	E6	Lack of training opportunities	[13]

P: Practices, A: Awareness, O: Organization, E: Education.

3   Research Methodology and Material

The current study employed a quantitative research design to identify and assess the main factors affecting the extensive use of BIM The research followed a multistage methodological framework consisting of the determination of causes comprising the affecting factors, design of a questionnaire, data collection and statistical analysis of the collected data.

Determination of the causes that will comprise the factors is the first stage of the current research. As a result of a comprehensive literature review, 46 possible causes were identified that directly related to the use of BIM, 13 related to BIM practices, 9 related to BIM awareness, 18 related to organization and 6 related to BIM education.

Based on a review of former studies on this subject, a questionnaire was composed and conducted with architects and engineers working in architectural offices and construction companies in Turkey that do not use BIM in their firms. The questionnaire consisted of 15 questions of which are two open-ended and 13 closed-ended question types. The first five questions of the questionnaire included questions to identify the participants' level of BIM knowledge, BIM awareness and their thoughts on BIM use in the industry. Four out of the 15 questions constitute main parts of BIM practices with 13 causes, BIM awareness with 9 causes, organizational structure with 18 causes and BIM education with 6 causes of the questionnaire that comprise a total of 46 causes using a 5-point Likert scale. In the last part of the questionnaire, socio-demographic questions (gender, education level, profession, sectoral experience, sector served, types of projects, the number of technical personnel in the company, city where lived/worked) were asked to determine the demographic characteristics of the participants.

The questionnaires were sent to 600 people via e-mail, consisting of architects and engineers from 07.07.2020 to 14.11.2020. A total of 152 questionnaires were returned and 11 of them were dismissed due to missing data. Finally, 141 completely completed were used as the material of the current study representing a response rate of 25.3%.

To determine the internal consistency among questions using a Likert scale in a survey, reliability should be measured [65]. To determine the internal consistency of questions based on participants' perceptions on the Likert scale, a reliability analysis was conducted on the 46 possible causes in the questionnaire.

The index of relative importance (IRI) was determined by taking into consideration the participants' responses based on the obstacles that affect the extensive use of BIM technology. The IRI is calculated as follows [66]:

$$IRI_k(\%) = \frac{5(n_5) + 4(n_4) + 3(n_3) + 2(n_2) + n_1}{5(n_5 + n_4 + n_3 + n_2 + n_1)} \times 100$$

where IRI_k (%) represents the perception of obstacles and is evaluated individually for regarding data (k) of respondents. The overall IRI for each impact considering all participants was determined for all sets of the effect levels using the weighted average of the IRI_k, as follows [67]:

$$Overall\ IRI(\%) = \frac{\sum_{k=1}^{k=5}(k \times IRI_k)}{\sum_{k=1}^{k=5} k} \times 100$$

where Overall IRI (%) represents the total weighted average percentage of the IRI for each obstacle.

Explanatory factor analysis (EFA), which is used to determine the complex relationships between the items and group items that are part of the composite concepts, and where no preliminary any assumptions are made about the relationships between the factors [68], is a technique in factor analysis [69] which the main purpose is to define the basic relationships between the measured variables. For the main purpose of the study, explanatory factor analysis was carried out to determine the factors affecting the prevalent use of BIM technology in the Turkish construction industry.

4 Research Findings and Discussion

4.1 Research Findings

The data obtained by the questionnaire applied to the determined sample group were analyzed with statistical methods. Within the scope of the research, reliability analysis, index of relative importance (IRI) and explanatory factor analysis were performed. Firstly, reliability analysis was conducted on 46 possible causes in the questionnaire and to the question about the level of use of BIM technology in the Turkish construction industry. Cronbach's Alpha coefficient was used as the "Internal Consistency Method" to measure the reliability of the scale in perception-based questions. As a result of the reliability analysis, Cronbach's Alpha Coefficient takes values between "0" and "1". If the Cronbach's Alpha Coefficient is less than 0.50, reliable unaccepted; If it is over 0.70 acceptable; If it is over 0.90, it means that the internal consistency is excellent [70]. Cronbach's Alpha Coefficient for this study was determined as $\alpha = 0.961$. According to this obtained value, the questionnaire is highly reliable.

IRI analysis was conducted to rank the relative importance of each obstacle, as shown in Table 2. While the most important obstacle was "lack of BIM related courses in higher education", the least important obstacle was the "thought of increasing design duration and cost".

To realize one of the main objectives of this study, it was important to identify the underlying factor structure. The responses to the 46 causes were taken as an input to the SPSS software and subjected to exploratory factor analysis using varimax rotation (eigenvalue $= 1$ cut-off) to identify the main factors. Items with a factor loading greater than 0.4 were determined to be such main factors [65]. The 8 factors obtained by exploratory factor analysis, and the causes located under factors named according to the contents of which reasons, and the factor loads are given in Table 2.

Table 2. Exploratory factor analysis.

Factors that cause BIM technology not used	Code of causes	Eigen value	% of variance	Factor loadings	Overall IRI	Average IRI (%)	Rank of factor
Factor 1- Awareness and knowledge level of BIM	A8	17.564	17.225	0.869	52.30	52.99	5
	A6			0.864	53.77		
	A4			0.862	56.43		
	A2			0.860	50.58		
	A3			0.857	54.34		
	A7			0.849	53.57		
	A5			0.843	54.49		
	A1			0.839	50.37		
	A9			0.833	51.13		
Factor 2- Lack of management support	O6	4.814	12.354	0.823	59.23	58.19	3
	O5			0.809	61.78		
	O4			0.766	58.62		
	O7			0.681	57.68		
	O8			0.678	55.78		
	O1			0.598	54.51		
	O3			0.559	61.66		
	O9			0.554	57.67		
	O2			0.490	56.84		
Factor 3- Problems with BIM transition process	O17	3.511	10.991	0.716	54.48	56.05	4
	O14			0.702	54.99		
	O16			0.676	51.81		
	O18			0.655	52.51		
	O13			0.604	62.18		
	O15			0.576	56.28		
	O12			0.556	54.00		
	O11			0.499	57.36		
	O10			0.478	60.84		

(continued)

Table 2. (*continued*)

Factors that cause BIM technology not used	Code of causes	Eigen value	% of variance	Factor loadings	Overall IRI	Average IRI (%)	Rank of factor
Factor 4- Lack of BIM education and training opportunities	E4	2.311	10.227	0.807	61.05	60.54	1
	E1			0.803	64.06		
	E2			0.800	62.75		
	E3			0.793	61.50		
	E6			0.682	57.10		
	E5			0.629	56.81		
Factor 5- BIM-based software problems	P11	1.851	7.631	0.785	48.81	51.86	7
	P13			0.780	49.09		
	P12			0.724	54.38		
	P10			0.670	57.32		
	P9			0.554	49.70		
Factor 6- Lack of incentives for BIM	P4	1.481	5.812	0.736	58.55	59.89	2
	P5			0.725	58.53		
	P6			0.508	62.61		
Factor 7- Lack of communication between project stakeholders regarding the use of BIM	P7	1.169	5.014	0.777	53.65	52.50	6
	P8			0.745	51.35		
Factor 8- Bias regarding BIM technology	P1	1.154	4.342	0.790	45.92	47.81	8
	P2			0.685	46.01		
	P3			0.543	51.52		
Total explained variance			73.597				
Kaiser–Meyer–Olkin (KMO) value	0.865						
Barlett's test of sphericity	Approx. chi-square					6345.315	
	df					1035	
	p					0.000	

KMO value is an indicator that indicates whether the size of the data set is sufficient for factor analysis, and it should be above 0.50 [71]. The Kaiser-Meyer-Olkin (KMO) test value for the analysis was 86.5% (0.865). Since the KMO test value is 0.865 > 0.50, it can be stated that the data set is large enough for factor analysis. When the Bartlett test (chi-square) values of the factor analysis were examined to test the integrity of the sample, it was obtained as $\chi^2 = 6345.315$ (p < 0.000). According to the obtained values, there is a high correlation between the variables, in other words, the data set is suitable for factor analysis.

Eigenvalue and Varimax rotation method were used in explanatory factor analysis. Scope of the study, variables with eigenvalues of 1 and greater than 1 were accepted as factors. Eight factors with an eigenvalue greater than 1 were obtained. 8 factors explain 73.597% of the total variance. The 46 possible causes affecting the prevalent use of BIM technology in the Turkish construction industry are grouped under 8 factors. Each factor was assigned a name corresponding to the nature of latent factors which load onto that particular component. The interpretations for each of these components are as follows:

Factor 1: Awareness and knowledge level of BIM

Factor 2: Lack of management support

Factor 3: Problems with the BIM transition process

Factor 4: Lack of BIM education and training opportunities

Factor 5: BIM-based software problems

Factor 6: Lack of incentives for BIM

Factor 7: Lack of communication between project stakeholders regarding the use of BIM

Factor 8: Bias regarding BIM technology

4.2 Discussion

In the current study, among the 8 factors affecting the extensive use of BIM in the Turkish AEC industry, "Lack of BIM education and training opportunities" has been determined as the most important factor according to the index of relative importance. It can be stated that the existence of BIM courses and academicians who have knowledge of BIM technology in undergraduate programs of universities is important. When similar studies on the subject in the literature are examined, this finding of the study is consistent with the finding in the study of Sarıçiçek [14], who stated that the lack of BIM education is the most important obstacle to the extensive use of BIM. In addition, while Sarıçiçek [14] emphasizes the importance of education of professionals in the sector; In the current study, it has been determined that the possession of BIM knowledge and skills before entering professional life has a significant effect on the prevalence of use. However, the studies of Ademci [12] emphasize the importance of training/consulting services in terms of BIM competence, and Olawumi and Chan [45], describe the high number of training programs as one of the most important factors in BIM success, also support this finding of the study.

The "Lack of incentives for BIM" factor emerged as the second most important factor. When the previous studies on the subject are examined, Erdik [16] emphasized the importance of the inadequacy of stakeholders and subcontractors regarding BIM in BIM adaptation. Additionally, the lack of BIM standards is among the important obstacles [11, 13]; Studies evaluating it as an important risk factor [23] support this finding of the current study.

The "Lack of management support" factor was determined as the third important factor. Corroborating this argument, Sarıçiçek [14] and Aladağ et al. [15] stated that the most important obstacle to the prevalent use of BIM is the high amount of initial investment costs. Like the example of Taiwan [36] and Singapore [37], management support is an important organizational factor in the use of BIM in Turkey. In addition, one of the organizational reasons under the mentioned factor is that BIM technology has not yet been included in the competitive environment in the Turkish AEC industry. Ademci (2018) and Erdem (2018) emphasized the importance of this issue in the use of BIM in their studies.

"Problems with BIM transition process" is another limiting factor in the prevalent use of BIM that placed at the fourth rank. Although previous studies [61, 72] identified this factor under the list of challenges and barriers to BIM implementation, this study revealed that this factor is one of the significant limiting factors for BIM implementation. The importance of the obstacles loaded under this factor "need for significant organizational structure change" [27], and "lack of employer knowledge on BIM and demand" [7, 11] were also emphasized by different researchers.

In the current study, "Awareness and knowledge level of BIM" was determined as the fifth factor among 8 factors affecting the extensive use of BIM in the Turkish AEC industry. When similar studies on the subject in the literature are examined, Akkaya (2012) emphasized the perception of BIM as only a program, and Sarıçiçek (2018) likewise emphasized the lack of awareness. The results support the findings of this study. Similarly, the factor of "Lack of communication between project stakeholders regarding the use of BIM" supports the findings of previous studies on the subject [6, 11, 34]. A differentiation is found regarding the lack of communication among stakeholders between former and current research. Sinoh et al. [73] stated that non-technical factors, such as communication, ranked higher than technical factors; however, communication among stakeholders ranked as the sixth place among eight factors. Sinoh et al. [73] focused on the Malaysian AEC industry. Although Malaysia and Turkey are developing countries, their cultures are different. Therefore, cultural dissimilarities may explain this differentiation.

Finally, the "Negative bias regarding BIM" factor includes the perception of increased time and project costs due to BIM transition and the extension of service scope for BIM-related tasks and procedures. This particular finding contradicts with the Kıvırcık's [11] study as it posits the existence of a positive impact of BIM on cost, duration and quality of design among the selected firms. The possible reason for this is the existence of a divide between Turkish firms towards BIM adoption, client portfolios and varying technological capabilities that is reflected in the study samples.

5 Conclusions

Although BIM has significant contributions to the AEC industry, various barriers in the Turkish AEC environment have negative impacts on pervasive adoption. This study revealed the key domains as (1) current BIM practices, (2) BIM awareness, (3) organizational dynamics, and (4) BIM education as the BIM negative drivers.

Half of the survey participants stated that although they know how to use BIM, the company they work for does not use or endorse BIM. It can be stated that the participants were aware of the use of BIM in the industry, albeit to a small extent.

Lack of BIM-related courses in higher education and lack of faculty members who have knowledge of BIM applications/technology in universities were listed as the most important obstacles among the education-related reasons. The connected eight factors for preventing the pervasive BIM implementation are given as:

- Awareness and knowledge level of BIM,
- Lack of management support,
- Problems with the BIM transition process,
- Lack of BIM education and training opportunities,
- BIM-based software problems,
- Lack of incentives for BIM,
- Lack of communication between project stakeholders regarding the use of BIM,
- Bias regarding BIM technology.

Furthermore, "Lack of BIM education and training opportunities", "Lack of incentives for BIM", and "Lack of management support" are the most important three factors limiting the prevalent use of BIM and therefore are worthy of attention. The following measures may be taken to mitigate the adverse effects of these factors.

Both universities and the government should take responsibility for the "Lack of BIM education and training opportunities". Related departments of universities, particularly architecture and engineering departments, should update their education curricula and increase the number of BIM-related courses. Higher education institutions and the government should collaborate to develop a national BIM curriculum to fulfill the need for BIM proficiency among graduates entering the workforce. This guarantees that graduates entering the AEC sector have the necessary skills and expertise to apply BIM to their businesses. The creation of such a curriculum may be a subject of future research.

During the early phases of BIM implementation, the government should actively promote local BIM demand by granting incentives and financial subsidies to the local AEC industry as well as selecting a few pilot projects to introduce BIM to the ACE industry.

Regarding "Lack of management support", it is recommended that the up-down management create a dedicated BIM department to handle or support BIM deployment in their projects in the long run. Moreover, top management in construction organizations is urged to address gaps in their employees' skill sets by supporting them in attending appropriate BIM seminars, workshops, or conferences to improve their BIM capacity and knowledge.

References

1. Popov, V., Juocevicius, V., Migilinskas, D., Ustinovichius, L., Mikalauskas, S.: The use of a virtual building design and construction model for developing an effective project concept in 5D environment. Autom. Constr. **19**(3), 357–367 (2010)

2. McGraw-Hill: SmartMarket report: BIM: transforming design and construction to achieve greater industry productivity. McGraw-Hill Construction, Bedford, Massachusetts (2008)
3. McGraw-Hill: SmartMarket report: The Business Value of BIM for Construction in Major Global Market: How Constructors Around the World Are Driving Innovation with Building Information Modeling. McGraw-Hill Construction, Bedford, Massachusetts (2014)
4. Jung, W., Lee, G.: The status of BIM adoption on six continents. World Acad. Sci. Eng. Technol. Int. J. Civil Environ. Eng. **9**(5), 512–516 (2015)
5. Elmalı, Ö., Bayram, S.: Adoption of BIM concept in the Turkish AEC industry. Iranian J. Sci. Technol. Trans. Civil Eng. **46**, 435–452 (2022)
6. Akcay, E.C.: Analysis of challenges to BIM adoption in mega construction projects. In: IOP Conference Series: Materials Science and Engineering, Creative Construction Conference (CCC 2021) 28th–30th June 2021, vol. 1218, no. 1, pp. 1–6, 012020. IOP Publishing, Budapest, Hungary (2022)
7. Tezel, E., Alatli, L., Giritli, H.: Awareness and use of BIM for FM: empirical evidence from Turkey. In: Jylhä, T. (ed.) The 20th EuroFM Research Symposium 16–17 June 2021, European Facility Management Network, pp. 1–93. EuroFM, Netherlands (2021)
8. Ozorhon, B., Karahan U.: Critical success factors of building information modeling implementation. J. Manage. Eng. **33**(3), 04016054, 1–10 (2016)
9. Koseoglu, O., Nurtan-Gunes, E.T.: Mobile BIM implementation and lean interaction on construction site: a case study of a complex airport project. Eng. Constr. Archit. Manag. **25**(10), 1298–1321 (2018)
10. Akkaya, D.: İnşaat Sektöründe Yapı Bilgi Modellemesi Hakkında İnceleme. Master Thesis, Istanbul Technical University, Istanbul (2012)
11. Kıvırcık, İ.: An Investigation into the Building Information Modeling Applications in the Construction Project Management. Master Thesis, Istanbul Technical University, Istanbul (2016)
12. Ademci, M.E.: An Analysis of BIM Adoption in Turkish Architectural, Engineering and Construction (AEC) Industry. Master Thesis, Mimar Sinan Fine Arts University, Istanbul (2018)
13. Başyazıcı, İ.U.: BIMgenius Türkiye BIM Raporu-Genel Eğilim ve Beklentiler, Research Report- 24 Dec 2018, P0001 (2018)
14. Sarıçiçek, T.: Türkiye'de Mimarlık Şirketleri İçin BIM Uygulama Yol Haritası. Master Thesis, Hasan Kalyoncu University, Gaziantep (2019)
15. Aladağ, H., Demirdögen, G., Isik, Z.: Building Information Modeling (BIM) use in Turkish construction industry. Procedia Eng. **161**, 174–179 (2016)
16. Erdik, M.: Yapı Sektöründe Yapı Bilgi Modellemesinin Adaptasyonu. Master Thesis, Balıkesir University, Balıkesir (2018)
17. Çağlayan, S.S.: Developing a Building Information Modeling (BIM) Effectiveness Model for The Turkish Construction Industry. Doctoral Thesis, Bogazici University, Istanbul (2020)
18. Yiğiter, F.: An Assessment of Building Information Modeling Implementation For The Turkish Transportation Infrastructure Industry. Master Thesis, Istanbul Technical University, Istanbul (2020)
19. Azhar, S., Nadeem, A., Mok, J. Y. N., Leung, B. H. Y.: Building information modeling (BIM): a new paradigm for visual interactive modeling and simulation for construction projects. In: Proceedings of 1st International Conference on Construction in Developing Countries: Advancing and Integrating Construction Education, pp. 435–446. Research & Practice, Karachi, Pakistan (2008)
20. Azhar, S.: Building Information Modeling (BIM): trends, benefits, risks, and challenges for the AEC Industry. Leadersh. Manag. Eng. **11**(3), 241–252 (2011)

21. Arayici, Y., Coates, P., Koskela, L., Kagioglou, M., Usher, C., O'reilly, K.: Building information modeling adoption and implementation for architectural practices. Struct. Surv. **29**(1), 7–25 (2011)
22. Wong, K., Fan, Q.: Building information modelling (BIM) for sustainable building design. Facilities **31**(3), 138–157 (2013)
23. Ugwu, O., Kumaraswamy, M.: Critical success factors for construction ICT projects- some empirical evidence and lessons for emerging economies. ITcon **12**, 231–249 (2007)
24. Morlhona, R., Pellerin, R., Bourgault, M.: Building information modeling implementation through maturity evaluation and critical success factors management. Procedia Technol. **16**(2014), 1126–1134 (2014)
25. Chien, K.-F., Wu, Z.-H., Huang, S.-C.: Identifying and assessing critical risk factors for BIM projects: empirical study. Autom. Constr. **45**(2014), 1–15 (2014)
26. Smith, D.K., Tardif, M.: Building Information Modeling: A Strategic Implementation Guide. Wiley, Hoboken, New Jersey (2009)
27. Khosrowshahi, F., Arayici, Y.: Roadmap for implementation of building information modeling in the UK construction industry. Eng. Constr. Archit. Manag. **19**(6), 610–635 (2012)
28. Lee, S., An, H., Yu, J.: An Extension of the Technology Acceptance Model for BIM-Based FM. Construction Research Congress, 21–23 May, pp. 602–611. West Lafayette, Indiana, United States (2012)
29. Sunil, K., Pathirage, C., Underwood, J.: Factors Impacting Building Information Modelling (BIM) Implementation in Cost Monitoring and Control. In: 13th IPGRC. 14–15 September, pp. 210–224. University of Salford, UK (2017)
30. Howard, R., Björk, B.C.: Building information modelling–experts' views on standardisation and industry deployment. Adv. Eng. Inform. **22**(2), 271–280 (2008)
31. Arayici, Y, Khosrowshahi, F, Ponting, A.M., Mihindu, S.A.: Towards implementation of building information modelling in the construction industry. In: Fifth International Conference on Construction in the 21st Century (CITC-V) "Collaboration and Integration in Engineering, Management and Technology", 20–22 May. Istanbul, Turkey (2009)
32. Succar, B.: Building information modelling framework: a research and delivery foundation to industry stakeholders. Autom. Constr. **18**, 357–375 (2009)
33. Suermann, P., Issa, R.: Evaluating industry perceptions of building information modeling. J. Inform. Technol. Construct. **14**, 574–594 (2009)
34. Eadie, R., Odeyinka, H., Brown, M., Mckeown, C., Yohanis, M.: An analysis of the drivers for adopting building information modeling. ITcon **18**, 338–352 (2013)
35. Won, J., Lee, G., Dossick, C., Messner, J.: Where to focus for successful adoption of building information modeling within organization. J. Construct. Eng. Manage. **139**(11) (2013)
36. Won, J., Lee, G.: Identifying the consideration factors for successful BIM projects. In: Conference of 17th International Workshop on Intelligent Computing in Engineering, EG-ICE 2010, pp. 1–6. Nottingham, United Kingdom (2010)
37. Arayici, Y., Coates, P.: Operational knowledge for building information modeling adoption and implementation for lean efficiency gains. J. Entrepren. Innov. Manage. **1**(2), 1–22 (2013)
38. Tsai, M.H., Mom M., Hsieh, S.H.: Developing critical success factors for the assessment of BIM technology adoption: part I. methodology and survey. J. Chinese Inst. Eng. **37**(7), 845–858 (2014)
39. Attarzadeh, M., Nath, T., Tiong, R.L.K.: Identifying key factors for building information modelling adoption in Singapore. Manage. Procure. Law **168**(MP5), 220–231 (2015)
40. Aibinu, A., Ventkatesh, S.: Status of BIM adoption and the BIM experience of cost consultants in Australia. J. Profession. Issues Eng. Educ. Pract. **140**(3), 3021–3110 (2014)
41. Liu, S., Xie, B., Tivendal, L., Liu, C.: Critical barriers to BIM implementation in the AEC industry. Int. J. Market. Stud. **7**(6), 162–171 (2015)

42. Bryde, D., Broquetas, M., Volm, J.M.: The project benefits of building information modelling. Int. J. Project Manage. **31**(2013), 971–980 (2012)
43. Boktor, J., Hanna, A., Menassa, C.C.: State of practice of building information modeling in the mechanical construction industry. J. Manag. Eng. **30**(1), 78–85 (2014)
44. Kivits, R.A., Furneaux, C.: BIM: enabling sustainability and asset management through knowledge management. Sci. World J. **2013**, 1–14 (2013)
45. Olawumi, T.O., Chan, D.W.M.: Critical Success Factors (CSFs) for Amplifying the Integration of BIM and Sustainability Principles in Construction Projects: A Delphi Study. COBRA 2018 Conference Paper, pp. 1–11 (2018)
46. Gu, N., London, K.: Understanding and facilitating BIM adoption in the AEC industry. Autom. Constr. **19**(8), 988–999 (2010)
47. Sacks, R., Dave, B.A., Koskela, L., Owen, R.: Analysis framework for the interaction between lean construction and building information modelling. In: Proceedings for the 17th Annual Conference of the International Group for Lean Construction, pp. 221–234 (2010)
48. Ahn, K., Kim, Y., Park, C., Kim, I., Lee, K.: BIM Interface for Full vs. Semiautomated Building Energy Simulation, vol. 68, pp. 671–678. Energy& Buildings, Elsevier B.V. (2014)
49. Lee, S., Yu, J., Jeong, D.: BIM acceptance model in construction organizations. J. Manage. Eng. **31**(3), 04014048, 1–13 (2014)
50. Antón, L.Á., Díaz, J.: Integration of LCA and BIM for sustainable construction. Int. J. Soc. Behav. Educ. Econ. Bus. Indust. Eng. **8**(5), 1378–1382 (2014)
51. Ofluoğlu, S.: Yapı Bilgi Modelleme: Yeni Nesil Mimari Yazılımlar. Mimar Sinan Fine Arts University, Informatics Department (2009)
52. Forbes, H.L., Ahmed, S.M.: Modern Construction – Lean Project Delivery and Integrated Practices. CRC Press, New York (2011)
53. Gambatese, J.A., Hallowell, M.: Enabling and measuring innovation in the construction industry. Constr. Manag. Econ. **29**(6), 553–567 (2011)
54. HM (Her Majesty's) Government: Building Information Modeling, Industrial Strategy— Government and Industry in Partnership. Government Report, London (2012)
55. Ding, Z., Zuo, J., Wu, J., Wang, J.Y.: Key factors for the BIM adoption by architects: a China study. Eng. Constr. Archit. Manag. **22**(6), 732–748 (2015)
56. Gokuc, Y.T., Arditi, D.: Adopting BIM in Architectural Design Offices. Interaction between Theory and Practice in Civil Engineering and Construction, pp. 533–538 (2016). ISBN: 978-0-9960437-2-4
57. Lindblad, H., Guerrero, J.R.: Client's role in promoting BIM implementation and innovation in construction. Constr. Manag. Econ. **38**(5), 468–482 (2020)
58. Ganah, A., John, G.: Suitability of BIM for enhancing value on PPP projects for the benefit of the public sector. In: Public Private Partnership International Conference 2013 Body of Knowledge, pp. 347–356. University of Central Lancashire, Preston, UK (2013)
59. Succar, B., Sher, W., Williams, A.: An Integrated Approach to Building Information Modeling Competency Assessment, Acquisition and Application. School of Architecture and Built Environment (2013)
60. Linderoth, H.: Understanding adoption and use of BIM as the creation of actor networks. Autom. Construct. **19**(1), 66–72 (2010)
61. Vass, S., Gustavsson, T.K.: Challenges when implementing BIM for industry change. Constr. Manag. Econ. **35**(10), 597–610 (2017)
62. Hochscheida, E., Halinb, G.: A Model to Approach BIM Adoption Process and Possible BIM Implementation Failures. Creative Construction Conference 2018, CCC 2018, 30 June–3 July, pp. 257–264. Ljubljana, Slovenia (2018)
63. Türkyılmaz, E.: YBM'nin Mimarlık Eğitim Programı ile Bütünleşmesi Üzerine Bir Çalışma. Megaron **11**(1), 78–88 (2016)

64. Akipek, F.O., Inceoglu, N.: Bilgisayar Destekli Tasarım ve Üretim Teknolojilerinin Mimarlıktaki Kullanımları. Megaron **2**(4), 237–253 (2007)
65. Nunnally, J.C., Bernstein, I.H.: Psychometric Theory. McGraw-Hill Construction, New York, NY (2007)
66. Zhao, Z.Y., Chen, Y.L.: Critical factors affecting the development of renewable energy power generation: evidence from China. J. Clean. Prod. **184**, 466–480 (2018)
67. El-Gohary, K.M., Aziz, R.F.: Factors influencing construction labor productivity in Egypt. J. Constr. Eng. Manag. **30**(1), 1–9 (2013)
68. Polit, D.F., Beck, C.T.: Nursing Research: Generating and Assessing Evidence for Nursing Practice. 9th edn. Wolters Klower Health, Lippincott Williams & Wilkins, Philadelphia, USA (2012)
69. Norris, M., Lecavalier, L.: Evaluating the use of exploratory factor analysis in developmental disability psychological research. J. Autism Dev. Disord. **40**(1), 8–20 (2009)
70. George, D., Mallery, P.: SPSS for Windows Step by Step: A Simple Guide and Reference, 11.0 Update. 4th edn. Allyn & Bacon, Boston (2003)
71. George, D., Mallery, P.: SPSS for Windows Step by Step: A Simple Guide and Reference. Allyn & Bacon, USA (1999)
72. Ganah, A., John, G.A.: Integrating building information modeling and health and safety for onsite construction. Saf. Health Work **6**(1), 39–45 (2015)
73. Sinoh, S.S., Othman, F., Ibrahim, Z.: Critical success factors for BIM implementation: a Malaysian case study. Eng. Constr. Archit. Manag. **27**(9), 2737–2765 (2020)

The Use of Building Information Modeling in Early Architectural Design: Case Studies with AEC Firms

Afif Eymen Nalbant(✉) ⓘD and Salih Ofluoglu ⓘD

Mimar Sinan Fine Arts University, 34380 Istanbul, Turkey
a.eymennalbant@gmail.com, salih.ofluoglu@msgsu.edu.tr

Abstract. Building Information Modeling (BIM) has gained an important place in AEC fields. However, the use of BIM in early architectural design processes is still a relatively less known and underused aspect of BIM by many design professionals. BIM offers important features such as free form modeling, building performance analyses and parametricism that are valuable for decision making in early design processes. This study aims at understanding the use of BIM in the early design process using case studies with AEC firms. To accomplish this goal semi-structured interviews were carried out with these firms, and the verbal data produced were analyzed with the content analysis method. As revealed from the findings of this study, BIM comes forward as a design development environment in which early design ideas transferred from other design media are improved.

Keywords: Building Information Modeling · BIM · Early architectural design · Design case studies

1 Introduction

Design is "an activity aimed at achieving certain desired goals without undesirable side and consequence effects" [1]. According to many researchers, design is considered one of the most complex intellectual processes of humans as a problem-solving activity. The act of design is also believed to be a process of producing solutions [2–5].

In the early stages of design, the architect defines the concepts and basic ideas of a building. Some of the activities inherent in the early design stages are identifying needs, assessing requirements, determining key issues, defining project specifications, establishing initial concepts, and evaluating proposals [6]. Initial ideas and organizing principles have an identifiable impact on the solution that extends throughout the entire design process [7]. Each design idea reflects the designer's understanding of the design problem and managing the process with his thoughts [8–10]. These early design stages involve a cyclical process that includes defining, interpreting and re-evaluating the design problem. This cyclical process relies on the cognitive skills of the designer, such as processing and transforming design information to produce creative design solutions.

Designers use various tools and media to achieve design tasks. Gänshirt divides design tools into six groups: observation, sketch, design drawing, model, calculation

© Springer Nature Switzerland AG 2022
O. Ö. Özener et al. (Eds.): EBF 2021, CCIS 1627, pp. 19–30, 2022.
https://doi.org/10.1007/978-3-031-16895-6_2

and verbalization [11]. Tool selection depends on the design task involved, the design idea and the design phase. Computers are heavily used in the context of design. Attempts to integrate the design process into computation and a knowledge base into Computer-Aided Design (CAD) have long been the focus of many design researchers [12–14]. CAD software has a graphical language consisting of lines and curves necessary to produce information including the formal geometry and spatial position of building elements.

Over the years, CAD tools were mainly used for drafting and documentation tasks in practice, their use in designing has been limited [15]. One of the drawbacks of CAD software is that it lacks semantic data incorporating alphanumeric characteristics of buildings elements such as material, cost, physical environment control data, etc. This alphanumeric data is important for creating real-world simulations and analyses in projects that feed design decision-making. Another shortcoming of CAD is related to project revisions. CAD continued to produce design representations such as plan, section, and view in the same order and with similar processes as the traditional paper and pen environments they replaced. Since these representations are created independently of each other, it is not easy to make consistent revisions covering all project documents, especially in large projects. Each project document needs to be handled one by one [15]. As design also constantly evolves, it should ideally take place in a cyclical process allowing frequent data flow at different stages. CAD software imposes a linear workflow making this data transition between stages difficult.

Building Information Modeling (BIM) software has been gaining acceptance in AEC fields. It creates a digital prototype for the actual construction with semantically rich information content, multidisciplinary interoperability of data and decision support in various stages of a project. It reflects an ideal that is aimed to be achieved for the building sector [15]. BIM also has important contributions to the early stages of design. It has an innovative approach that allows designers to control project cost and environmental performance starting from the first stage of the lifecycle. It helps the designer visualize and analyze their design and related materials and technologies before the building physically exists [17]. It creates an opportunity for sustainability measures and performance analysis throughout the design process [18]. In addition, it offers a collaborative design environment between stakeholders and an effective database of interoperable objects spanning the entire project lifecycle [19, 20].

2 BIM and Its Utilization in Early Design Stages

The early phases of any building project are potentially the most vibrant, dynamic and creative phases. At this stage, designers from all disciplines interact to achieve optimal design solutions. The decisions taken at the early design stage directly affect a significant part of the decisions to be taken in the later stages of the design process. They have a great potential to improve outcomes such as reducing costs and increasing customer satisfaction [21, 22].

As a promising platform for the early design stage, BIM has evolved from the development of CAD to create integrated management of multidisciplinary information generated throughout the life cycle of the project [23]. BIM is perceived as a set of technology, methodology and processes that can support integrated design and project delivery processes and offer significant advantages compared to existing information technologies

[24]. Unlike traditional CAD, BIM uses building components such as walls, columns, floors, doors, windows, and many other building components to make (object-based) models. In addition, various features are embedded that support comprehensive types of information such as geography, material, area, typology, and user information [23].

BIM allows project stakeholders to transfer, manage and store information in a virtual environment during the life adventure of the building (design, construction, operation, demolition). It creates consistent, workable, coordinated data in the building design and application processes, influences decision-making processes thanks to its parametric working feature, produces high-quality application drawings, provides cost control and allows testing the design on building performance issues [24].

In a BIM platform, at the earliest stages of design, projects from all disciplines are overlapped in 3D, and problems are identified and likely larger problems can be prevented in the future. Design coordination is an activity that combines designs from all disciplines to achieve total quality control standards of the work [25]. The design coordination process usually begins after the conceptual design and preliminary description of the building systems have been completed [26]. It is seen as a kind of final review phase where possible errors can be detected. The effectiveness of design coordination is more efficient when the project is developed early.

BIM can provide digital and real-time feedback to the designers and enable them to test and develop their work at every stage of the design in line with the conditions they want. The processes of performing analyses, evaluating the feedback and developing the design can be continued cyclically. In the search for satisfactory solutions, it is ensured that aesthetic, function and performance development can be maintained in a coordinated manner [27].

Quantity survey is one of the main elements of the construction business, such as the approximate cost of the building or the project process planning [28]. It is the data required from the preliminary design stage to the end of the project. BIM-based quantity data; It has been reported that the project provides simpler, more detailed and accurate cost estimations, reducing time and expenses [29]. In order to examine the calculated difference between the quantities obtained with modeling tools and traditional methods, it is possible to quickly obtain the quantity data in the models created using BIM tools [30].

During the design phase, BIM can also contribute to the development of building through various methods. The first method is to create 3D masses for conceptual design with the geometric modeling commands. These 3D masses can be transformed into BIM objects afterwords. The second method is to produce forms supported by parametric/generative design principles. A parametric design interface is a relatively new paradigm in the field of CAD and BIM, as the mechanisms which are capable of producing design alternatives are controlled by certain rules or limits, regardless of the modeling and visualization skills of designers [31]. The third method is to utilize sustainability analyses including solar, wind and energy studies for early design forms. These analyses, also called building performance analyses, allow the design decisions to be reviewed and to create more sustainable designs [15].

3 Case Studies

3.1 Research Methodology

This study examines how BIM is used in the early stage architectural design process through case studies. The case study research methodology was used to collect data in this study. It focuses on understanding the dynamics' presence in environments [32]. It is an efficient method for investigating a specific phenomenon, such as a program, a person, a process, an institution, or a social group. A case study may include single or multiple cases and offer in-depth analysis or multiple levels of analysis about the lim-ited cases selected [33, 34]. It is a general practice to conduct case studies with a small number of cases to produce an in-depth analysis [35].

Four architectural firms were selected as cases for this study. These firms are some of the leading Turkish AEC firms that utilize BIM in many projects at different scales for many years (see Fig. 1 and Fig. 2). In line with the scope of this study, the research was confined to the early design phase use of BIM by these firms.

The interviews were held at the firms' offices. Generally, interviewing is often pre-ferred as a way of collecting data in the field of social science and the case study re-search methodology [32]. In this study, the interviews were conducted in a semi-struc-tured manner with open-ended questions. The verbal data obtained from the interviews were recorded in a phonoscope and transcribed into text manually. When analyzing data, the content analysis method was used. It is the process of analyzing qualitative data obtained from various sources, making quantitative evaluations and extracting meaning from the data [36, 37]. It involves characterizing and comparing transcript doc-uments collected from the interviews. This process was completed in the NVivo soft-ware, a data analysis software produced by the QSR International firm.

The verbal data was transcribed into the Microsoft Word file format; then, imported into NVivo for graphical analysis. NVivo facilitates the processes of coding in data analysis, revealing themes, presenting results visually and numerical analysis of quali-tative data. The coding was done within the Nvivo to analyze the data. All of the firms interviewed are defined as a "case" in Nvivo. Coding was carried out by dividing the interview content into the categories such as (1) Management of the early-stage archi-tectural design process (2) BIM Uses in Early Design Stages and (3) Strengths and weaknesses of BIM in early design phases. Content analyzes were carried out by creat-ing a subcode (child node) of the categories. All these relationships are graphed using NVivo's "hierarchy chart" feature.

3.2 Results and Analyses

According to the content analysis the most frequently used words in the interviews were "information" and "time" (Fig. 3). The fact that "time" and "information" are also con-sistent with the nature of Building Information Modeling. This outcome can be inter-preted in a way that BIM is an information-focused process, and it represents the timely exchange of information by all project stakeholders.

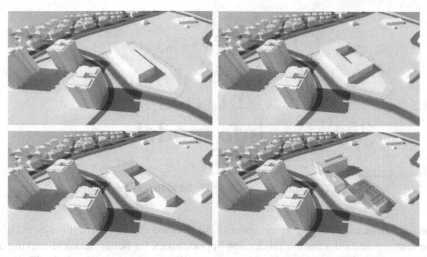

Fig. 1. Design progress on different masses using energy analysis by Firm 3

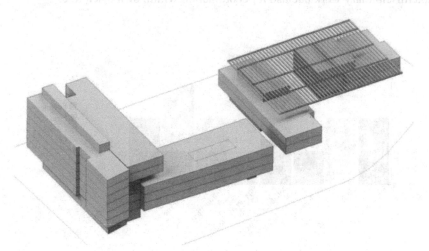

Fig. 2. Sun study on a proposed design by Firm 3

The survey included a question about the general use of BIM by firms. As revealed, BIM helps the decision-making process in different phases of the project life-cycle including the early design phase (Fig. 4). As stated by an interviewee "unpredictable information for problems and their solutions" can be obtained through BIM. The interview results show that many firms use software other than BIM at the beginning of their design work. They switch to BIM after reaching a certain stage for advanced analysis, assessing design control, creating accurate schedules and more precise project docu-mentation. Most firms expressed that BIM is a virtual construction site in which all building-related activities are pre-analyzed before the actual construction. They believed that the lifecycle representation of the building involving all project phases was one

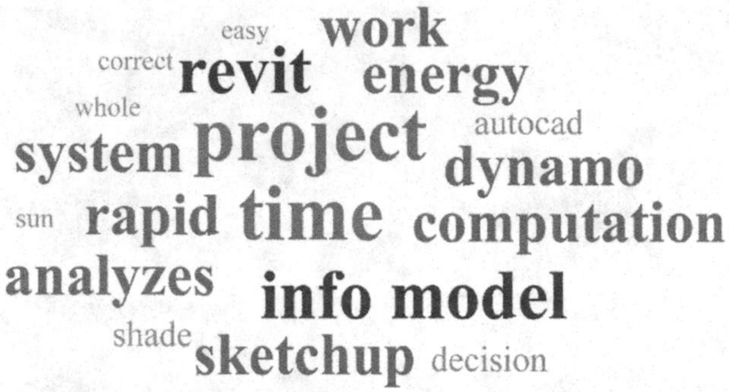

easy **work**
correct **revit** **energy**
whole
system **project** autocad
dynamo
sun **rapid time** computation
analyzes info model
shade **sketchup** decision

Fig. 3. The word cloud result produced in the content analysis

of the important uses of BIM. Interviewees also stressed that multidisciplinary collabo-rative features and information production opportunities for better decision-making are essential aspects of BIM. They added that the coordination feature is not only sig-nificant for interdisciplinary work but also for coordination within own discipline.

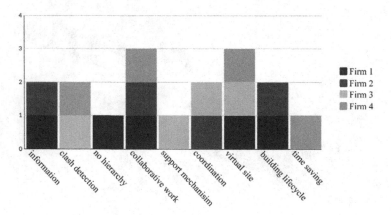

Fig. 4. BIM uses by the firms

Another question examined the type of software used in the firms. For most of the firms, Autodesk products such as Revit, Navisworks and BIM360 Docs are primary BIM plat-forms. Occasionally, firms appear to introduce other software when deemed necessary. Dynamo, the visual programming environment by Autodesk, is also used by the firms, for productivity-related tasks in project documentation rather than design-related purposes (Fig. 5).

Firms were also asked about the design media they used and the flow of their design work (Fig. 6, 7). Traditional paper-based sketches are still the main design media for these firms. Physical models as another traditional medium also appear to have their uses in the design process. Following the creation of the design in traditional mediums, firms showed different attitudes toward the use of digital tools. According to Firm 1,

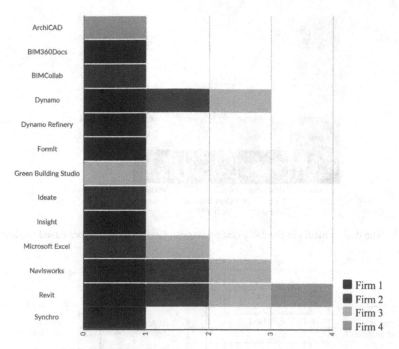

Fig. 5. The type of software used in the early design stages

BIM is a "working method. It is a system that excludes all traditional methods and has sociological effects." Firm 1 and Firm 4 stated that they move to digital media with BIM. Firm 2 and Firm 3 preferred working with CAD software after the hand-drawn sketches. CAD systems are still found more flexible and easier to use for design tasks as they imitate graphic environments presented in paper-based media. According to Firm 1, which uses BIM at every stage, "Modeling the design geometry and transferring it to the digital environment is still difficult in the BIM environment. (3D) Modeling a building takes longer than drawing it. It is necessary to use more than one software."

In some projects, BIM is used in the early stages for supporting design decisions with information specific to that task. As stated by Firm 4, the digital proficiency of the designer is also determining factor in choosing design media. Firm 2 explained the transition process to BIM as such "… after the decisions regarding form, space organization and the volume are made, BIM is used for developing design ideas and alternatives." Firms that do their first design work with traditional mediums, move to BIM at the late design stages. They move to BIM for informed decisions. Firm 3 states that "The early-stage architectural design process can be very different according to the subject, content and intensity of the design. If you know what to do, then it will be easy to switch to BIM, but if it is not known what to do, it is necessary to make models, sketch, try and repeat. A lot of analyses are required."

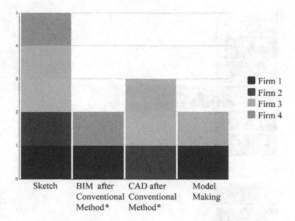

Fig. 6. The design media in the early design stages (* refers to pen-paper based media)

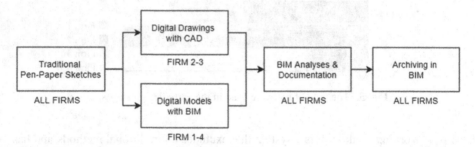

Fig. 7. Preferences for the design and documentation media in the project processes

Firm 2 and Firm 5 emphasized the importance of working with all stakeholders in the early stages of design with BIM. Firm 2 expressed that "the basis of BIM, and thus its greatest advantage, is based on "coordinated knowledge generation with the participation of different stakeholders." Firm 1 and Firm 4 stated that BIM provides a significant benefit in existing situation modeling and analyses. According to Firm 1 conventional tools do not take environmental conditions into account. Firm 1 and Firm 3 said that "the BIM offers a great benefit for incorporating environmental factors such as sun, wind, shadows into the design process". Firm 1 and Firm 3 believed that BIM is important for energy analysis in the early design stages. However, Firm 3 also stressed that: "The features of the BIM such as energy modeling and wind analysis should show how it is integrated into the context and urban infrastructure. Furthermore, we are not sure of the accuracy of the analysis outputs (Table 1)."

Table 1. BIM uses in early the design phases by the firms interviewed

	FIRM 1	FIRM 2	FIRM 3	FIRM 4
Design authoring			X	X
Existing situation modeling and analysis	X			X
Quantity surveying		X	X	
Energy analysis	X		X	

The next question examined the strengths and weaknesses of BIM in comparison with other digital environments. Firm 1 and Firm 3 expressed that BIM contributes to the early-stage architectural design process for existing situation analysis, quantity surveying, documentation, energy analysis and coordination (Table 2). Firm 3 and Firm 4 emphasized the BIM's contribution to 3D mass design. They both stated that the ability to model 3D geometrical models called masses is beneficial for design studies. Firm 3 also emphasized the variability of the design process, saying that "choosing the right tool for the situation is important. When information is not needed, the need for BIM decreases. For this reason, BIM and early-stage architectural design processes do not converge at certain points." The same firm claimed that, "at present, BIM conveniently benefits construction documentation for architectural design offices in terms of revision and coordination."

Table 2. Strengths and weaknesses of BIM in early design phases

Strengths	Weaknesses	Potentials
Efficient collaboration	Rigidity	Energy analysis
Existing condition analysis	Time	Integration with CAD tools
Working with conceptual masses		
The support of computational design tools		

4 Findings

Despite some of the drawbacks concerning design-related capabilities of existing BIM software, the research findings reveal that BIM still helps early design and design development tasks in the following areas:

1. **Testing the sustainability of design alternatives with energy analysis,**
   The ability of BIM environments to analyze and simulate through early design models for sustainability distinguishes BIM from other tools and environments and highlights it as an important working environment for design [24].

2. **Assessing the context utilizing the site and existing condition analysis,**
   BIM is effective for site analysis, site utilization planning and modeling the site conditions. In early project stages, BIM can be used to assess site conditions and characteristics and to make decisions about organizational relationships and building layout [38].
3. **Generating the design intent conceptual mass in 3D,**
   For the early stages of design, a 3D model is created at the LOD 100 level, which corresponds to the conceptual design level. This environment encourages working with 3D geometries from the start in contrast to transforming 2D views into 3D as in CAD platforms [39].
4. **Developing design alternatives with generative design methods,**
   Generative design helps to produce a pool of solutions for design problems within the framework of defined rules. In the BIM environment, this feature is being integrated into various software or offered with visual programming tools. In this way, the role of BIM in finding the preliminary design idea increases.
5. **Creating an environment for efficient collaborative design,**
   BIM software offers foresight for the planning and implementation of the project and reduces project risks. Many participants collaborate in model formation processes by making the process dynamic and detailed [16].
6. **Coordinating early-stage design decisions with documentation,**
   In BIM, documenting the design and showing its constructibility can help all project stakeholders. This is possibly one of the strongest aspects of BIM in comparison to CAD software. Both geometric and non-geometric information can be retrieved from models for documentation purposes in different phases of a project.

5 Conclusion

As supported by the research results in this study, BIM has an important place in the early stage architectural design process, especially in data-intensive processes. By incorporating all the geometrical and semantic data and interpreting that through analyses, BIM acts as a facilitator in the designer's decision-making. While CAD concentrates on form building and 2D project documentation, BIM actively supports decision-making in multidimensional project contexts. These new design development methods also help designers with new perspectives on design methods. In the interviews, BIM is seen as particularly important in terms of providing information and coordination as opposed to CAD software.

This research showed that BIM is often used as a design development environment rather than creating the initial design idea. It contributes to the development of the design idea and the production of alternatives from it. One drawback of BIM as revealed in this study is that it still lacks flexibility in geometric modeling; often other software are introduced into projects to achieve the desired geometrical tasks useful for designing. BIM as an early design tool is expected to improve with the availability of easy and intuitive interfaces with performative, parametric and generative design tools.

References

1. Rittel, H.W., Webber, M.M.: Dilemmas in a general theory of planning. Policy Sci. **4**, 155–169 (1973)
2. Akin, Ö.: Models of Architectural Knowledge - An Information Processing Model of Design. Carnegie Mellon University, College of Fine Arts, Pittsburgh (1979)
3. Liu, Y.T.: Is designing one search or two? A model of design thinking involving symbolism and connectionism. Des. Stud. **17**(4), 435–449 (1996)
4. Oxman, R.: Cognition and design. Des. Stud. **17**(4), 337–340 (1996)
5. Gero, J.S., Mc Neill, T.: An approach to the analysis of design protocols. Des. Stud. **19**(1), 21–61 (1998)
6. Macmillan, S., Steele, J., Austin, S., Kirby, P., Spence, R.: Development and verification of a generic framework for conceptual design. Des. Stud. **22**(2), 169–191 (2001)
7. Rowe, P.: Design Thinking. The MIT Press, Cambridge, MA (1987)
8. Oxman, R.: Design by re-representation: a model of visual reasoning in design. Des. Stud. **18**(4), 329–347 (1997)
9. Kryssanov, V.V., Tamaki, H., Kitamura, S.: Understanding design fundamentals: how synthesis and analysis drive creativity, resulting in emergence. Artif. Intell. Eng. **15**, 329–342 (2001)
10. Stempfle, J., Badke-Schaub, P.: Thinking in design teams-an analysis of team communication. Des. Stud. **23**(5), 473–496 (2002)
11. Gänshirt, C.: Sechs Werkzeuge des Entwerfens. In: Cloud-Cuckoo-Land – International Journal of Architectural Theory, No. 1/1999. http://www.cloud-cuckoo.net/openarchive/wolke/deu/Themen/991/Gaenshirt/gaenshirt.html. Accessed 8 Sept 2021
12. Coyne, R.D., Rosenman, M.A., Radford, A.D.: Knowledge-based design systems (1990)
13. Carrara, G., Kalay, Y.E.: Past, present, future: process and knowledge in architectural design. In: Carrara, G., Kalay, Y.E. (eds.) Knowledge-Based Computer-Aided Architectural Design, pp. 389–395. Elsevier, Amsterdam (1994)
14. Kalay, Y.E.: Design, Architecture's New Media: Principles, Theories, and Methods of Computer-aided Design, vol. 11. MIT Press (2004)
15. Pektas, S.T.: Cognitive styles and performance in traditional versus digital design media. Computation: The New Realm of Architectural Design [27th eCAADe Conference Proceedings], pp. 769–772 (2009)
16. Ofluoğlu, S.: Yapı Bilgi Modelleme: Gereksinim ve Birlikte Çalışılabilirlik, Mimarist, vol. 49, pp. 10–12 (2014)
17. Bryde, D., Broquetas, M., Marc, J.: the project benefits of building information modelling (BIM). Int. J. Project Manag. **31**(7), 971–80 (2013). (Elsevier Ltd and APM IPMA)
18. Schueter, A., Thessling, F.: Building Information Model-Based Energy/Exergy Performance Assessment in Early Design Stages, Automation In Construction (2008)
19. Plume, J., Mitchell, J.: Collaborative design using a shared IFC building model- learning from experience. Autom. Constr. **16**, 28–36 (2007)
20. Kubba, S.: Handbook of Green Building Design and Construction: LEED, BREEAM, and Green Globes. UK: Butterworth Heinemann (2012)
21. Attia, S., De Herde, A.: Early design simulation tools for net-zero energy buildings: a comparison of ten tools. In: Conference Proceedings of 12th International Building Performance Simulation Association (2011)
22. Bogenstätter, U.: Prediction and optimization of life-cycle costs in early design'. Build. Res. Inform. **28**(9), 376–386 (2000)
23. Yoon, S. Park, N., Choi, J.: A BIM-Based Design Method for Energy-Efficient Building. Seoul, IMS, and IDC, pp. 376–381 (2009)

24. Krygiel, E., Nies, B.: Green BIM: Successful Sustainable Design with Building Information Modeling. Wiley (2008)
25. Staub-French, S., Khanzode, A.: 3D and 4D modeling for design and construction coordination: issues and lessons learned. ITcon **12**, 381–407 (2007)
26. Liu, H., Ming, L., Mohamed, A.-H.: BIM-based integrated framework for detailed cost estimation and schedule planning of construction projects. In: ISARC. Proceedings of the International Symposium on Automation and Robotics in Construction, vol. 31. Vilnius Gediminas Technical University, Department of Construction Economics & Property (2014)
27. Kymmell, W.: Building Information Modeling: Planning and Managing Construction Projects with 4D CAD and Simulations. McGraw Hill Professional (2008)
28. Leonardo, G., Silvio, M., Sérgio, S., Márcio, F.: Trends and challenges for design management in Brazilian building industry: case studies in São Paulo (2005)
29. Tulke, J., Nour, M., Beucke, K.: Decomposition of BIM objects for scheduling and 4D simulation. In: eWork and eBusiness in Architecture, Engineering and Construction, pp. 667–674. CRC Press (2008)
30. Wu, S., Wood, G., Ginige, K., Jong S. W.: A technical review of BIM-based cost estimating in UK quantity surveying practice, standards and tools. J. Inf. Technol. Construct. **19**, 534–562 (2014)
31. Lee, J.H., Gu, N., Ostwald, M.J., Jupp, J.: Understanding cognitive activities in parametric design. In: Zhang, J., Sun, C. (eds.) CAAD Futures 2013. CCIS, vol. 369, pp. 38–49. Springer, Heidelberg (2013). https://doi.org/10.1007/978-3-642-38974-0_4
32. Eisenhardt, K.M.: Building theories from case study research. Acad. Manag. Rev. **14**, 532–550 (1989)
33. Cohen, L., Manion, L.: Research Methods in Education, 4th edn. Routledge, London (1994)
34. Yin, R.K.: Case Study Research Design and Methods, Second Edition, Thousand Oaks. Sage, CA (1994)
35. Gerring, J.: The case study: what it is and what it does. In: The Oxford Handbook of Comparative Politics (2007)
36. Bauer, M.W.: Classical content analysis: a review. In: Bauer, M.W., Gaskell, G. (eds.) Qualitative Researching with Text, Image and Sound, pp. 131–151. Sage Publication, London (2003)
37. Saldana, J.: The Coding Manual for Qualitative Researchers. SAGE Publications, Great Britain (2009)
38. Bonenberg, W., Wei, X.: Green BIM in Sustainable Infrastructure, Procedia Manufacturing, vol. 3 (2015)
39. Eastman, C., Teicholz, P., Sacks, R., ve Liston, K.: BIM Handbook: A Guide to Building Information Modeling for Owners, Managers, Designers, Engineers, and Contractors. Wiley, Hoboken, NJ (2011)

BIM for Project and Facilities Management

BIM-Based Value Engineering: Creating a Plug-In System for Time Saving and Quantity Management

Kerem Kabaca(✉) and Cansu Yalnız

Rönesans Proje Mühendislik A.Ş., Istanbul, Turkey
{kerem.kabaca,cansu.yalniz}@ronesans.com

Abstract. The recent advancements in BIM methods emphasize the effective time usage for project-producing phases. Especially various capabilities of plugins and coding provide an opportunity to create customized solutions for BIM applications. From a specific viewpoint, value-engineering processes require project-based solutions and plug-ins can be developed as catalyst tools for facilitating this important phase and related BIM tasks. Encountered issues should be considered an opportunity to save time in the next project. Considering the in-house BIM project experiences, Ronesans Construction Project Company has evaluated the BIM-related issues that were faced on the projects to create specific solutions by producing new plugins. In addition, all team members are trained to improve their knowledge to increase working efficiency, which is also an advantage that saves time. Every generated plugin or update is shared with the team synchronously. This study presents a case study on a room related plug-in that has been utilized within the firm. Such use patterns, features and user responses are reported to show the effectiveness of customized tools for specific BIM tasks such as Room-Related Surfaces.

Keywords: Roombook · BIM parameters · Cost management · Time saving · Value engineering · BIM plug-in

1 Introduction

Digitalization has been defined as the process of changing analog to digital form, also known as digital enablement [1]. Digitalization has affected the operational processes of companies due to the provided opportunities for efficiency [2]. This trend has recently become mandatory to be successful in the competitive markets for many sectors [2]. The construction sector is one of them that has also been affected by the rapid advancement of technology [3]. Many software platforms have been implemented in the project production phases to work more efficiently. Besides, design and delivery methods also have changed due to the continuous digital improvements in the Architecture, Engineering, and Construction (AEC) industry [3]. Many organizations work collaboratively in the AEC industry to finalize projects. In line with that, the information management and exchange process become crucial [4]. Therefore, there have been some improvements

© Springer Nature Switzerland AG 2022
O. Ö. Özener et al. (Eds.): EBF 2021, CCIS 1627, pp. 33–52, 2022.
https://doi.org/10.1007/978-3-031-16895-6_3

regarding the common working way and collaboration considering all relevant disciplines [4]. Building Information Modeling (BIM) is the most profound development of the digital transformation in the AEC industry that provides a common platform to work collaboratively [4]. In addition, BIM is defined as both a method and process where the physical features and information of every element of the project are digitalized regarding its required level of detail [5]. Created information model includes nD building information ranging from geometry, spatial relationships, light analysis, geographic information, quantities and properties of building components product's material, specification, fire rating, U-value, fittings, finishes, costs, and carbon content [3]. Thus, all designers and engineers could monitor and manage the required parameters [3]. In addition, error minimization, improving productivity, supporting quantity, cost, scheduling and safety management are significant enhancements provided by BIM usage [6]. There are many software tools utilized in BIM processes to achieve the indicated potential. The BIM field clusters a group of professionals who specialize in developing software, hardware, equipment, and networking systems necessary to increase the efficiency, productivity, and profitability of AEC sectors. These include organizations that generate software solutions and equipment of direct and indirect applicability to the design, construction, and operation of facilities [7].

Although there are many tools to use, the software is inadequate in some cases. Such cases unlock the opportunity for new Plug-in creation, it's even crucial for some situations to better utilize the system [8]. Plugins are created due to improve the capabilities of the existing software considering specialized tasks [9]. Scripting Language and Application Program Interfaces (API) are two methods that allow for the creation of new tools for the Revit Software [8]. There are many software providers such as Autodesk App Store [10], AGACAD [11], Kiwicodes [12], RevitWorks [13], IdeateSoftware [14], RTVTOOLS [15]. Besides, there are almost 797 plug-ins that have been utilized in the construction industry [16]. In addition, many construction firms have started to create their personnel plug-ins [8]. For instance, Thornton Tomasetti has created CORE platform for research and development regarding the software [17]. Bentley is another example that created the plug-ins for sharing and accessing the models [18]. In addition to the private R&D efforts, there are also academic studies regarding the plug-in creation for the detected issues. For instance, Revit Add-in has been developed for parametric modeling of bridge abutments in a master thesis [19] and another plug-in has been created for the electrical equipment placement to achieve repetitive works efficiently in a doctoral dissertation [20].

Plug-in creation for time and cost-saving and to achieve more efficient usage could be considered a value engineering (VE) approach of the BIM phases. Value engineering is defined as a structured problem-solving process based on function analysis to improve the value of a system. Value is also defined by a ratio of function to cost and consequently, it can be increased by either improving the function or reducing the cost [21]. The VE study is conducted by a team of members with multi-disciplinary experience and expertise [21]. Value engineering is a management approach that can significantly improve the function and value of projects and eliminate unnecessary costs [22]. Information, function analysis, creativity, development and evaluation, presentation, and implementation are the phases that need to be followed during the value engineering processes [23].

The study aims to demonstrate the similarities between the Renaissance Construction Company's plug-in production phases and the value engineering phases.

The selection of the predicted finishing work materials by the designers before the construction documentation phase is a performance considering the cost management that today's project companies often try to reveal. The BIM parameters are being used to manage outputs of the finishing materials and these parameters are starting to differ for each company's standards. Therefore, the design companies need to add additional compatible and integrated systems into the main BIM software. In these circumstances, the architects and engineers can easily integrate into the Project producing process with predefined BIM settings. When the main BIM software like Revit is analyzed, there isn't any solution in the default systems to connect the material information of wall coverings, ceilings, floors, and skirtings, which are the four basic components of closed room volumes with the room families. This study mentions an integrated plug-in system with predefined features that were created by Renaissance Construction. At the end of the study, it is aimed to present practical results with the automation of cost estimation and preparing bills of quantities (BOQ) in the BIM software.

2 Methodology

The Room-Related Surface plugin is presented as a case study in this article. Autodesk Revit software and the plugin which was produced by Renaissance Construction will be used in this case. The plug-in usage was designed based on Revit system families. It generates families and automatically enters parameter values into them step by step with coding language C# (C Sharp). Autodesk Revit has a .NET API which means it can be used any of the .NET compliant programming languages (C#, VB.NET, F#...) to develop a plug-in. While each language has its own relative benefits, C# is the natural choice for this guide: it is easy-to-learn, easy-to-use and leverages the power of the underlying. So, the C# was chosen in order to generate plug-in as a general-purpose, multi-paradigm programming language which is used for RCP tools plug-in [24].

This chapter aims to investigate the role and ways of usage of plug-in BIM system, and its effect on the company's BIM working process. In addition, the study also explains the schematic organizational chart of the firm in order to tell how Ronesans company approaches the problems. The indicated plug-in abilities in the introduction part are shown based on the sample project. Then, the time-saving benefits of the plugin are presented with a man/hour comparison between the classical usage of the software and the plugin-based one. In addition, a short survey was conducted to understand the BIM users' perception to the plugin and coding usage in the BIM process.

The tools features of plug-in: (see Fig. 1) (1) To generate system families (wall, floor, ceiling); (2) to copy parameter values into the generated families. (computer-readable statement); (3) to generate exported list on.xls format from generated families.

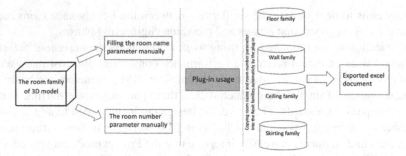

Fig. 1. The tools of features of plug-in with steps

3 The BIM Implementation Perspective in Ronesans

Ronesans Construction produces construction projects using BIM as an integrated and multidisciplinary system. All related disciplines such as architecture, structure, and MEP are integrated through BIM platforms. Besides, a common Revit server has been established for the project teams. Two project teams exist within the structure of Ronesans Construction; Ronesans Proje-Mühendislik (located in Turkey) and Renaissance Construction Project (located in Russia). There is also an R&D team that works on the BIM process for research and development. The software provides every team member to be free of location, Due to the opportunities of BIM. Indicated teams work collaboratively in the projects. BIM meetings are organized to discuss the goals or to train the team regarding updates. BIM R&D team prepares required families, templates, or plugins based on the remaining team members' experiences or requests. Thus, Ronesans Construction creates "needs-oriented solutions of the company" for project BIM processes (see Fig. 2).

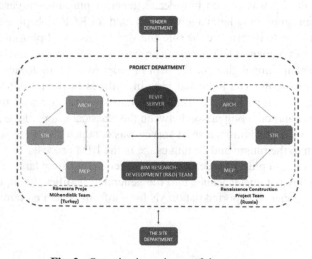

Fig. 2. Organization schema of the company

The projects are developed from the start of the tender phase. Therefore, after initial documents and models are received from the client, the Tender team shares them with the Project Team of Renaissance Construction for updates and BOQ preparations. During that process, the project team updates the model with parameters and prepares BOQ schedules for tender documentation. At that point, plugin creation is required due to inadequate software capabilities. The Revit software cannot provide a connection between the Rooms and the elements around. For instance, there is no room numbering parameter value inside any of the Revit elements. At that point, the plug-in provides to enter room numbering parameter into the Revit elements automatically. Thus, the connection is provided between the Rooms and the elements rapidly. The indicated issue is the reason for the creation of the Room-Related Surfaces Plugin by the Design Team.

The Plug-In Production Progress of the R&D Team: All design team members can work on the Revit server synchronously (see Fig. 1). During that process, if the team members face any software-based issue, they share it with the R&D team. Then, indicated issues are discussed at the meeting platforms to find the best solutions. After all, the R&D team provides solutions accordingly.

4   Plug-In Development Process Considering VE Phases

Plug-in production is a value engineering point of view for the BIM process. When examining the Room Related Surface plugin production process, it is seen that every step follows value engineering phases [23] (see Fig. 3).

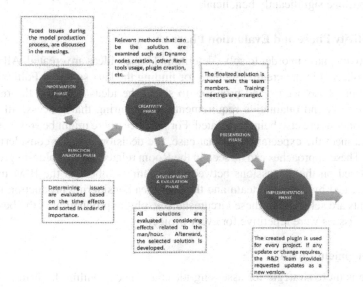

Fig. 3. Value engineering phases and reflection into the plugin production.

4.1 Information Phase

The purpose of the information phase is to define the status of the project and to determine its possibilities for development. In addition, many workshops have been arranged to discuss the status [23]. Considering the Room related surface plugin production process, BIM and design development meetings can be accepted as the workshops for the information phase of VE since BIM-related requirements and issues are discussed. The tasks related to the Project are defined in the meetings. All Project teams organize to finalize the job tasks. During that process, the issues related to the BIM Program Usage are defined and the R&D team is informed. Afterward, BIM meetings are arranged between the Project Team and the R&D Team to analyze the problems.

4.2 Function Analysis Phase

The Function Analysis Phase aims to state the needs of the Project Process. Defined functions are evaluated and classified to find the best options [23]. If the R&D team's approach is considered; the determined complications in BIM meetings are prioritized based on the order of importance. While they are working on classification, repetitive work causing time-wasting are mainly being considered. To exemplify, command usage can be analyzed in many projects, per that minimizing the time-wasting of repetitive commands can be defined as an issue. A room-Related surface plugin is produced for facilitating repetitive commands. Without the plugin, it takes time to add room name and room number parameters into the wall and floor elements or create wall and floor elements based on the room edges. Besides, entering a parameter manually can cause some negative results such as missing parameter, wrong parameter entering, letter mistake in parameter. Indicated mistakes affect schedules and quantities. Therefore, the produced solutions become significantly beneficial.

4.3 Creativity Phase and Evaluation Phase

In the creativity phase in order to solve determined issues, ideas are created. All possible ideas are collected in the creativity phase for finding the best solution. Following that, the evaluation phase occurs and proposes to select the ideas based on the resources, man/hour effects and qualitative requirements [23]. During that process, all relevant alternative options are also being evaluated. For instance, there might be some outsource plugins that meet the expectation, in that case, the decision is made considering cost-efficiency. These approaches can be seen in the Room related surface plug-in production process. Based on the discussions between the team members in the BIM meetings, ideas are created by the R&D team and the best idea considering production time and requirements are selected. In these circumstances, plugin production is the best option because the issues were repetitive for every project.

4.4 Development Phase

This phase is more strategic for assessing ideas and needs within the firm [23]. After the decision for the specific plug-in development the BIM R&D team develops plug-in prototypes for testing and user feedback. Following the project team's feedback, the plugin is updated and finalized for deployment.

4.5 Presentation Phase

The finalized solution and relevant information are shared with the project team and comparison results are assessed in this phase [23]. Considering the Room Related Surface Plugin's processes; after the plugin testing process is finalized, the relevant information is shared with the project team members in the meetings, and additional meetings are arranged to train the team.

4.6 Implementation Phase

This phase aims to realize the expected advantages of the new methodology [23]. When the plugin production process is examined; Room-related surface plugin usage provided time gains and prevented the user errors during the parameter filling. This situation demonstrates that the predicted advantages of the plugin are achieved. In the following part, a comparison between the usage with the plugin and without the plugin is shown as a case study.

5 Room-Related Surface Plug-In Usage Process

In the first stage, the room families and the masonry walls are defined in the Revit model with closed volumes, in order to start working with the plug-in. The masonry walls and their finishing covers are modeled by using two separate family types (see Fig. 4).

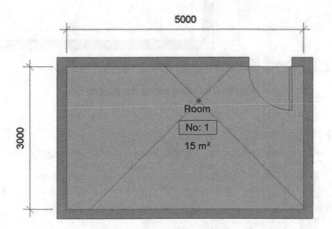

Fig. 4. The model status to implement the plug-in

The critical unit that has a function in an architectural design is the room. So the plug-in focuses on preparing finished works for these critical unites. The plug-in has 3 features known as creation families, copying values of parameters, and a creation list otherwise known as a Roombook (see Fig. 5).

0001   Walls Finishes   room -> walls   XLS roombook   Search room's tags   Who? select elements   Duplicate View
1-Ceration finishes   2-Copying values   3-Creation list
as a roombook

Fig. 5. All features of plug-in

The first feature of the plug-in is the automatic creation of models with predefined families (wall coverings and floors) along with the room boundaries (see Fig. 6, 7, 8).

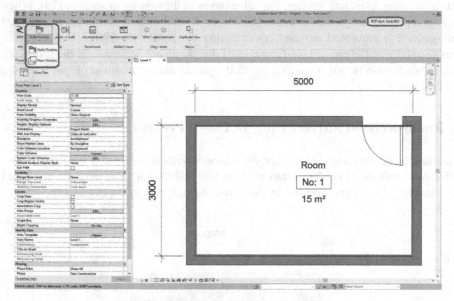

Fig. 6. The interface of the plug-in

Fig. 7. The initial feature of plug-in for the automatic creation of wall finishes

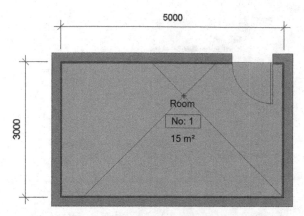

Fig. 8. Created wall claddings with the plug-in.

On the other hand, the parameter values of these elements are linked with the information of rooms. Rooms may have a lot of information, but the main variables are the name and number of the room, in order to provide requirements for the Roombook. In this case, the second feature of the plug-in is to insert room names and numbers into the parameters of model elements such as wall coverings, floors, ceilings and stairs (see Fig. 9, 10).

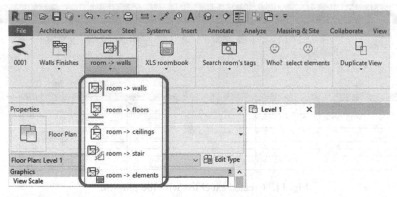

Fig. 9. The second feature of the plug-in is to automatic insertion of room names and numbers into the finished elements in the model.

The third feature is the creation of an Excel spreadsheet known as a Roombook. All rooms can be listed with a quantity of wall coverings, floors, ceilings and skirtings as areas by the plug-in. The standards of the Renaissance Construction are indicated in Excel. For example, the layout of the list, language of text are defined by the plug-in (see Fig. 11). All these automations provide serious benefits in terms of time and data management.

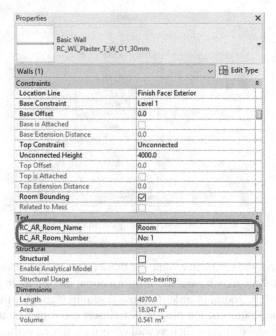

Fig. 10. Already copied values of parameters into the wall family with plug-in.

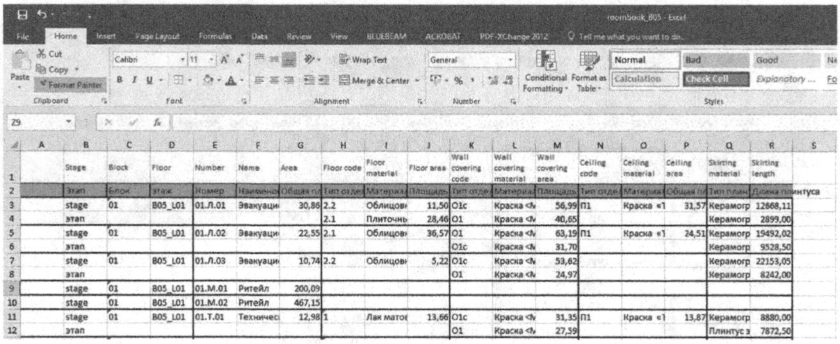

Fig. 11. Created excel list with the plug-in.

6 Case Study

There are a few factors such as the time saving and simplicity, which have advantages in the performance of plug-in usage. A sample project has been selected, in order to test the efficiency of the plug-in. The Project has the following characteristics: Total area of project: 229.021 m². The functions of building: Business center, shopping The total floor and height: 62 floors, 258,75 m.

Three staff members worked with the same method in the same model in order to eliminate comparing problems of personal performance. Considering the personal performance of professionals, it demonstrated that the use of the plug-in helped to eliminate factors such as negative personal performance and working efficiency which were observed across the samples. Almost everyone completed the same work with the plug-in at the same time. As predicted, the accuracy of method entries depends on subjective performance when using manual Revit methods. However, the plug-in creates this process and eliminates such problems with automation.

The first process of the proposed method is to create all wall coverings using the plug-in (see Fig. 12 and 13). The height of walls can be changed in the settings of plug-in. This setting is also provided to create a skirting, a wall or a floor which it can be followed the user steps below. Pre-intervention status of the model -as seen without wall covering- before the use of the plug-in (Fig. 12).

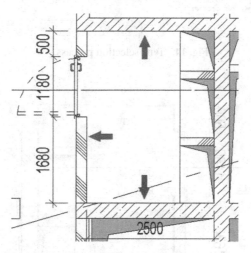

Fig. 12. Before using the plugin.

Fig. 13. Wall creation step of the plug-in.

At the same time, the family name can be recognized with requested any rules. Actually, in the regular process, this type of rules for a family name should be defined by the companies. So, the company standards as the code of the family name is created inside of the plug-in automatically (see Fig. 14).

All information about family names, material names are so critical in order to submit correct data. These automated processes ensure accuracy in a document like BOQ where data needs to be extremely accurate. The aim with the plug-in is to provide the automation accuracy. The software provides the information of quantity on the walls and the floors according to all separate rooms (Figs. 15, 16, 17, 18 and 19).

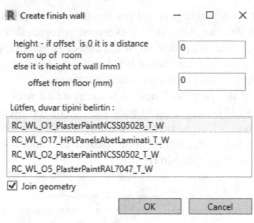

Fig. 14. Type selection process.

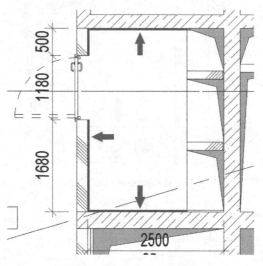

Fig. 15. After the plugin usage

6.1 Plug-In Usage Comparison

When the task is defined as adding wall cladding by type considering room naming and numbering parameters for 5 rooms; the time comparison chart in Fig. 20 shows that the plugin decreases the time usage almost by half. In line with the sample project, there are 500 rooms where the walls were created with the same method. Resulting, a 20 h of working time saved for 500 rooms. Besides, the plugin can be used for every project and provides error minimization.

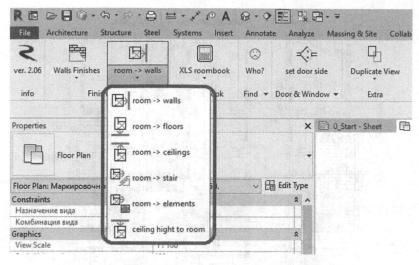

Fig. 16. Parameter adding process.

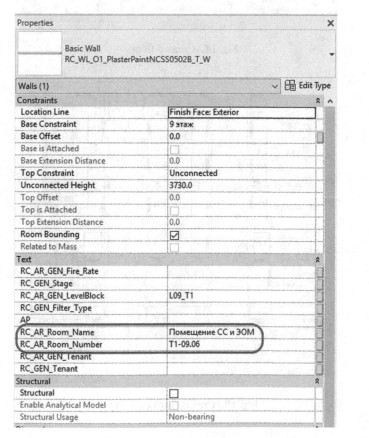

Fig. 17. After the plugin usage.

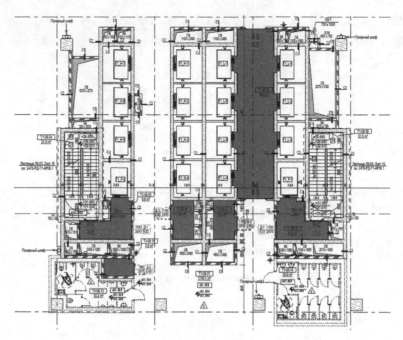

Fig. 18. Created floors

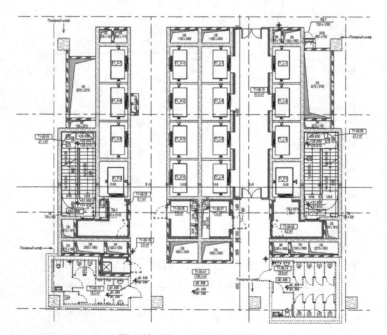

Fig. 19. Created wall claddings

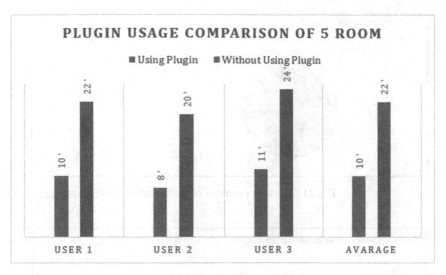

Fig. 20. Plugin usage comparison

6.2 Survey Results

BIM User's points of view regarding plug-in usage was examined with a compact survey. Questions were prepared to evaluate considering the parameters such as users BIM experience, utilized software, plug-in usage rate, plug-in production rate, coding usage rate and users deduce from the plugin usage. While making the survey, the attendees were mostly chosen from different companies. In the survey, 21 BIM users responded to the questions. The professions of the users were mainly architects, civil engineers, and BIM managers. Considering that both the case study results and survey results are in line with each other, the results of the survey can be considered as valid. In the first pie chart below, it can be seen the working positions of the users (see Fig. 21), and in the second pie chart, BIM usage experience is shown (see Fig. 22). In the first pie chart below, it can be seen the working positions of the users (see Fig. 21), and in the second pie chart BIM usage experience is shown (see Fig. 22). In addition, all participants are using Autodesk BIM tools (see Fig. 23). It is seen that all participants have the experience to evaluate the BIM processes.

19 participants use plugins during the working process (see Fig. 22). 9 of the attendees' companies have produced their plugin solutions (see Fig. 23). It is determined that the experienced BIM users are aware of the plug-in usage and almost half of the companies tried to solve the issues by considering the plugin creation (Figs. 24 and 25).

18 participants indicated that coding is used during the project production processes in the company's (see Fig. 26). In addition, 17 of the attendees plan to learn coding (see Fig. 27). This indicates a shift in the job descriptions and professional profile of AEC workforce.

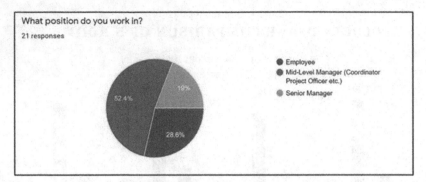

Fig. 21. Working positions of the attendees.

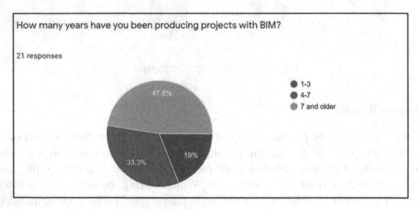

Fig. 22. BIM experiences of the attendees.

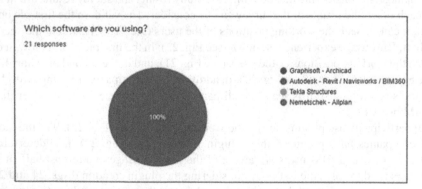

Fig. 23. BIM software preferences of the attendees.

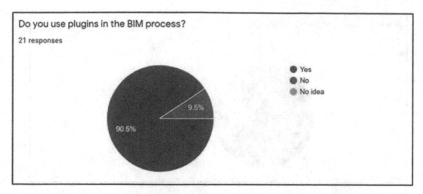

Fig. 24. Plugin usage percentages of the attendees.

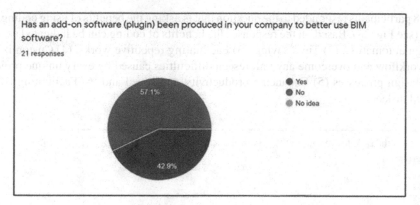

Fig. 25. Company based plugin production percentage.

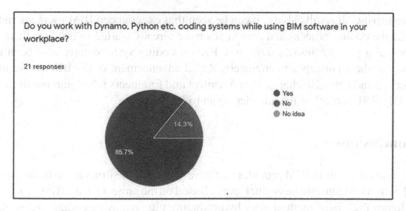

Fig. 26. Coding system usage percentages of the attendees.

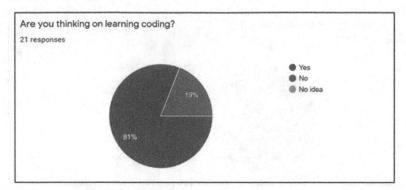

Fig. 27. Percentages of the attendees who plan to learn coding.

18 participants responded to the question that is asking the benefits of using coding on BIM (see Fig. 28). Based on the responses the benefits of coding can be indicated as: (1) Design automation, (2) Time-saving, (3) Facilitating repetitive works, (4) Customizing the workflow and overcome any unforeseen difficulties caused by every unique project and design processes (5) Enhancing productivity and speed and (6) Facilitating BOQ related tasks.

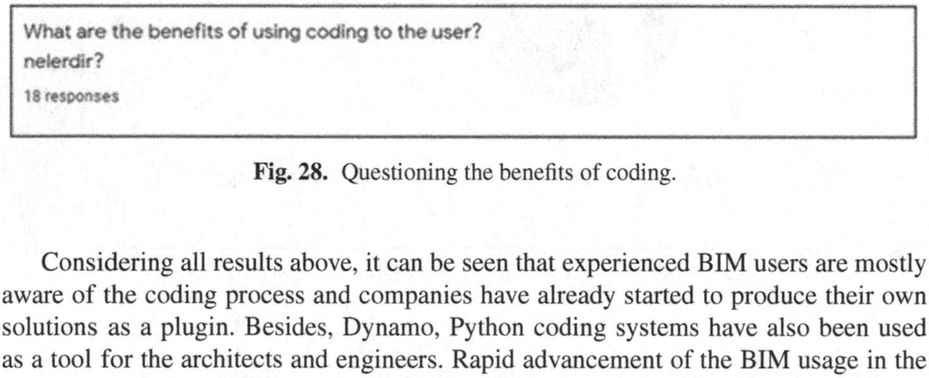

> What are the benefits of using coding to the user?
> nelerdir?
>
> 18 responses

Fig. 28. Questioning the benefits of coding.

Considering all results above, it can be seen that experienced BIM users are mostly aware of the coding process and companies have already started to produce their own solutions as a plugin. Besides, Dynamo, Python coding systems have also been used as a tool for the architects and engineers. Rapid advancement of the BIM usage in the construction industry also changed the Architect and Engineers job requirements as seen in Fig. 27; %81 percent of the attendees plan to learn coding.

7   Conclusions

Recent advancements in BIM provides vast advantages for the firms in the business scale as well as users at team and individual levels. Based on the project needs, BIM task groups can enhance their BIM methodology by producing plugins, using coding and scripting interfaces like Dynamo, Python. Due to the inadequacy of the generic BIM platforms for specific purposes, demand oriented plugin production is inevitable [8, 16]. Different from conventional BIM users, large companies need to create their own solutions to proceed efficiently. This approach can be exemplified as the value engineering for the

BIM processes when examining the Room Related Surface plug-in production process. It is evident that every step follows value engineering phases. As provided in the case study, the Ronesans Construction Company's need-oriented plugin production approach is consistent for efficient BIM usage. Considering the potential savings from the VE tasks, the firm realized the potentials of VE at the design development, work drawing, and construction documentation phases through need-oriented plugins. Time-savings is the main achievement of the firm with this tailor-made approach.

In addition, BIM user experience, utilized software, plug-in usage rate, plug-in production rate, coding usage rate and time deductions from the plugin usage parameters were examined through the short survey. Considering the survey results, it is determined that plugin and coding solutions provide numerous advantages for the project production phases. The advantages can be listed as; design automation; time-saving; facilitating repetitive tasks; customizing the workflow; overcoming any unforeseen difficulties caused by production processes; enhancing productivity and speed; facilitating BOQ-related tasks. On the other hand, many experienced BIM users in the construction industry want to learn coding for increased efficiency. Therefore, it is expected that job descriptions may change for architects and engineers in the near future. Also, the results show that many construction companies that work with BIM approach, have already started to produce their own need-oriented plugin solutions for their own BIM implementation frameworks. This compact study illustrated the applicability of customized software solutions for a large business enterprise and provided evidence for similar implementations of plug-in based software utilizations.

References

1. www.gartner.com. Accessed 07 Apr 2022
2. Parviainen, P., Tihinen, M., Kääriäinen, J., Teppola, S.: Tackling the digitalization challenge: how to benefit from digitalization in practice. Int. J. Inf. Syst. Proj. Manag. 5(1), 63–77 (2017)
3. Ghaffarianhoseini, A., et al.: Building Information Modelling (BIM) uptake: clear benefits, understanding its implementation, risks and challenges. Renew. Sustain. Energy Rev. 75, 1046–1053 (2017)
4. Liu, Y., Van Nederveen, S., Hertogh, M.: Understanding effects of BIM on collaborative design and construction: an empirical study in China. Int. J. Project Manage. 35(4), 686–698 (2017)
5. Ranjbaran, Y., Moselhi, O.: 4D-based value engineering. In: Construction Research Congress 2014: Construction in a Global Network, pp. 1606–1615 (2014)
6. Chen, L., Luo, H.: A BIM-based construction quality management model and its applications. Autom. Constr. 46, 64–73 (2014)
7. Succar, B.: Building information modelling framework: a research and delivery foundation for industry stakeholders. Autom. Constr. 18(3), 357–375 (2009)
8. Kensek, K.: BIM: enhancing workflows with add-ins. Technol. Arch. Des. 5(2), 244–246 (2021)
9. Ali, B., Zahoor, H., Nasir, A.R., Maqsoom, A., Khan, R.W.A., Mazher, K.M.: BIM-based claims management system: a centralized information repository for extension of time claims. Autom. Constr. 110, 102937 (2020)
10. https://apps.autodesk.com/en. Accessed 10 Apr 2022
11. https://agacad.com/. Accessed 10 Apr 2022

12. http://www.kiwicodes.com/. Accessed 07 Apr 2022
13. https://www.revitworks.com/. Accessed 09 Apr 2022
14. https://ideatesoftware.com/. Accessed 12 Apr 2022
15. https://www.rtvtools.com/. Accessed 10 Apr 2022
16. Silva, J.D., Mussi, A.Q., Ribeiro, L.A., Silva, T.L.: BIM software plug-ins: an alternative to optimize design processes from the perspective of performance and sustainability. J. Civil Eng. Arch. **11**(3), 249–264 (2017)
17. http://core.thorntontomasetti.com/. Accessed 12 Apr 2022
18. https://www.bentley.com/en/products/product-line/building-design-software/i-model-plu gin-for-revit. Accessed 10 Apr 2022
19. Georgoula, V., Vilgertshofer, S.: Development of an Autodesk Revit Add-in for the Parametric Modeling of Bridge Abutments for BIM in Infrastructure, Master Thesis, Technical University of Munich, Germany (2018)
20. Huang, L.: Revit Plugins for Electrical Engineering Improvements in Buildings: Lighting Power Density and Electrical Equipment Placement, Doctoral Dissertation, University of Southern California, Los Angeles (2018)
21. Zhang, X., Mao, X., AbouRizk, S.M.: Developing a knowledge management system for improved value engineering practices in the construction industry. Autom. Constr. **18**(6), 777–789 (2009)
22. Park, C.S., Kim, H.J., Park, H.T., Goh, J.H., Pedro, A.: BIM-based idea bank for managing value engineering ideas. Int. J. Project Manage. **35**(4), 699–713 (2017)
23. Rad, K.M., Yamini, O.A.: The methodology of using value engineering in construction projects management. Civil Eng. J. **2**(6), 262 (2016)
24. https://knowledge.autodesk.com/search-result/caas/simplecontent/content/my-first-revit-plugoveview.html#:~:text=Autodesk%20Revit%20has%20a%20.,the%20power%20of %20the%2underlying%20. Accessed 10 Apr 2022
25. Gordian. https://www.gordian.com/resources/value-engineering-for-construction/. Accessed 31 Aug 2021

Leveraging Prefabricated Construction Supply Chain Management Through Building Information Modelling

Kherun Nita Ali[✉], Aimi Sara Ismail, Norhazren Izatie Mohd, Shamsulhadi Bandi, Mohd Azwarie Mat Dzahir, and Hamizah Liyana Tajul Ariffin

Faculty of Built Environment and Surveying, Universiti Teknologi Malaysia, Johor, Malaysia
b-kherun@utm.my

Abstract. Prefabricated construction has been promoted as an innovative process in the Architecture, Engineering, and Construction (AEC) industry to reduce construction time and waste. Despite its capability, the adoption of prefabricated construction in Malaysia remains low due to the fragmented delivery processes among a large number of project stakeholders. Building Information Modelling (BIM) has a high capability to address these issues by centralising, coordinating, and visualising the design, timeline, and related costs for the supply chain management. Thus, this research aims to develop a process map that integrates BIM in prefabricated construction supply chain management. A 28-storey commercial building was selected as a case study to evaluate and visualise the supply chain management. A total of 405 precast families were created to develop a BIM Level of Detail (LOD) 300 model in Revit®. This model was utilised to (1) develop a work programme in Oracle® Primavera and (2) simulate the four-dimensional (4D) and five-dimensional (5D) BIM analysis in Navisworks® Manage. A process map was developed based on this case study and further validated by six expert panels. High mean scores ranging from 4.06 to 4.58 out of 5.00 were obtained for the validation process, affirming the feasibility of BIM integration in prefabricated construction to improve the supply chain management process. Generally, the experts agreed that the process map could be applied in other projects depending on the nature and suitability of the projects. Thus, future works include testing the process map in other case studies. This study contributes to a formalised process in preparing, coordinating, and simulate relevant information for prefabricated construction supply chain management.

Keywords: Building Information Modelling · Prefabricated construction · Supply chain management

1 Introduction

There is a growing interest in the Architecture, Engineering, and Construction (AEC) industry in applying the prefabrication approach to improve the construction processes. Prefabrication has been acclaimed as one of the means of reducing construction waste,

© Springer Nature Switzerland AG 2022
O. Ö. Özener et al. (Eds.): EBF 2021, CCIS 1627, pp. 53–68, 2022.
https://doi.org/10.1007/978-3-031-16895-6_4

where one of the earliest studies had reported up to 84.7% of wastage reduction saving for common construction materials [1]. Over a decade, other studies have explored and affirmed the effectiveness of prefabricated construction in reducing waste, especially timber formwork waste [2–5]. A recent study reported that this approach contributes to a 15.38% reduction in construction waste [6]. In definition, prefabricated construction refers to two main activities: the fabrication of components in a factory, commonly known as off-site fabrication, and the assembly of components on a construction site [7].

The prefabrication approach was introduced in Malaysia in the early 1960s with its early implementation in housing development [8]. Its implementation evolved towards high rise buildings, lightweight railway trains, and building complexes in the 1990s and early 2000s [9]. Although prefabricated construction promotes the minimisation of construction time by 50%, it was reported that the adoption rate is still low, with only 42% of public projects and 70% of private projects implementing this approach over the decade [10].

The Construction Industry Development Board (CIDB) had introduced the Construction Industry Transformation Programme 2016–2020 (CITP 2016–2020), where one of its strategic thrusts aimed to improve the construction industry through the acceleration of prefabricated construction [11]. While the outcomes of CITP have yet to be published, the management issues in handling prefabricated construction projects have been widely discussed in recent times [12]. Managing such projects is more complex than conventional ones as it deals with high initial investment and intricate delivery processes [13]. The fragmented delivery processes among many project stakeholders are considered one of the main challenges in implementing prefabrication approach in construction projects [14, 15].

An efficient supply chain management process has the potential in addressing these issues [11, 16]. An effective supply chain management is capable of accelerating the adoption of prefabricated construction. Building Information Modelling (BIM) has been identified as one of the key enablers in construction supply chain management [17]. Digitalisation through BIM is beneficial in improving information exchange, decision-making processes, and on-site production [18, 19].

Henceforth, this study aims to provide a process map that integrates BIM in the supply chain management of prefabricated construction projects. This study focuses on identifying the supply chain management in a prefabricated construction project, followed by simulating the 4D and 5D BIM analysis.

The remainder of this paper is organised as follows. In the next section, past studies are reviewed to discuss issues in construction supply chain management in the prefabrication industry and the capability of BIM as an enabler. The research methodology is presented in Sect. 3. Section 4 discusses the development and validation of the process map. The conclusion is set out in the final section.

2 Related Works

Issues related to prefabricated construction supply management and BIM implementation are reviewed in this section. The issues provide the direction of developing the process map for this study.

2.1 Prefabricated Construction Supply Chain Management

A supply chain consists of all activities involved in the delivery of products or services. The number of organisations or individuals involved in the flow of products or services from a source to a customer directly influences the depth of a supply chain [20]. A construction supply chain comprises all construction business processes from the client's requirements, design, and construction to maintenance, replacement, and decommissioning [21]. Managing a construction supply chain involves planning and controlling human resources as well as utilising suppliers' resources, infrastructures, and services to meet the client's requirements.

Supply chain management is an approach that originated and blossomed from the manufacturing industry. One of the earliest implementations of this approach was in the Just-In-Time delivery system in Toyota Production [22]. It was reported that hundreds of millions of dollars had been saved through supply chain management in the manufacturing industry [23]. Supply chain management can be defined as "the systematic, strategic coordination of the traditional business functions and tactics across these business functions within a particular company and across businesses within the supply chain, for the purpose of improving the long-term performance of individual companies and the supply chain as a whole" [24].

Construction supply chain management revolves around the management of information and the flow of materials and monetary funds throughout the development of a construction project. It is a system where project stakeholders could coordinate and exchange information to deliver the project [25]. In this system, the supply chain describes the workflow between building owners, designers, consultants, main contractors, subcontractors, and suppliers to create the proposed building [26]. Construction supply chain management aims to improve construction productivity, create a competitive advantage, and satisfy the client's requirements at the most reasonable cost [27].

A construction project can be divided into several phases depending on its suitability [23, 28–30]. Commonly, a construction project consists of five phases: concept phase, procurement phase, production phase, installation phase, and completion phase. During the concept phase, feasibility studies are conducted to identify the client's requirements [28]. A good communication platform is needed as financing issues are discussed in the concept phase. Complete drawings and specifications are made available for tendering purposes. In the procurement phase, the materials needed for the buildings are identified accordingly. A detailed design that is aligned with the concept design is proposed. The quantity, cost estimation, and specific requirements of the materials are also defined in this stage. A wide variety of information is exchanged during this stage. Typically, the information is fragmented due to the inefficiency of paper-based documents as the medium for information exchange [31].

The main contractor is then responsible for the production phase where the materials are classified as either off-the-shelf materials or prefabricated. The identification of local and imported materials is also included in this stage. The main contractor is accountable to request quotations from suppliers or subcontractors in selecting the appropriate parties [32]. The historical data of subcontractors and suppliers from previous projects is essential for better decision-making [33]. In prefabricated construction, the activities include the procurement, purchasing, and manufacturing of the components according to the material scheduling [34].

Next, the installation phase marks the commencement of the construction works. The site organisation and subcontracting works are coordinated with the material scheduling [30]. Architects and consultants should ensure that the materials or components are similar to the original design and delivered precisely on time [28]. It is common for the design or requirements to be revised during this stage. Therefore, the information must be exchanged and coordinated efficiently between construction parties. In conjunction with this, the main contractor is responsible for making decisions related to the on-site operations, such as the transportation system, site layout planning, and component handling [32]. The cooperation between the main contractor and subcontractors is crucial in assuring the construction's schedule, cost, and quality.

After the installation phase, project handover is carried out or also known as the winding-up phase. The operation and maintenance activities are then conducted [28]. The building owners should keep information such as as-built drawings and specifications for future references. Thus, it is advantageous to create a platform to manage and store this information to be accessible whenever necessary.

2.2   The roles and Challenges in Construction Supply Chain Management

Since supply chain management is adopted from the manufacturing industry, its roles in the AEC industry need to be defined to suit its purpose. The AEC industry's nature differs from the manufacturing industry because it contains different stakeholders to conduct numerous construction activities [35]. Four major roles of supply chain management in the AEC industry are identified where it can be focused on the supply chain itself, on the construction site, or both [23, 36–38].

Firstly, the construction supply chain management aims to improve the relationship between site activities and supply chain. The material transfer from off-site manufacturing to on-site assembling could lead to various concurrent activities [39]. The main aim of supply chain management is to avoid errors and reduce the duration of the activities. The main contractor has the strongest influence to efficiently administer the flow between manufacturing, delivery, and assembly [40]. Secondly, construction supply chain management aims to enhance the supply chain by reducing logistics, delivery, and inventory costs. The prefabricated suppliers can adopt this focus to improve their decision-making skills and overall performance [25]. The third focus of construction supply chain management is to achieve a wider concurrency between activities with better planning [25]. However, it can be quite challenging due to many technical dependencies. The fourth focus is to integrate and improve supply chain management in component production. Supply chain management enhances the flow expeditiously with a lower consumption rate of resources and ensures efficient layout management both on and off-site material transfer within the network [39].

The construction supply chain is known to be fragmented, which has a direct effect on productivity, cost, and schedule [41]. There are three ways fragmentation could occur in the AEC industry [41–43]. First, fragmentation occurs in the construction phases. There is a separation of information delivery within the construction phases. Secondly, fragmentation exists in different groups of project actors due to poor communication.

Thirdly, fragmentation arises due to a lack of understanding and standardisation between projects. Although fragmentation commonly occurs in a construction project, there is a strong connection or interdependence between each fragment [42]. As the activities, processes, and operations overlap between phases and actors, efficient information exchange is crucial in addressing the fragmentation issues [44].

2.3 Capabilities of Building Information Modelling (BIM) in Construction Supply Chain Management

BIM revolutionalises the AEC industry by granting a single digital platform for information management and exchange, coordination, and collaboration [45]. The integration of BIM in construction supply chain management is necessary to facilitate inter-organisational communication [46]. The attainment of this integration is regarded as the panacea for better performance and achievement of long-term objectives [31]. Integrated systems that assist collaboration and coordination could allow timely knowledge and information sharing [47]. Seamless and timely information exchange is the most critical success factor in integrating BIM in construction supply chain management [13].

The main principle of construction supply chain management is to recognise the integral management of suppliers and other relevant parties in delivering valuable products or services through a centralised and coordinated platform [48]. BIM is a crucial collaborative system that could facilitate the construction supply chain in achieving integrated practice [31]. A centralised platform for digital information exchange could eliminate the inefficiency of information flow in the supply chain [49]. Past studies reported improved design coordination, effective communication between stakeholders, and risk reduction through BIM adoption as potential issues could be detected earlier [13, 50]. In prefabricated construction, an integrated BIM-based construction supply chain management helps in reducing the procurement and fabrication time [13] as the overall activities are well-coordinated [51].

BIM solutions can create and operate on digital databases where changes could be managed efficiently and coordinated in all parts [45]. This information could be utilised as lessons learnt, which are beneficial among supply chain actors for continuous improvement [52, 53]. Interoperability is a primary component in facilitating information exchange. Interoperability refers to data competency between different BIM platforms to support a collaborative working environment among project participants for better design and construction management workflow [45]. In RIBA Plan of Work 2020, interoperability and collaboration issues are emphasised where architectural and engineering information must be spatially coordinated before providing detailed information for manufacturing and construction [54]. This coordination provides visualisation for designers in analysing multiple design solutions [45, 55].

In addition to interoperability, standardisation plays an important role in implementing BIM successfully in prefabricated construction projects. Standardisation is acquired through classification systems that organise entities based on the design, construction, and management processes [56]. Object libraries can be generated from the entities and further utilised for information management [57]. The most common BIM classification systems are OmniClass™ and Uniclass™ [58]. The purpose of each classification system determines the most appropriate classification to be applied in a BIM model [59].

BIM application could act as an early-cautioning and problem-solving mechanism for the supply chain network [52]. BIM-based collaboration using 4D and 5D could enhance the communication environment, for instance, the change of building materials could be simulated in the design stage to observe the effects on costs and time [60]. A project team often encounters various problems related to budget, work schedules, risks, and uncertainties during the construction or installation phase. These hurdles could impact the safety and quality of the project. Thus, a 5D model could be developed for budget controlling [61]. Through the 5D BIM application, design mistakes or omissions could be identified, and cost amendments could be conducted accordingly. Potential solutions to any conflicts and clashes could also be visualised and developed during the coordination process [55]. In summary, the information in a BIM model along with the 4D and 5D BIM analysis is beneficial in facilitating seamless prefabricated construction supply chain management.

3 Methodology

Based on the knowledge gaps, this paper attempts to achieve the following objectives:

1. To identify the necessary information for prefabricated construction supply chain management in a BIM-based environment.
2. To develop and validate a BIM-based process map for prefabricated construction supply chain management.

A design science research (DSR) methodology was adopted in this study to achieve the research objectives through an objective-centred solution [62]. This study was motivated by a research collaboration between academia and industry to develop an artefact in the form of a process map. The artefact was constructed through a qualitative case study approach and further demonstrated and validated.

A 28-storey commercial building was selected as a case study, courtesy of the construction developer involved in this research collaboration. Since this building was not built through a prefabrication approach and BIM models are commonly considered intellectual property [45], the building design was remodelled in Revit® 2020 to model the prefabricated components. All techniques and approaches in this study acted as the basis in developing the BIM-based process map for prefabricated contruction supply chain management. Subsequently, this process map was validated by six experts consisting of one planning manager, one BIM coordinator, two civil engineers, and two quantity surveyors. The process map was validated in terms of its usability, accuracy, reliability, and improvement to existing practice based on a $1 - 5$ Likert scale (1: strongly disagree, 5: strongly agree). Their feedbacks and suggestions were also acquired during the validation process.

4 Results and Discussion

A process map was developed which includes the overall tasks that were carried out in this study from the modelling process until simulation process. The development and validation of the process map are discussed in the following subsections.

4.1 Development of Process Map

Figure 1 presents a process map that consists of 3D, 4D, and 5D modelling. The 3D modelling represents the creation of necessary information including object geometries and semantic information, the 4D modelling represents the simulation and manipulation of time-related information, and the 5D modelling represents the simulation and manipulation of cost-related information. The process map was implemented in the case study, where the problems and challenges faced were used as lessons learnt to improve the sequence of tasks in the process map.

In this study, the design process initiated with the 3D modelling where project and families were created in Revit. This process was highly iterative in this study due to the challenges in designing a whole building with prefabricated components. The first challenge was to determine the maximum dimension for the components to avoid logistics issues. It was determined that the length of a component should not be more than 15 m, and the span should not be more than 4 m. The second challenge emerged during the modelling process in Revit. Generally, Revit contains system families and loadable families. System families such as wall, floor, room, and topography family pre-existed in Revit while loadable families are created in separate files and loaded into the building model. Loadable families consist of building components such as doors, windows, columns, and beams. It was analysed that the system families were not suitable to be applied for prefabricated construction as they were built upon the parametric modelling technique. Thus, all components were created using the loadable families option. The application of loadable families posed another challenge where the families must be created with precise dimensions as they were not adaptive to design changes, unlike system families. The families and their respective parameters were equipped with accurate and reliable information for the supply chain management.

A total of 405 families were created in this study comprising six categories: precast column, precast beam, precast slab, precast wall, precast stairs, and precast ramp. Each family was assigned an OmniClass™ Number, OmniClass™ Title, and a specific code name for standardisation purposes. The standardisation of building information was essential to ensure accurate information exchange for the supply chain management. OmniClass™ classification system was chosen as Revit contain a built-in OmniClass™ taxonomy file in all families [63]. Generally, the code names represented the family types, relevant dimensions, and even the shape of families in some instances. For instance, the precast column families were divided into 'CR' (rectangular column) and 'CS' (square column). An overview of the families is presented in Fig. 2.

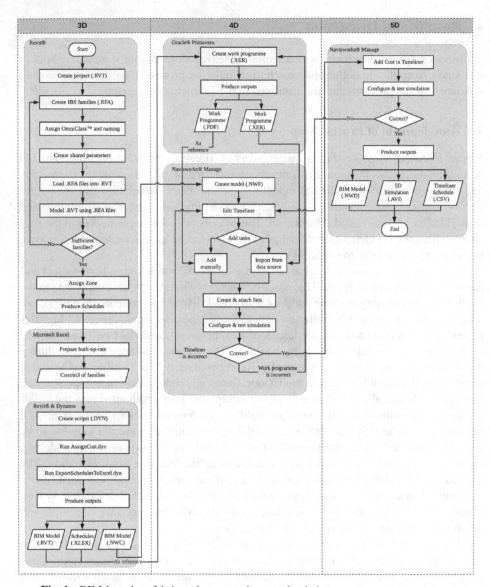

Fig. 1. BIM-based prefabricated construction supply chain management process map

The relevant information was stored in shared parameters to allow the utilisation in multiple families and projects. Seven groups of parameters were created in this study in which three groups were created for dimension-related information while four groups focused on cost-related and construction management-related information. These parameters were added into the project or relevant families to be used for the scheduling process. The example of shared parameters in a stairs family is illustrated in Fig. 3.

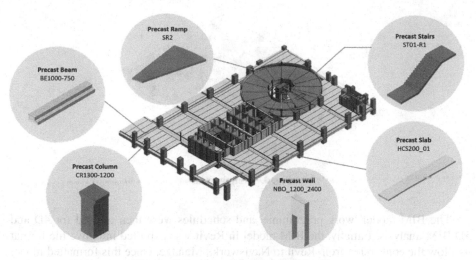

Fig. 2. Overview of prefabricated families

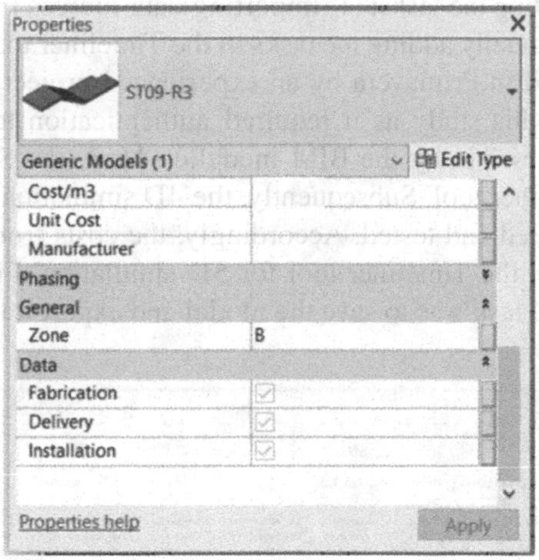

Fig. 3. Example of shared parameters in a stairs family

The costs of prefabricated components were obtained through the preparation of built-up rate for the prefabricated families. Dynamo scripts were developed to automatically add and calculate the costs of all prefabricated components as well as exporting the schedules into Microsoft Excel. The completed BIM model and the schedules acted as references for creating a work programme in Primavera, which marked the start of 4D modelling. A zoning technique was applied to simulate a more practical construction work sequence. It could promote a better construction process by managing the delivery, storage, and installation of the components. Figure 4 provides an example of a floor level that was divided into four zoning areas.

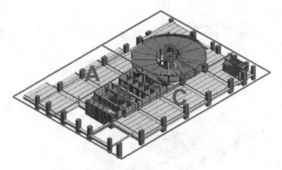

Fig. 4. Zoning areas

The BIM model, work programme, and schedules were then utilised for 4D and 5D BIM analysis. Initially, the BIM model in Revit was exported into.nwc file format to allow the conversion from Revit to Navisworks Manage. Once this formatted model was loaded into Navisworks Manage, it was saved as .nwf file format. The construction tasks were then added into the Timeliner tool in Navisworks Manage. There were two options available in adding the tasks: (1) importing data sources from Microsoft Project or Primavera, (2) or manually adding the tasks in the Timeliner tool. Although the work programme was created in Primavera by an experienced project manager, the second option was chosen in this study as it required authentication to import the file and Primavera was not accessible by the BIM modeller. Next, the Sets were created and attached into the Timeliner tool. Subsequently, the 4D simulation of construction tasks was automatically created and tested. Accordingly, the costs from the schedules were added into each task in the Timeliner tool for 5D simulation. Figure 5 illustrates the timeliner tool. The final task was to save the model and export it to necessary files.

Active	Name	Status	Planned Start	Planned End	Task Type	Attached	Total Cost
☑	⊟ B2 Slab		1/1/2019	23/1/2019			
☑	B2 Slab - Zone A		1/1/2019	4/1/2019	Construct	Sets->Basement & Car Park->B2->B2 Slab & Beam->B2 Slab & Beam - Zone A	
☑	B2 Slab - Zone B		5/1/2019	9/1/2019	Construct	Sets->Basement & Car Park->B2->B2 Slab & Beam->B2 Slab & Beam - Zone B	
☑	B2 Slab - Zone C		10/1/2019	14/1/2019	Construct	Sets->Basement & Car Park->B2->B2 Slab & Beam->B2 Slab & Beam - Zone C	
☑	B2 Slab - Zone D		15/1/2019	18/1/2019	Construct	Sets->Basement & Car Park->B2->B2 Slab & Beam->B2 Slab & Beam - Zone D	
☑	B2 Slab - Zone E		19/1/2019	23/1/2019	Construct	Sets->Basement & Car Park->B2->B2 Slab & Beam->B2 Slab & Beam - Zone E	
☑	⊟ B2 Column		24/1/2019	9/2/2019			
☑	B2 Col - Zone A		24/1/2019	26/1/2019	Construct	Sets->Basement & Car Park->B2->B2 Col->B2 Col - Zone A	
☑	B2 Col - Zone B		28/1/2019	30/1/2019	Construct	Sets->Basement & Car Park->B2->B2 Col->B2 Col - Zone B	
☑	B2 Col - Zone C		31/1/2019	2/2/2019	Construct	Sets->Basement & Car Park->B2->B2 Col->B2 Col - Zone C	
☑	B2 Col - Zone D		4/2/2019	6/2/2019	Construct	Sets->Basement & Car Park->B2->B2 Col->B2 Col - Zone D	
☑	B2 Col - Zone E		7/2/2019	9/2/2019	Construct	Sets->Basement & Car Park->B2->B2 Col->B2 Col - Zone E	

Fig. 5. Timeliner tool in Navisworks Manage

Six outputs were produced through the implementation of process map: BIM model (.rvt), schedules (.xlsx), work programme (.xer), BIM model (.nwd), 4D and 5D simulation video (.avi), and timeliner schedule (.csv). The BIM model in Revit could provide standardisation of information that can be used throughout the project lifecycle from the concept phase until winding up phase. Since the schedules in Microsoft Excel and the BIM model in Navisworks Manage were exported from Revit, all parties could coordinate and exchange information accurately. The schedules could be utilised for the procurement, production, and installation processes. The work programme, time-liner schedule, and the BIM model in Navisworks Manage could be used to plan and track the progress on and off-site efficiently. In addition to this, all project stakeholders could visualise and review the construction through the simulation video, improving the communication between parties.

4.2 Validation of Process Map

The process map was validated by six experts based on its usability, accuracy, reliability, and improvement to existing practice. The process map was first explained to the experts along with the demonstration of BIM modelling in Revit and BIM simulation in Navisworks Manage. Subsequently, the experts validated the process map by providing feedbacks and filling out a questionnaire consisting of Likert scale questions (1–5).

The validation results indicate high mean ratings ranging from 4.06 to 4.58 out of 5.00, as shown in Table 1. The experts believed that proficiency in BIM, especially in Revit and Navisworks Manage, is required to utilise the process map comprehensively. One of the experts suggested that a user manual should be produced to accommodate the implementation of the process map. This suggestion could be further explored in future works.

An expert, a BIM modeller, commented that the flow of activities for 3D, 4D, and 5D visualisation might vary according to the construction projects. Another expert also stated that while this process map could be applied to other projects, adjustments to the flow of activities will be inevitable to suit the nature of the projects. This expert highlighted that although the fundamental principle of a design process remains unchanged, differences could occur in terms of the site location, storage availability, and the prefabricated components' specifications. In another point of view, an expert emphasised that precast manufacturers usually used Tekla Structures for their design. Nonetheless, this expert agreed that Revit is commonly applied among various construction parties; thus, a much more reliable platform compared to Tekla Structures.

Table 1. Mean ratings for validation

Criteria	Description	Mean
Usability	To assess the overall display, flow of activities, and the ability to use the process map	4.29
Accuracy	To assess the accuracy of the flow of activities and outputs produced in the process map	4.30
Reliability	To assess the reliability of the process map to be applied to other construction projects	4.58
Improvement to existing practice	To assess the efficiency of the process map to assist construction players in improving the supply chain management	4.06

Lastly, the ability of the process map to improve the existing practice was validated with a mean score of 4.06. One of the experts stated that BIM application could assist in monitoring the supply chain management for the fabrication, delivery, and installation. Another expert suggested that the workability of the process map could be tested in other projects. An expert highlighted that the 3D, 4D, and 5D modelling should be explicitly described to ensure proper implementation of the process map.

5 Conclusion

This paper presents a process map that integrates BIM in prefabricated construction supply chain management. Through the development of the process map, it is concluded that the design process is an important phase to enable the integration of BIM in the prefabricated construction supply chain management. This is because seamless coordination, visualisation, and communication are only achievable if the project stakeholders could utilise accurate and standardised information in the BIM model. Thus, four crucial aspects to be addressed during the modelling process are identified as the following:

- Prefabricated components are confined to dimension limits due to logistics and transportation purposes. Therefore, it is vital to determine the allowable dimensions of the components before designing.
- Creating prefabricated components in a BIM model differs from conventional projects as BIM software applications are built upon a parametric modelling technique. The components must be modelled through loadable families in Revit.
- As the loadable families are not adaptive to changes, an iterative process in designing the building is inevitable. Standardisation through the application of the OmniClass™ classification system and code naming should be applied to allow information tracking for any design changes.
- Planning the procurement, manufacturing, and delivery of prefabricated components could be a challenging process. Thus, a zoning technique should be applied to segregate the workflow and construction sequence.

The process map could act as a specific guideline for stakeholders to implement BIM efficiently in prefabricated construction projects. Designers could refer to this process map to create necessary information for the supply chain management. The BIM outputs comprising the BIM models in Revit and Navisworks Manage, work programme, detailed schedules, 4D and 5D simulation, and a timeliner schedule could provide accurate and well-coordinated information throughout the entire project lifecycle. While the validation results affirm the feasibility of the process map, future studies may include applying the process map in other case studies to test its workability further.

Acknowledgement. The authors would like to thank Universiti Teknologi Malaysia (VOT number: 4C288) and IJM Construction Sdn. Bhd. For supporting this study.

References

1. Tam, V.W.Y., Tam, C.M., Zeng, S.X., Ng, W.C.Y.: Towards adoption of prefabrication in construction. Build. Environ. **42**(10), 3642–3654 (2007)
2. Jaillon, L., Poon, C.S., Chiang, Y.H.: Quantifying the waste reduction potential of using prefabrication in building construction in Hong Kong. Waste Manage. **29**, 309–320 (2009)
3. Tam, V.W.Y., Hao, J.J.L.: Prefabrication as a mean of minimizing construction waste on site. Int. J. Constr. Manag. **14**(2), 113–121 (2014)
4. Osman, N.A., Lee, N.C.C.: Evaluating the material waste reduction by using prefabrication in building construction in Kuala Lumpur. INTI J. Spec. Ed. Built Environ. **2016**, 1–6 (2016)
5. Eghbali, S.R., Azizzadeh, A.R., Mofrad, B.A.: Construction waste generation in the iranian building industry. Civil Eng. Infrastruct. J. **52**(1), 1–10 (2019)
6. Lu, W., Lee, W.M.W., Xue, F., Xu, J.: Revisiting the effects of prefabrication on construction waste minimization: aA quantitative study using bigger data. Resourc. Conserv. Recycl. **170**, 105579-1–10 (2021)
7. Smith, R.E.: Prefab Architecture A Guide to Modular Design and Construction. Wiley (2010)
8. Thanoon, W.A., Lee, W.P., Kadir, M.R.A., Jaafar, M.S., Salit, M.S.: The essential characteristics of industrialised building system. In: International Conference on Industrialised Building Systems, pp. 283–392. Kuala Lumpur, Malaysia (2003)
9. Din, M.I., Bahri, N., Dzulkifly, M.A., Norman, M.R., Kamar, K.A.M., Hamid, Z.A.: The adoption of Industrialised Building System (IBS) construction in Malaysia: the history, policies, experiences and lesson learned. Proc. Int. Symp. Autom. Robot. Construct. **29**, 1–8 (2012)
10. CIDB: Upskilling the Industry. CIDB Heights Industrialised Building System The Path to Enhanced Productivity. Construction Industry Development Board, Kuala Lumpur, Malaysia (2016)
11. CIDB: Construction Industry Transformation Programme 2016–2020. In: Malaysia CIDBC, editor. Kuala Lumpur, Malaysia: Construction Industry Development Board (CIDB) Malaysia (2015)
12. Zairul, M.: Opening the pandora's box of issues in the Industrialised Building System (IBS) in Malaysia: a thematic review. J. Appl. Sci. Eng. **25**(2), 297–310 (2021)
13. Mostafa, S., Kim, K.P., Tam, V.W.Y., Rahnamayiezekavat, P.: Exploring the status, benefits, barriers and opportunities of using BIM for advancing prefabrication practice. Int. J. Constr. Manag. **20**(2), 146–156 (2018)
14. Nawi, M.N.M., Lee, A., Nor, K.M.: Barriers to Implementation of the Industrialised Building System (IBS) in Malaysia. Built Hum. Environ. Rev. **4**, 22–35 (2011)
15. Zakaria, S.A.S., Gajendran, T., Rose, T., Brewer, G.: Contextual, structural and behavioural factors influencing the adoption of industrialised building systems: a review. Architect. Eng. Des. Manag. **14**(1–2), 3–26 (2017)
16. Liu, Y., Dong, J., Shen, L.: A conceptual development framework for prefabricated construction supply chain management: an integrated overview. Sustainability **12**(5), 1878 (2020)
17. Chen, Q., Hall, D.M., Adey, B.T., Haas, C.T.: Identifying enablers for coordination across construction supply chain processes: a systematic literature review. Eng. Construct. Architect. Manage. 1–31 (2020)
18. Chen, P.-H., Nguyen, T.C.: A BIM-WMS integrated decision support tool for supply chain management in construction. Autom. Constr. **98**, 289–301 (2019)
19. Magill, L.J., Jafarifar, N., Watson, A., Omotayo, T.: 4D BIM integrated construction supply chain logistics to optimise on-site production. Int. J. Construct. Manage. 1–10 (2020)

20. Fitriawijaya, A., Hsin-Hsuan, T., Taysheng, J.: A blockchain approach to supply chain management in a BIM-enabled environment. In: Haeusler, M., Schnabel, M.A., Fukuda, T. (eds.) Intelligent & Informed - Proceedings of the 24th CAADRIA Conference – vVol. 2. pp. 411–20. Victoria University of Wellington, Wellington, New Zealand (2019)
21. Xue, X., Wang, Y., Shen, Q., Yu, X.: Coordination mechanisms for construction supply chain management in the Internet environment. Int. J. Project Manage. 25(13), 150–157 (2007)
22. Arntzen, B.C., Brown, G.G., Harrison, T.P., Trafton, L.L.: Global supply chain management at digital equipment corporation. Interfaces 25(1), 69–93 (1995)
23. Vrijhoef, R., Koskela, L.: The four roles of supply chain management in construction. Eur. J. Purch. Supply Manage. 6(3–4), 169–178 (2000)
24. Mentzer, J.T., Keebler, J.S., Nix, N.W., Smith, C.D., Zacharia, Z.G.: Defining supply chain management. J. Bus. Logist. 22(2), 1–25 (2001)
25. Charehzehi, A., Chai, C., Yusof, A., Chong, H., Loo, S.C.: Building information modeling in construction conflict management. Int. J. Eng. Bus. Manage. 9, 1–18 (2017)
26. Nguyen, P.T., Nguyen, V.N., Pham, L.H., Nguyen, T.A., Nguyen, Q.L.H.T.T., Huynh, V.D.B.: Application of supply chain management in construction industry. Adv. Sci. Technol. Res. J. 12(2), 11–9 (2018)
27. Souza, D.V.S., Koskela, L.: On improvement in construction supply chain management. In: 20th Annual Conference of the International Group for Lean Construction, pp. 1–10. San Diego, California, USA (2012)
28. Behera, P., Mohanty, R.P., Prakash, A.: Understanding construction supply chain management. Product. Plan. Control 26(16), 1–19 (2015)
29. Hall, D.M., Algiers, A., Levitt, R.E.: Identifying the role of supply chain integration practices in the adoption of systemic innovations. J. Manag. Eng. 34(6), 1–14 (2018)
30. Le, P.L., Elmugharabi, W., Dao, T., Chaabane, A.: Present focuses and future directions of decision- making in construction supply chain management: a systematic review. Int. J. Construct. Manage. 1–19 (2018)
31. Vrijhoef, R.: Supply Chain Integration in the Building Industry. IOS Press, Netherlands (2011)
32. Sandanayake, Y.G., Dissanayake, T.B., Oduoza, C.: Construction supply chain resilience in catastrophic events. In: Oduoza, C.F. (ed.) Risk Management Treatise for Engineering Practitioners. IntechOpen, London, UK (2018)
33. Tandale, S.C., Sonavane, J.R., Ghorpade, K.H.: Survey for supplier selection in construction supply. CIKITUSI J. Multidiscipl. Res. 6(3), 19–24 (2019)
34. Luo, L., Jin, X., Shen, G.Q., Wang, Y., Liang, X., Li, X., et al.: Supply Chain management for prefabricated building projects in Hong Kong. J. Manage. Eng. 36(2) (2020)
35. Yadav, S., Ray, G.S.: Supply chain management in flyover projects in India. J. Construct. Develop. Countries 20(1), 25–47 (2015)
36. Wibowo, M.A., Sholeh, M.N.: The analysis of supply chain performance measurement at construction project. Procedia Eng. 125, 25–31 (2015)
37. Papadopoulos, G.A., Zamer, N., Gayialis, S.P., Tatsiopoulos, I.P.: Supply chain improvement in construction industry supply chain improvement in construction industry. Univ. J. Manage. (2016)
38. Zeng, W., Tse, M.Y.K., Tang, M.: Supply chain quality management: an investigation in the Chinese construction industry. Int. J. Eng. Bus. Manage.ment 10, 1–16 (2018)
39. Luo, L., Qiping Shen, G., Xu, G., Liu, Y., Wang, Y.: Stakeholder-associated supply chain risks and their interactions in a prefabricated building project in Hong Kong. J. Manage. Eng. 35(2) (2019)
40. Broft, R.D., Koskela, L.: Supply chain management in construction from a production theory perspective. In: 26th Annual Conference of the International Group for Lean Construction, pp. 271–281. Chennai, India (2018)

41. Amade, B., Akpan, E.O.P., Ubani, E.C., Amaeshi, U.F.: Supply chain management and construction project delivery: constraints to its application. PM World J. **5**(5) (2016)
42. Bankvall, L., Dubois, A., Bygballe, L.E., Fahre, M.: Interdependence in supply chains and projects in construction. Supply Chain Manage. Int. J. **15**(5), 385–393 (2010)
43. Riazi, S.R.M., Zainuddin, M.F., Nawi, M.N.M., Musa, S., Lee, A.: A critical review of fragmentation issues in the construction industry. J. Talent Develop. Excell. **12**(2), 1510–1521 (2020)
44. Hoeber, H., Alsem, D.: Life-cycle information management using open-standard BIM. Eng. Constr. Archit. Manag. **23**(6), 696–708 (2016)
45. Eastman, C., Teicholz, P., Sacks, R., Liston, K.: BIM Handbook A Guide to Building Information Modeling for Owners, Managers, Designers, Engineers, and Contractors, 3rd edn. Wiley, New Jersey, US (2018)
46. Succar, B., Sher W, Williams A. Measuring BIM Performance: Five Metrics Measuring BIM performance: Five metrics. Architectural Engineering and Design Management 8(June 2014), 120–42 (2012)
47. Xue, X., Shen, Q., Fan, H., Li, H., Fan, S.: IT supported collaborative work in A/E/C projects: a ten-year review. Autom. Constr. **21**, 1–9 (2012)
48. Briscoe, G., Dainty, A.: Construction supply chain integration: an elusive goal? Supply Chain Manage. Int. J. **10**(4), 319–326 (2005)
49. Arayici, Y., Coates, P., Koskela, L., Kagioglou, M., Usher, C., Reilly, K.O.: Technology adoption in the BIM implementation for lean architectural practice. Autom. Constr. **20**(2), 189–195 (2011)
50. Robson, A., Boyd, D., Thurairajah, N.: UK construction supply chain attitudes to BIM. In: 50th ASC Annual International Conference Proceedings, pp. 1–8. Virginia Tech, Washington D.C (2014)
51. BIS: Supply Chain Analysis into the Construction Industry - A Report for the Construction Industrial Strategy. Department for Business Innovation & Skills,London, UK (2013)
52. Meng, X., Sun, M., Jones, M.: Maturity model for supply chain relationships in construction. J. Manag. Eng. **27**(April), 97–105 (2011)
53. Poirier, E.A., Forgues, D., Staub-French, S.: Understanding the impact of BIM on collaboration: a Canadian case study. Build. Res. Inform. **45**(6), 681–695 (2017)
54. RIBA: RIBA Plan of Work 2020 Overview. RIBA, London, UK (2020)
55. Grilo, A., Jardim-Goncalves, R.: Value proposition on interoperability of BIM and collaborative working environments. Autom. Constr. **19**(5), 522–530 (2010)
56. Ekholm, A.: A conceptual framework for classification of construction works. J. Inform. Technol. Construct. **1**, 1–25 (1996)
57. Siebelink, S., Voordijk, H., Adriaanse, A.: Developing and testing a tool to evaluate BIM maturity: sectoral analysis in the dutch construction industry. J. Construct. Eng. Manage. **144**(8), 05018007 (2018)
58. OmniClass: http://beta.omniclass.org/. Accessed 29 Sept 2021
59. Afsari, K., Eastman, C.: A Comparison of construction classification systems used for classifying building product models. In: 52nd ASC Annual International Conference Proceedings, pp. 1–8. Provo, Utah, US (2016)
60. Zou, Y., Kiviniemi, A., Jones, S.W.: A review of risk management through BIM and BIM-related technologies. Safe. Sci. **97**(Special Issue), 88–98 (2017)
61. Luong, L.P., Amin, C., Thien-my, D.: BIM contributions to construction supply chain management trends: an exploratory study in Canada. Int. J. Construct. Manage. 1–19 (2019)

62. Peffers, K., Tuunanen, T., Rothenberger, M.A., Chatterjee, S.: A design science research methodology for information systems research. J. Manage. Inform. Syst. **24**(3), (2007)
63. Update OmniClass Taxonomy File. https://knowledge.autodesk.com/support/revit-products/troubleshooting/caas/CloudHelp/cloudhelp/2020/ENU/Revit-Troubleshooting/files/GUID-BA0B2713-ADA0-4E51-A7CD-85D85511F3ED-htm.html. Accessed 29 Sept 2021

A Simplified Guide on BIM Integration to Mitigate Facilities Management Risks of Modular Construction Projects

Sabah Khodabocus⬡ and Senem Seyis⁽⊠⁾ ⬡

Ozyegin University, Istanbul, Turkey
sabah.khodabocus@ozu.edu.tr, senem.seyis@ozyegin.edu.tr

Abstract. Building Information Modelling (BIM) has been upscaling throughout the years being highly interoperable. In modular construction, projects have limited scope for alterations at later stages because of exorbitant costs. It is preferable to start with an accurate and well-established platform that will automatically clear obstacles at later stages. As with any project, risks are to be encountered. In this study, Facilities Management (FM) risks are analyzed and BIM-linked approaches are brought together as a guide. The input was derived from a literature review and given the limited studies performed in this scope, interviews with six experts who also validated the outputs have boosted overall quality. Since the modular sector has not yet witnessed early FM integrations with BIM platforms, this investigation had as aim to pave the path for this subject. For modular construction projects to perform to their full efficacy, early involvements are the key. In the study, subcategories that involve maintenance of module and space management, energy analysis, quality and safety were deemed as major contributors to FM risks if not handled correctly. Being interconnected, cost, scheduling, and quality equally impact the project. For instance, without prior planning for accessing faulty facilities, the facility manager in charge would dedicate more time to figure out another path that could hinder designated quality standards. BIM integration acts as visual aid and database containing project attributes. This study forms simplified guides with suggestions on BIM platforms that modular construction projects can adopt for tackling FM risks while early integrating designers with facilities managers.

Keywords: Modular construction · Off-site construction · Facilities management · Building information modeling · Risk management

1 Introduction

The construction industry has experienced a major upgrade with a growing interest in modular construction. In the past, conventional construction methods have reigned over for the majority of the Architecture, Engineering and Construction (AEC) industry's timeline. Nowadays, traditional methods of construction do not meet the expectations of society while causing an increase in the construction period, loss of materials, low-quality outputs, and a rise in construction cost [1]. This has in turn diverted a lot of

O. Ö. Özener et al. (Eds.): EBF 2021, CCIS 1627, pp. 69–83, 2022.
https://doi.org/10.1007/978-3-031-16895-6_5

attention to more efficient methods such as off-site construction which is also called modular construction. If carried out properly, modular construction deems as a faster, more efficient, cheaper, and eco-friendly method that has the capabilities to tackle labor issues in the construction industry [2]. Moreover, modular projects ensure that the majority proportion of a project is achieved off-site before being transported to the site and completing the finishes.

However, the implementation of 'stick-built' methods in modular construction has resulted in the inability to witness the efficiency of this highly capable method of construction. Modular construction is deemed as a technique enabling fruitful outcomes in a short time span. Having the ability to replicate modules and with all organizational levels involved at a workstation, considerable time is saved. Being under a roof, most of the time, hinders various health and safety hazards, weather limitations, scheduling issues, and quality impacts. But as with any project, the probability of risk occurrence exists even though not severe. To maximize the correct implementation of this highly powerful construction technique, it is of utmost importance to have structured guidance for individuals in the industry at all organizational levels.

Building Information Modelling (BIM) has often been labeled as a platform enabling digital visualization of the physical and functional properties of a building [1]. In modular construction incorporated with BIM, the organization of activities like planning, design-analysis, development of drawings, fabrication schedules, and construction schedule is facilitated [3]. The choice of linking BIM in this study is justified by the platform's ability to accurately portray the location of components, for example, in a module along with the relevant documentation; based on the virtual BIM collaboration database, forming part of the digital twin model. Introducing facilities management (FM) early in the project will potentially reduce the efforts for maintenance during the operational phase of facilities while simultaneously mitigating risks. This area of study has few initiatives that were undertaken in the construction industry [4]. BIM being model-centric and having an object-driven core, its nature reduces the low-value production-related activities performed by the designer [3]. There is also a limited number of investigations that have applied BIM to deal with FM risks in modular construction projects [5]. Hence, the research objective of this study is to provide a guide regarding incorporating BIM to ease the integration of facilities management at the design stage of modular construction projects for tackling FM risks.

2   Research Methodology

This study has pursued a qualitative research structure which consists of a systematic literature review and semi-structured open-ended interviews. Figure 1 below demonstrates the stepwise process adopted in this study.

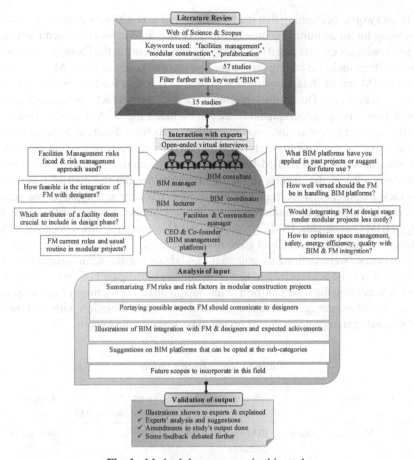

Fig. 1. Methodology process in this study

In performing the systematic literature review, criteria considered for the literature consisted of any year range, English language, journal articles and conference proceedings. The search for eligible literature was performed via Web of Science and Scopus. These platforms ensured grasping all recent and updated literature on the specified topic. Keywords such as "facilities management", "modular construction" and "prefabrication" were initially inserted. With the results attained from 57 articles, the search within this pool of studies was further narrowed down with the keyword "BIM". A specific list of 6 articles was directly linked to the scope of this investigation. Hence, conference proceedings were taken on board the literature review adding to the journal articles found. After thoroughly analyzing the abstracts, the studies were confirmed and added to the input source of this investigation. Mendeley was used to store and navigate through the literature.

It is also worth mentioning that the literature hunt was still very narrow, and this has led to opting for an additional source of input. Hence, interaction (i.e.; semi-structured interviews) with six experts aided to fill the gaps encountered in the literature review. The selection criteria included having more than 5 years of experience in the AEC sector with a focus on BIM and modular construction as well as at least a Bachelor's degree in engineering or architecture. Due to the ongoing pandemic, the interactions were all virtually executed, and experts' geographical locations included the USA, Canada, Turkey and Australia, and Saudi Arabia. Interviewing with experts from different countries ensures the collation of various insights that may aid in identifying particular issues on the facilities management risks in the BIM-based modular construction projects. The choice for adding those six specific experts in the input source driving the goal of this study is due to their qualifications, current role in the AEC industry and applaudable years of experience in the sector as demonstrated in Table 1 Interviewee's profile below. BIM Manager, BIM Consultants, BIM Coordinator, BIM Lecturer, Facilities management and Construction Manager, and a Chief Executive Officer for a BIM management platform, with experience, were defined as potential candidates for the semi-structured virtual interviews. It is to be acknowledged that all members of the panel of experts have come across implementing the BIM platform in the design phase for a smooth-running project. However, facilities managers were not included yet in collaboration with designers, in modular construction projects, based on the experience of the experts.

Table 1. Interviewee's profile

Expert no.	Qualifications	Job position	Years of experience in AEC	Country
E1	MSc Architecture	BIM consultant & Lecturer	6	Australia
E2	BSc Mechanical Engineering, MBA	BIM coordinator	18	Turkey
E3	MSc Civil Engineering	BIM consultant	10	Canada
E4	MSc Construction Management	BIM project manager	10	Turkey
E5	BSc Mechanical Engineering, MBA	Facilities & Construction manager	29	Saudi Arabia
E6	MSc Civil Engineering	CEO & Co-founder (BIM management platform)	22	USA

Further to the input received, simplified illustrations were formed for the sub-divisions which are maintenance of module & space management, energy efficiency, quality guarantee & safety in operation. These are further elaborated in Sects. 4.1–4.3. To ensure the quality of output, the illustrations were shared with the experts for validation. Upon this phase, critical reviews were received. Those were debated further in Sect. 4.4 and amendments in the study's outputs were undertaken as needed.

3 Facilities Management Risks and Risk Factors of Modular Projects

Every project comes with risks and risk management approaches help tackle the latter to mitigate unwanted consequences. While cost and schedule risks in BIM-based investigations have been attracting a lot of interest, facilities management risks were significantly overlooked [5]. Hence, this study has as an initiative to pave the path for dealing with the latter with a more efficient approach by including BIM platforms. Table 2 below shows the identified risks and the risk factors in modular construction projects based on virtual open-ended interviews with three experts.

Table 2. FM risk and risk factors based on experts' interactions

FM risk category	Risk factors
Space conflicts	Inaccessibility to heating, ventilating and air conditioning (HVAC) Lack of storage space for machinery
Cost overruns	Maintenance at the operational stage demands a lot of input if no prior consideration is given at the design stage
Schedule delay	Increased time required for the fixtures due to no set plan for the facility manager to reach the faulty facility or access the documents
Halted functionality	Efforts to find the previous record of maintenance, stopping the functionality of the facility until fixed
Quality impaired	Without a history of material initially used at the design stage, FM will look for reachable alternatives and, in some cases, not meet initial standards
Health and safety hazards	Occupants' health affected by improper facility setups No planned emergency evacuations

Given the fact that most modular construction projects are established to a large percentage within common compounds, individuals from every organizational level of the project find themselves at common workstations giving rise to undesirable inconveniences due to lack of planning. With an integrated use of knowledge management and BIM, failure root causes are detected which could help deal with FM risks at the starting phase itself [6]. At the same time, while having input from the FM team, the design team can allocate space as per the requirement for accessibility to components such as heating, ventilation, and air conditioning (HVAC). Similarly, space should be allocated for the storage and operation of machinery and emergency evacuations areas [4]. This early consideration shall diminish the investment that would be otherwise required in the future stages such as operational.

Cost overruns are a project's biggest obstacle. The factors which negatively impact cost, as identified in the investigation [2], include lack of data regarding components, history archives, inadequate consideration for fire hazards early on, and lack of organization in the documentation. This statement fits in line with the concept of this study regarding the early and well-established inclusion of the mentioned contents. Risks do pose cost overruns regardless of which category is being dealt with. With an analysis of risk factors, detailed insight is achieved to reach the root cause.

Space conflict risk is interconnected to the cost overrun and scheduling risks. Maintenance of components without prior set plans will require a guide at the operational stage for FM to be able to successfully handle the faulty element. Upon handling the issues, documents such as warranty, manuals, and maintenance records contribute to smoothing the path a facility manager sorts out. Unless a very well-arranged platform was early on established with all attributes, the functionality of the related component will be halted. It should also be acknowledged that with limited content about a facility, the maintenance procedure shall have a goal to resolve the issue in the least time possible. This in turn indicates that quality can be at risk. Without the know-how on which specifications were taken into consideration for meeting quality standards at the design phase, the facility manager is left with the most convenient choice to integrate the option deemed as the most feasible in that period.

As a faulty facility demands the attendance of a facility manager instantly, the common strategy of work lacks a pre-defined path for reachability. This leads to time dedication in figuring out the latter as well as halted functionality. With such a dilemma, the most preferable option for the facility manager is to find alternatives as per the availability. A crucial lacking here is the quality standard initially promised. As such, the cost involved, time spent, and quality impairs each demonstrates how they are interlinked.

Furthermore, the health and safety of occupants, which is a very delicate aspect, can be prone to drawbacks with improper facilities' setup [7]. Having individuals perform tasks whereby they have no expertise can lead to undesirable consequences. When it comes to the health and safety of all individuals and occupants in a project, a significant dedication to prioritize the latter is expected in the AEC industry. Integration of facility managers at the design phase, which is meant to create a solid foundation for the upcoming stages of a project, will ensure that there is little to no degree of ignorance regarding the health hazards. Perhaps, the use of interfaces to predict safety measures could attend to this risk outstandingly.

4   Achievements from Facilities Management Inclusion at the Design Stage of Modular Construction

Facilities managers have responsibilities to ensure the proper functioning of services and management of overall building performance. Modular constructed projects consist of a different overall flow as compared to conventional construction. During site development, modules are being constructed simultaneously and a team deals with inventory intakes with labor forces at each workstation. As compared to conventional construction, the site is developed, and the team then proceeds with the construction of the building [2]. Being very fragmented and dependent on each stage's completion to proceed, the conventional method of construction has a slot for tackling each risk. However, in the modular construction process, with the simultaneous ongoing of major processes, the risks that are encountered have a narrow gap for mitigation in the fast-paced approach. Figure 2 below shows the common flow of modular constructed projects alongside FM-related risks coming along each phase. With the integration of FM in the design stage, the identified risks can be largely hindered. This is indicated in Fig. 3 whereby the benefits which will be seen during the maintenance phase are shown. The concepts for achieving Fig. 2 and 3 were based on literature review and interviews with experts. It can be deduced that the integration depicted has noteworthy aspects when it comes to boosting overall quality while achieving the project in the promised timeline and within the budget.

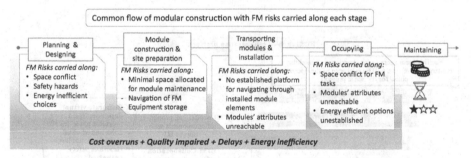

Fig. 2. The common flow of modular construction with FM risks faced

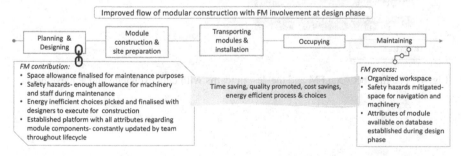

Fig. 3. The improved flow of modular construction with FM integration at the design stage

5   BIM Integration Process with FM and Design Team

BIM's linkage to the collaboration between designers and facility managers is mainly in the form of a visual platform and a collaborative database which will be of utmost usage throughout the lifecycle of the modular construction project. In this study, the thorough input gathering from literature reviews and interactions with experts in the industry has enabled derivations of concise illustrations on what content is to be communicated early on and how the BIM collaboration platform will handle the latter. Due to each project coming with its own specificities, accuracy in software to incorporate was not investigated to a large extent. Nevertheless, by familiarizing the team with the idea of this workflow and BIM inclusion, a shift in mindset shall automatically lead to more efficient task execution. The design team is responsible for analyzing the chosen FM personnel based on their contributions at design team meetings, education level, training taken, experiences and work ethics [8]. Furthermore, achievements of adopting such a workflow are also stated based on the findings in this study. To achieve the latter successfully, facilities managers with experience in past maintenance issues should collaborate in the development of a database alongside design professionals. The designers are in the best position to translate the operational insight into the optimized design considerations [9]. It is crucial for clients also to provide more incentives and clarity for the successful collaboration of FM and designers. A general idea of the expected connections and phases is portrayed in Fig. 4. This illustration was mounted upon analyzing the systematic literature review and semi-structured interviews in this study.

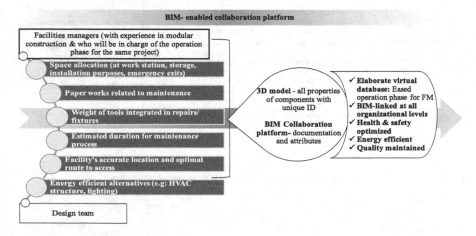

Fig. 4. The link between FM and the design teams with data exchange and achievements

5.1 Maintenance of Modules and Space Management

Having a 3D model of the building using Revit, which is often the default platform for modeling [10], FM maintaining the structure will have access to the properties of each component along with the exact location and reachability. Adding on to the latter, a specific route can be planned out to access the facility [11]. Often known as 'walk-through', it is possible for users to virtually navigate through the 3D model and select specific components to view its properties. On top of this, the safest and most efficient path to take in reaching the faulty element is also provided to the FM. By so doing, time otherwise spent to figure out access to the faulty facility and the hazards on the way are significantly reduced. Further, it will be of advantage to know beforehand what equipment or aid is needed to accommodate the maintenance process. For example, the location height of the latter is accurately available in the 3D model, hence the provision for accessibility can be made accordingly.

Once the core of the matter is tackled, documentation and paperwork come next. By having a fully prepared platform from the design stage with BIM–enabled collaboration (e.g., ShareBIM, Archibus, and CAFM), each facility will be allocated a unique ID or code which upon scanning leads to the availability of all documentation. This renders the planning stage for a facility manager smoother by being virtual and more estab-lished. Paper works include but are not limited to, warranty documents, user manuals, maintenance history reports, and vendors' details [4]. Once the facility is attended by a facility manager, the latter will also be responsible to insert the modifications details, date, and current performance in the BIM-enabled collaboration platform. Figure 5 below depicts the flow of BIM integration for handling the maintenance process more efficiently. This figure was derived based on the study's methodology which included open-ended interviews with experts and an analysis of the literature review. This process shown is expected to be repeated throughout the project's lifecycle which will hence lead to fewer redesigning issues and costs incurred.

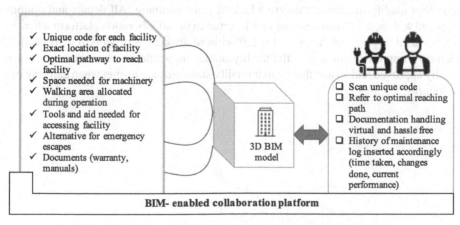

Fig. 5. The flow of BIM integration for maintenance efficacy

5.2 Energy Efficient Approach

The establishment of energy analysis pre-construction is deemed an expensive/unaffordable task and requires the validation of various energy-efficient alternatives. Thus, many projects are carried out without prior consideration of energy analysis [4]. With the usage of BIM, the collaboration platform and 3D model shall render the task more efficient and organized by providing relevant details hassle-free. An example of energy analysis software that can be used is Autodesk Revit or ArchiCAD. The latter is among the most popular software for BIM design and has the Industry Foundation Classes (IFC) certification of buildingSMART [12]. With the possibility of data loss, a federation environment, e.g., Solibri, can be used. Hereafter, the design team and FM shall create detailed energy-efficient alternatives including but not limited to HVAC, roofing, lighting, and internal and external walls, based on their previous experiences.

When it comes to making decisions concerning HVAC alternatives, efficient material choices and design structure, the early-on lifecycle cost analysis is of utmost importance for clarity to avoid any long-term effects [13]. Energy analysis software such as Autodesk Insight and EnergyPlus provides a wide array of options for external and internal walls meeting energy-efficient standards. Similarly, energy-efficient lighting options can be investigated by both parties and come to a final choice that fits the project's demands as well. The inclusion of FM having experience can act as a guide for deduction of cost analysis more accurately at the design stage. Moreover, a wide portion of the construction industry has gotten rid of the thought to deliver a facility at its lowest cost, instead, there is a greater urge to consider the cost over the whole life of the facility [8].

Once the energy analysis is performed, an energy consultant comes into play to validate the proposal so that the latter can be finalized for construction [4]. This step is crucial to guarantee that the tested alternatives are suitable for the project's criteria and shall not pose upcoming hurdles with huge cost overruns. The process of performing an energy analysis with validation at the design phase is shown in Fig. 6 below; derived from this study's methodology process. The latter can simultaneously aid in eradicating the risk of quality impairment due to a lack of prior planning. All details and options discussed with both FM and designers are inserted in the collaboration platform whereby no individual or phase of the project is left without awareness of workflow. If needed, when reverting for maintenance, the facility managers would know exactly the choice initially approved and ensure that similar quality standards are re-met when carrying out the fixtures.

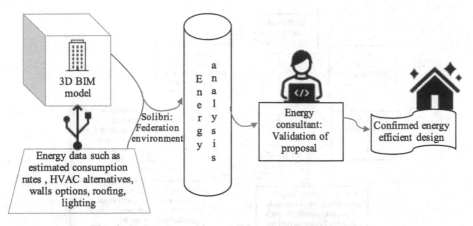

Fig. 6. Pathway to achieve validated energy-efficient design

5.3 Quality Guarantee and Safety in Operation

The use of BIM in the early stages of a modular construction project eliminates conflicts occurrence while acting as a clear visual guide for FM. BIM and FM integration has resulted in a centralized system where it is easier to access and maintain all components in a building [11]. The cost that would otherwise be needed to individually attend to the components can be avoided in this case. As mentioned earlier, BIM platforms are visual aids to FM with colored components and simplistic representations which ease spotting faulty elements. FM need not go through intensive training for understanding the models. This boosts the confidence of the FM team to adopt the platform and be sure of the workflow along with what to input at which stage. Any changes deemed necessary by FM shall be instantly effective on the BIM model and the concerned elements which saves a considerable amount of time as opposed to editing each element one by one. With automated possibilities, human errors are eradicated, and consistency develops in the quality standards.

The safety aspect of a project is a fundamental consideration that is directly linked to the performance of the structure and the well-being of occupants at later stages. With faulty installations or choices, the occupancy stage can face major setbacks. These can directly impact occupants and lead to a chaotic project which shall demand more financial input and lead to halted functionality. While having a project fully entrusted to BIM platforms, as an example, fire evacuation plans can be simulated in the 3D models early on. Once parameters such as time and route for exiting the building are retrieved, FM and designers can come to a consensus on where to place smoke or fire detectors. Similarly, assembly points and the optimized path for reachability are pre-decided meticulously. Since this process is based on the technical platform and not individuals' previous experiences, the accuracy of results is of higher reliability [11]. Figure 7 below demonstrates the linked scopes with the BIM 3D model and relevant outputs which optimizes quality; as concluded from experts' interactions and the literature review forming part of the methodology process.

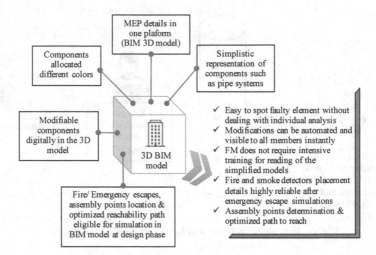

Fig. 7. Scopes directly linked to 3D model for quality and safety assurance

5.4 Analysis of Validations from Experts

The outputs of this study were shown to the panel of 6 experts (i.e., BIM Manager, BIM Consultant, BIM Coordinator, BIM Lecturer, Facilities management and Construction Manager, and a Chief Executive Officer for a BIM management platform) for validation. Table 3 below depicts comments from experts about the main subject targeted with an in-depth focus on some elements, along with the action taken in this investigation accordingly. As expected, experts have fully agreed on the integration of FM with the design team to mitigate possible FM risks. It was suggested that the client could provide better incentives for this successful integration. The statement of FM having no BIM knowledge has not been evaluated fully. The target of such integration should be tackling this issue to some extent, upon adoption by project team members. All suggested platforms were investigated and added accordingly to the simplified figures in the output for each sub-section. As for highway rules, the scope of this study dealt with indoor spaces management and maintenance, hence this point did not lead to alterations in the output. For energy analysis, it was pointed out by an expert that BIM models would not support live energy analysis. With due respect to the statement, this study suggests that EnergyPlus and Autodesk Insight could be used with the BIM model to achieve energy analysis. Another point that was debated is the fact that changes such as displacement of objects in the space would not be updated in the BIM model. The minute details are believed to not cause significant obstacles to the optimized path for reaching a facility.

Table 3. Comments during validation step from experts regarding output of study

Validation of study's outputs			
Main subject	**In-depth focus topics**	**Experts' comments**	**Action taken**
FM & designers' collaboration	Feasibility	Yes, should be integrated into the work culture	✓
	How to successfully achieve this collaboration	Greater incentive from client	📄
		FM operators have no BIM knowledge	⚠
	FM roles add-on	Integrate CAFM with BIM	📄
		Archibus for workplace management	📄
Maintenance and space management	Same FM team to be at Operational phase later	Highly recommended	✓
	Optimized path/ walkthrough to reach a facility	If includes an optimized path outside the structure, consider highway rules for modular projects	⚠
	FM add-on responsibility to update BIM platforms after maintenance	New responsibility should be reminded to FM during the briefing	📄
Energy efficiency		Industrially not aware of what equipment to be used in the actual project	✓
	Energy analysis & approval by energy consultant	Very essential to have prior energy analysis	✓
		BIM models would not support live energy analysis	⚠
		Energy data and analysis is not a commonly briefed requirement for designers and contractors	⚠
	ArchiCAD & Revit usage	Major data loss, includes a federation environment, e.g: Solibri	📄
Safety	Emergency escape Simulation to optimize placement of fire & smoke detectors	Assembly points determination to be considered too	📄
Quality		Should be added to FM responsibility and briefed early on	✓
	FM inserting data regularly after tasks	Post design handover concern: Orientation changes (e.g: relocation of a chair in another room) won't be updated on BIM model	⚠

 Validation received Amendments to output done Reconsideration/ being debated

6 Conclusion

The facilities aspects of a project are usually not thought of until the operational phase is reached. This is the reason why abundant projects witness hurdles at the later stages and the financial demands to tackle those issues are unbearable on many occasions. In this study, sub-categories that fall under the Facilities Management of buildings are each analyzed. These sub-topics: maintenance of modules & space management, energy efficiency, quality, and safety, each involves FM risks which are also taken into consideration for tackling. The integration of BIM is portrayed with the FM and design team along with suggestions on which BIM platforms deem suitable for usage. BIM-linked approaches that could help in mitigating the risks according to which sub-topic they fall into, were discussed in Sect. 4 of this paper. From a wider point of view, having FM work with the design team and contribute to sharing content based on experience could diminish those risks. This is deemed as crucially important since modular construction projects' modifications at later stages would be unaffordable and not as flexible.

Space management, quality guarantee, energy-efficient measures, and safety considerations are major sub-topics requiring attention early on. This investigation has shown how BIM collaboration platforms and an energy analysis software guide can maintain the quality of workflow consistently. In turn, the lifecycle of the structure is well-established and minimal chances for future alterations exist. With the high collaboration possibilities when a project starts from scratch with BIM, each organizational level is well versed in overall processes. Additionally, the built-in intelligence of BIM authoring tools decreases any design discrepancies [3]. The main take from this investigation would highly emphasize modular projects to integrate their FM efficiently with BIM platforms, at the design stage, and ensure that the same team will be responsible during the operational stages.

The contributions of this study consist of illustration guides for each sub-category analyzed (i.e., maintenance of modules & space management, energy efficiency, quality, and safety) to visually create a flow of the process for key decision-makers. Being still a new subject in the modular construction sector, this investigation is believed to simplify the approach to tackling FM risks by early involvement of facility managers with the designers, with BIM integration. Moreover, with qualitative results, understandability levels of mostly all organizational bodies in the project shall be high. Based on the experience of experts and academic content, the outputs have grasped both the industry and academic perspectives, making for reliability in the content. The unique value is indicated by the study's goals of tackling FM risk in modular construction with early involvement and BIM integration for a solid foundation throughout the lifecycle. Furthermore, focus on the four subcategories which have major impacts on overall project success were investigated separately.

In future studies, specific guides could be established with accurately defined software within the BIM family and the inclusion of the whole lifecycle risks will be a beneficial contribution to the industry. In the hunt for BIM-linked measures, options such as laser scanning, Radio Frequency Identification (RFID), Augmented Reality (AR), and Virtual Reality (VR) amidst others have applaudable potential. Case studies that include the usage of those guides would then be reliable sources of validation. Clear evidence is also retrievable regarding cost analysis and how early FM integration via BIM platforms opts in favor of cost control. As every project consists of varied criteria, the best-fit integrations need to be discussed and consensus should be reached with all organizational levels. To further support this, decision-making platforms produced based on systematic and credible methodologies would be highly useful.

References

1. Borjeghaleh, R.M., Sardroud, J.M.: Approaching industrialization of buildings and integrated construction using building information modeling. Procedia Eng. **164**, 534–541 (2016)
2. Lee, J.-S., Kim, Y.-S.: Analysis of cost-increasing risk factors in modular construction in Korea using FMEA. KSCE J. Civ. Eng. **21**(6), 1999–2010 (2017). https://doi.org/10.1007/s12205-016-0194-1
3. Singh, M.M., Sawhney, A., Borrmann, A.: Modular coordination and bim: development of rule-based smart building components. Procedia Engineering, Elsevier B.V., vol. 123, pp. 519–527 (2015)
4. Wang, Y., et al.: Engagement of facilities management in design stage through BIM: framework and a case study. Adv. Civil Eng. **2013**, 30836 (2013)
5. Darko, A., et al.: Building information modeling (BIM)-based modular integrated construction risk management – critical survey and future needs. Comput. Indust. **123** (2020)
6. Motamedi, A., Hammad, A., Asen, Y.: Knowledge-assisted BIM-based visual analytics for failure root cause detection in facilities management. Automation in Construction. Elsevier B.V., vol. 43, pp. 73–83 (2014)
7. Ali, A.S., et al.: The effect of design on maintenance for school buildings in Penang Malaysia. Struct. Surv. **31**(3), 194–201 (2013)
8. Enoma, A.: The role of facilities management at the design stage. Association of Researchers in Construction Management. In: Proceedings of the 21st Annual Conference, pp. 421–430. ARCOM, United Kingdom (2005)
9. Fatayer, F.A., et al.: Investigation of facilities management practices for providing feedback during the design development and review stages. Int. J. Build. Pathol. Adapt. **37**(5), 597–614 (2019)
10. Kensek, K.: BIM guidelines inform facilities management databases: a case study over time. Buildings **5**(3), 899–916 (2015)
11. Chong, H.Y., et al.: Improving quality and performance of facility management using building information modeling. In: Luo, Y. (eds.) Cooperative Design, Visualization, and Engineering. CDVE 2014. LNISA, vol. 8683, pp. 36–43 . Springer, Cham (2014). https://doi.org/10.1007/978-3-319-10831-5_6
12. Bonomolo, M., Di Lisi, S., Leone: Building information modeling and energy simulation for architecture design. Appl. Sci. (Switzerland) **11**(5), 1–32 G (2021)
13. Paya-Marin, M.A., Lim, J., Sengupta, B.: Life-cycle energy analysis of a modular/off-site building school. Am. J. Civil Eng. Archit. **1**(3), 59–63 (2013)

A Proposal of a BIM and AR Integrated Application Against Fall Risks in Construction Projects

Merve Aksu$^{(\boxtimes)}$ ⓘ and Salih Ofluoğlu ⓘ

Mimar Sinan Fine Arts University, 34380 Istanbul, Turkey
mervveaksu@gmail.com, salih.ofluoglu@msgsu.edu.tr

Abstract. The construction sector carries many risk factors in terms of occupational safety. Many studies reveal that the use of Information and Communication Technologies (ICT) is effective in reducing losses in the construction sector. Lately, BIM (Building Information Modeling) has been deployed as one of the working methodologies to tackle and automate safety measures in the construction industry. Apart from other methodologies, safety information and risk factors are often identified during the project design phases in BIM. Fostered with Augmented Reality (AR) and Virtual Reality (VR) technologies, BIM can also efficiently visualize such risks to prevent them. This study proposes a mobile application called AG-IGU that incorporates a BIM-supported AR environment against the risk of falling, which is the most common accident in construction projects.

Keywords: Building Information Modeling (BIM) · Occupational safety · Fall risk · Augmented Reality (AR) · Mobile applications

1 Introduction

Occupational safety is one of the risk factors in construction that causes time and cost losses. The use of Information and Communication Technologies (ICT) is considered effective in reducing losses in the construction sector and in other sectors [1], but it is often inadequately used in the construction sector [2].

Building Information Modeling (BIM) has been recently considered one of the encouraging technologies and working methodologies for tackling occupational safety issues [3]. BIM is increasingly used in the construction industry and provides a common platform for all project disciplines incorporating design, construction and management processes. The BIM working method also supports the principle of Lean Construction, which is a method of planning and controlling a project to improve its performance, from design to construction. Both BIM and lean construction have basic principles of minimizing cost, increasing efficiency and maximizing value creation [4, 5].

BIM-enabled occupational safety is often described as 8D BIM in which risk factors are included in a BIM model as an additional dimension. BIM incorporates a framework that detects risk factors at the design stages of a project and prevents the time and cost

O. Ö. Özener et al. (Eds.): EBF 2021, CCIS 1627, pp. 84–97, 2022.
https://doi.org/10.1007/978-3-031-16895-6_6

losses that can take place. This is different from other methods that deal with occupational safety. Unlike BIM they tend to address occupational risks outside the project design process causing unavoidable human and capital losses [2].

BIM is commonly used in conjunction with visualization technologies to address occupational safety problems in projects. As such, mixed reality technologies are utilized in AEC fields for some time, and they have become gradually matured to be deployed in the visualization of BIM models. Among these, Augmented Reality (AR) technologies have recently begun to be effectively used in the field of occupational [6].

This study proposes a mobile environment that incorporates a BIM-supported Augmented Reality framework to prevent the risk of falling which is the most common type of accident in construction projects. The AR technology, in particular, allows the interaction of BIM models in a physical environment and in real-time. It has considerable potential for identifying risky scenarios in construction projects.

2 Occupational Safety in the Construction Sector

Occupational safety is to raise the physical, mental and social conditions of employees in all professions to the highest level, to maintain them in this way, to protect them from diseases that may be caused by working conditions, to place them in the most appropriate occupational environments and to prevent the dangers caused by factors that are against health during work. Occupational accidents pose a risk to human health, loss of workforce that may occur as a result of death or injuries, and can cause psychological and financial difficulties for both the employee and the employer [7].

The "Occupational Health and Safety" (OHS) is seen as a necessity supported by certain standards and various regulations. Standards and regulations on occupational safety are based on similar principles, and countries have adopted these regulations in their own management forms over time. In the United States, the "Occupational Health and Safety Department" (OSHA), the "National Institute of Occupational Health and Safety" (NIOSH) under the Ministry of Health and Education carry out activities in this field. In the UK, the Occupational Health and Safety Commission (HSC), General Directorate of Occupational Health and Safety (HSE) and British Standards Institute (BSI) operate related to Occupational Safety. The standardization system published by BSI and called OHSAS 18001 is an international OHS (Occupational Health and Safety) management system certification. In Turkey, the Ministry of Labor and Social Security implements the "Occupational Health and Safety Directorate". The OHSAS 18001 certificate is translated into Turkish and used as the TS 18001 standard.

The construction industry is one of the leading sectors in terms of occupational accident rates. Risk factors in the construction industry cause the project to take longer than planned and exceed the calculated cost. The report from HSE (Health & Safety Executive) showed that the construction industry causes more fatal injuries and cost losses each year than any other industry due to the lack of safety in the construction industry [8, 9].

Many factors such as incorrect use of the equipment, insufficient use of technology, environmental conditions, psychological, social and physical reasons can cause work accidents [10]. Figure 1 shows the occupational accidents in the construction sector in

Turkey. As seen, accidents caused by falls from a height are the most common occupational accidents in Turkey. This accident type is also the highest encountered one in the world [11]. Table 1 illustrates the subgroups of fall risk in the world. Among the areas at risk of falling, it appears that the rate of falling from floor and platform edges, scaffolding, building gaps and roofs is the highest [12].

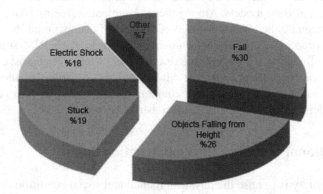

Fig. 1. Distribution of common work accident types in Turkey [11].

Table 1. The distribution of the fall accident type subgroups [12].

No.	Human Fall - Subgroups	Death		Injury		Total	
	Accident Type	Number	%	Number	%	Number	%
1	Flooring - From Platform Edge	248	35,7	190	24,1	438	29,6
2	Scaffolding	139	20,0	236	30,0	375	25,3
3	Building Spaces	99	14,3	71	9,0	170	11,5
4	Roofs	76	11,0	71	9,0	147	9,9
5	Level Falls	11	1,6	61	7,8	72	4,9
6	Hand Ladder	21	3,0	40	5,1	61	4,1
7	Electric - Telephone Poles	19	2,7	38	4,8	57	3,8
8	Fixed Construction Ladders	14	2,0	22	2,8	36	2,4
9	Freight Elevators	11	1,6	4	0,5	15	1,0
10	Holes and Pits in the Ground	9	1,3	6	0,8	15	1,0
11	Other Fall Types	47	6,8	48	6,1	95	6,4
	Total	694	100,0	787	100,0	1481	100,0

3   Existing Studies for Occupational Safety in the Construction Sector

There are a number of studies addressing occupational safety in construction projects [13–15]. These studies often focus on risk analysis and security planning and measures.

Studies focusing on safety planning generally consist of integrating occupational safety training into the work program. When the existing security measures are examined, personal protective equipment (PPE) comes as the most advanced measure. In addition to these, other technologies used for occupational safety; 3D/4D computer-aided design, laser scanning, QR code, RFID, robotics and automation, UAVs (Unmanned Aerial Vehicles), WSDs (Wearable Sensing Devices), sensors and alarm systems are the most commonly used technologies for on-site production and control [6].

The limited adoption of technology is seen as one of the potential risks that cause low safety performance in the construction industry [16]. Most recent studies investigate and propose technology-based solutions for identifying and taking measures against risks. As such, the use of Building Information Modeling (BIM) for occupational safety studies is a popular research topic lately [17–19].

Building Information Modeling (BIM) and related technologies have been utilized in AEC practice since the early 2000s. A Building Information Model is a three-dimensional model consisting of graphic (geometry/shape, etc.) and alphanumeric (material, cost, physical environment control, etc.) data related to the building, ensuring the common use of this model by project stakeholders. This three-dimensional model can be used in processes that include the entire life cycle of the project such as planning, design, project design, construction and operation [20]. The information in a building information model can be used in different project contexts such as design/construction documents (2D), multidisciplinary coordination (3D), scheduling (4D), cost estimation (5D), sustainability and engineering analysis (6D) and facilities management (7D). The 8D BIM is a relatively new use of BIM for occupational health and safety, and it is still evolving. For instance, the work safety regulations in ISO19650, which is a series of international standards that define the collaborative processes for the effective management of information, are planned to be integrated with BIM applications.

One noteworthy feature of BIM is that helps identify and design health and safety risks early in the project. It is possible to do Prevention Through Design (PtD) with BIM to profile the hazard, provide safe design recommendations and control field risk [21]. BIM and Design For Safety (DfS) are relatively new studies taking place today. DfS refers to the determination of security zones that may pose risks for the project and taking necessary security measures during the project design phase. The BIM working method ensures that the project is located on a single platform from the concept stage to the construction stage and most of the health and safety information can be created directly in this environment [3].

Some of the studies that use BIM for Occupational Safety are explained here. Zhang et al. proposed a control system that includes occupational safety criteria in the project process by creating a business plan structure integrated with BIM to reduce the possibility of occupational accidents. The system checks the model automatically, finds the gaps and slab edges in the wall, covers the slab edges and wall gaps with railing and visualizes the measures in the 4D time plan [22]. Hongling et al. investigated a system to automatically identify unsafe design areas in construction. This study proposed a code system for security measures to match BIM components [23]. Tekbas and Guven also conducted a study intended to prevent fall hazards in construction projects automatically. The "Automatic Fall Safety Control" (AFSR) tool developed in the study analyzes the 3D model and identifies the risky areas in the building. In this study, the as-built model is compared with any model in the construction phase of the project, and spaces that are not surrounded by walls are perceived as risk zones [24].

There are also studies exploring the use of mixed reality technologies such as Virtual Reality (VR) and Augmented Reality (AR) in the context of occupational safety in construction. Mixed Reality software offers an immersive realistic working environment for BIM content.

The AR technology, in particular, has the interesting notion of displaying virtual in a real environment and opens up new possibilities for the construction sector. It enables the user to interact with up-to-date project information through 3D models in a real context (the construction site) to cope and correct the problems before they physically exist in the real-time visualization of a project [25, 26]. There are various studies that investigate the use of AR for presentation, visualization and educational purposes in architecture for field inspections and occupational safety in the construction industry and facilities management [26–30].

AR technologies have also been gaining importance in the field of occupational safety. It can be used to simulate risky situations that may occur in the project area and to increase the awareness of employees. AR creates a unique learning opportunity for the inexperienced and construction-interested individuals by providing the opportunity to find and correct the flaws of a project in a safe and risk-free environment [31].

Most studies examining the integration of occupational safety and AR are theoretical without much practical implementation. The practical uses are generally for operational intent such as the use of personal protective equipment, tower crane and operator training. For example, one study offers a working framework for construction safety education, which includes mobile-based AR and VR experiences. This study consists of three stages: the dissemination of safety information, the identification of the dangers and the implementation of the necessary measures [32]. Another study introduced the Pro-Vis AR mobile application offering occupational safety training such as crane safety [33]. In a different study, heavy construction equipment management and operator training were introduced. A virtual construction site environment with materials and instructions was created and operator training was provided in an augmented reality environment [34].

4   The Proposal of the AG-IGU Application for the Fall Risk in Construction Projects

One of the shortcomings of existing methods of dealing with occupational safety in construction is that they concentrate on the construction phase outside the project processes. As a result, occupational safety consists of written rules and safety information communicated to employees during the construction phase, and this approach when implemented alone often increases safety risks. During the project phase, the written safety information of the project should be converted into a computer-readable format and the project team should be involved in this process. It is beneficial to visualize or simulate the safety measures organized in the computer environment in 3D. In this process, the safety information added to the BIM working model becomes permanent and can be reproduced. Visualization technologies such as AR and VR increase perceptibility before the project construction phase.

The proposed study aims to handle the occupational safety risks in the early stages of the project and to reduce the safety problems that may occur in the field. For this purpose, it proposes a mobile application called AG-IGU. AG-IGU is the aconym for Augmented Reality Construction Safety Application in Turkish (Arttırılmış Gerçeklik İnşaat Güvenlik Uygulaması). It integrates BIM-AR technologies to visualize the construction risks and help with measures to be taken. The application has been prepared for the risks of falling, which is one of the most common occupational safety problems. The mobile application facilitates access to project information. It can be utilized by all the project stakeholders everywhere. It is supported by Augmented Reality to visualize project data in real construction contexts. This approach is intended to increase the retention mind rate of the information by offering an effective user experience.

In this study, a Building Information Model is used to determine the regions at risk of falling. The necessary safety measures for the risk areas are determined by a designated project member or different project stakeholders. A library of 3D BIM objects of safety measures is modeled and stored in a common platform to be accessed in future projects. The process can be added to a BIM implementation plan to ensure its implementation. In addition to BIM software, the Unity development platform by Unity Technologies is used for the simulation of BIM project models and objects having safety measures. In the mobile application interface, occupational safety measures can be placed on the 3D model interactively by project stakeholders using pre-modeled library elements.

The AG-IGU application uses a simple, rectangular, five-story building shell below to illustrate the working concept, but it can accommodate different types, multi-storey and large-scale projects. However, in large projects, when the number of shafts, stairs and elevators increases in large-scale projects, manually adding safety measures can cause a considerable amount of time. The mobile application will allow practical placement of the safety measures to be selected from the application interface on the shaft, staircase and facade openings in the BIM model.

4.1 The AG-IGU Software Architecture

The AG-IGU application involves different modeling, development and AR software platforms. Figure 2 shows the steps and applications deployed in the development process of the Augmented Reality project and a mobile application. Some additional steps added within the scope of the study are modeling and controlling safety measures in a 3D architectural model, creating written rules informing the user about these measures and developing the user interface design with objects for safety measures.

Step 1: Modeling and Editing Models: The 3D project information and the measures to be taken against the risk of falling are modeled in BIM. A predefined ready-made project in the application is also made available for use. In the prototype, the safety measures of an existing project are modeled and checked. Autodesk Revit is used as a BIM modeling environment due to its widespread use in the building sector and support with mixed reality applications. The model is exported into FBX format and opened in 3DS Max software; the model check is made with a few simple commands and saved

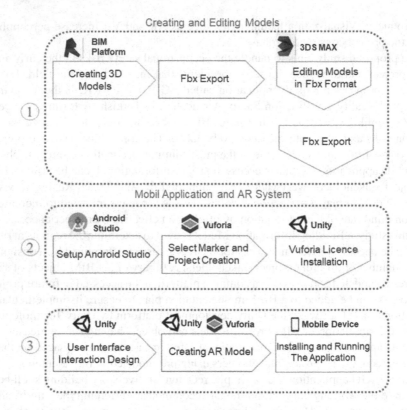

Fig. 2. The AG-IGU software architecture schema

as an FBX file again. When planning the Augmented Reality application of a project, it is sufficient to have only the necessary information in the model. All other unused information causes the application to slow down. For this reason, BIM metadata such as sheets, cost and quantity lists, levels, templates, etc. are eliminated by exporting the project into FBX format. The data referred to as metadata belong to a BIM project. 3DS Max is utilized to edit the model for the Unity game engine and to solve the problems that may occur with the model in Unity. In 3DS Max, operations such as surface normals of the model, material controls and checking the gaps in the model are performed.

Step 2: Importing AR Model: The license key is obtained by creating the project title on the web page of the Vuforia application developer and the pointer is selected from the database. After the project is saved in FBX, it is opened in Unity; the license key from Vuforia is added to Unity. Vuforia is a software development tool for mobile devices that enables the creation of Augmented Reality applications and provides Application Programming Interfaces (APIs) through the Unity game engine that offers an immersive real-time 3D experience. Android Studio is also included in the system architecture to allow printing a mobile application with the Vuforia plug-in from the Unity program,

Step 3: Developing the Mobile Application: After matching the model and the pointer in Unity, the user interface design is developed. In addition, necessary codes are added for the placement of safety measures in risk zones, written safety rules and buttons for switching them on and off. The platforms used for Unity generally support the C # programming language which is Unity's integrated programming language. While developing the mobile application, the C # is used to add the interface features. When the application is completed, the project file belonging to the Android operating system of the mobile application is received in Unity and opened on mobile devices.

4.2 The Working Methodology of AG-IGU

The AG-IGU application can be operated on a computer using a viewing software such as Unity Hub or launching it on an Android device by downloading its application. When the Android software is downloaded and run on mobile devices, a screen appears that allows the user to make a selection of the pointer first. An object in the real environment can be selected as a pointer without using any QR code for practical use. In this case, the user must define a pointer by selecting an image from the mobile device's database or taking a photo of an object in the current environment.

After selecting the pointer, the user must select the BIM model to be mapped with the pointer via the model selection button on the application interface. The models to be used in the application must be available in FBX format on a mobile device or the Web. Upon the model selection, the model matched with the pointer is displayed on the mobile device in the real environment.

The purpose of the mobile application is to show the precautions to be taken against the risk of falling in the AR environment and to model the elements of these precautions interactively. In a completed architectural project, railings belonging to MEP (Mechanical Electrical Plumbing) related shafts, facade gaps and stairwells are built. However, the risk of falling in these areas continues during the construction phases. When dealing with these risks the structural modeling phase was considered more appropriate as it virtually reflects the construction period accurately. Therefore, the model chosen for the application does not contain architectural elements that could block risky areas.

In order to avoid display problems in the AR environment, the BIM model to be used in the mobile application must be Watertight (waterproof) and Manifold. Manifold geometry is geometry that can unfold into a 2D surface with all face normals facing the same direction. In the manifold model, all surfaces of each object in the model must be closed, that is, it must be a Watertight object. The steps below are for control purposes and are the steps that facilitate the operation of the mobile application (Fig. 3).

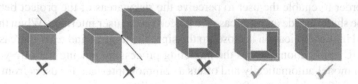

Fig. 3. Manifold geometry schemas [35].

Figure 4 shows the safety elements for the risk of falling modeled in Revit. They consist of covers for shafts, safety nets used for facade openings, and guardrails used for staircases. After the pointer and the selected model are matched in the AG-IGU mobile application, safety elements are automatically modeled through the buttons on the user interface and written safety measures are displayed on the user's screen. Upon selecting a safety element, the written rules of that safety measure are displayed on the user's screen for a set period, and then 3D safety elements are modeled according to the standard in the written rule. Both the written safety rules and 3D elements help the user understand safety issues in text and visuals.

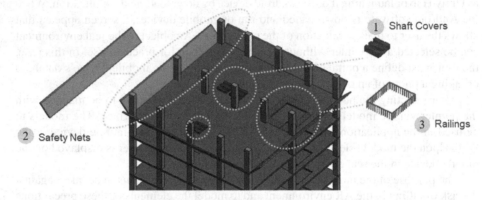

Fig. 4. Safety measures on the revit model

There are two other inputs for user interaction in the mobile application. The first one is the model selection button that enables the creation of an AR medium for more than one project in the application. The second one is the button that provides the transparency setting for the columns. The reason for the reduction of the opacity of the columns is to facilitate the visualization of risky areas corresponding to the column alignment and to increase their visibility.

Figure 5 shows the application's user interface, and Fig. 6 shows the steps followed in the mobile application. The user can record the last state of the model by taking a screenshot from the screen incorporating written safety rules and a 3D model.

The mobile application allows the selection of more than one BIM model in the database. The same safety measures are used for each project at this stage of implementation. In order to enable the user to perceive the risky areas of the project better, signs showing the shaft, facade and staircase are placed on the user interface. When the mobile device used in the application is closer to the sign, the models and texts increase in size. The AG-IGU application reduces the modeling process by placing the safety elements on the BIM model automatically and offers a common interface for users from different disciplines. Within the scope of the study, the application was developed based on fall risk, the most common type of risk, but the application can also be geared toward other types of occupational accidents.

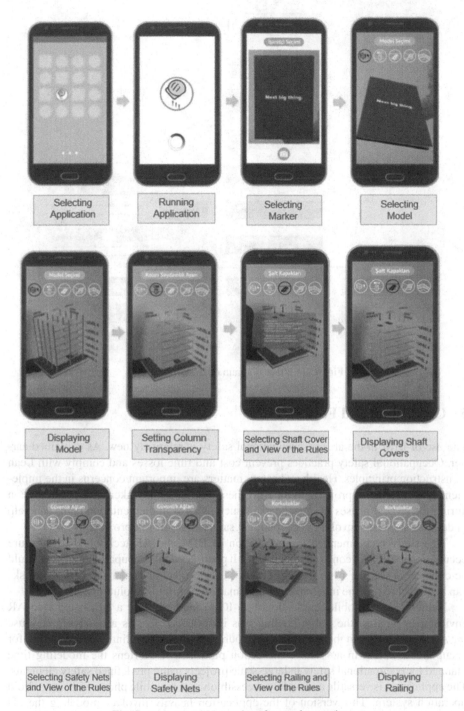

Fig. 5. The AG-IGU user interface and operations

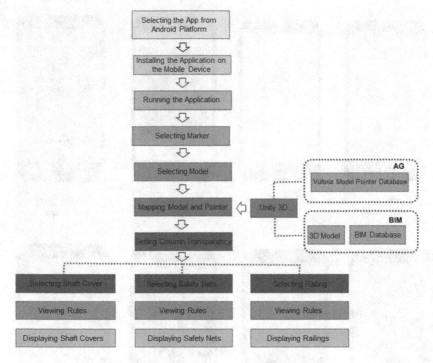

Fig. 6. Interface diagram of the application.

5 Conclusion and Future Scope

The use of BIM in the area of occupational safety is relatively new. As explained earlier. Occupational safety practices prevent cost and time losses and comply with Lean Construction principles. Health and safety matters are important concerns in the implementation of BIM in projects. With BIM these issues can be taken into consideration during the project phases and mechanisms such as BIM implementation plans can help to delegate the tasks involving occupational safety measures in projects.

This study recommended the integration of BIM and AR technologies to ensure occupational safety in construction projects. It postulated that occupational safety should be considered starting from the early phases of a project and many construction risks can be prevented by the integration of information technology solutions.

In the study, a mobile application (AG-IGU) incorporating a BIM-supported AR environment against the risk of falling was introduced. This is a relatively new use for AR technologies in the AEC fields, encouraging multidisciplinary collaboration for occupational safety in a visual construction platform. It shortens the modeling time planned for occupational safety in large-scale projects using predefined safety elements. The application is versatile and widely accessible via any mobile phone with an Android operation system. This version of the application heavily involves modeling the 3D safety elements for all possible scenarios and cases. For future versions, such elements are planned to make available as downloadable objects updated according to regulations.

References

1. Dehlin, S., Olofsson, T.: An evaluation model for ICT investments in construction projects. Electron. J. Inform. Technol. Construct. **13**(May), 343–361 (2008)
2. Karakhan, A., Alsaffar, O.: In safety management technology's role. Profession. Safe. J. **64**, 2017–2020 (2019)
3. Ganah, A.A., John, G.: Integrating building information modeling and health and safety for onsite construction. Saf. Health Work **6**(1), 39–45 (2015)
4. Yongge, X., Cheng, Q.: Lean cost analysis based on BIM modelling for construction project. Appl. Mech. Mater. **457–458**, 1444–1447 (2014)
5. Alizadehsalehi, S., Hadavi, A., Huang, J.C.: BIM/MR-lean construction project delivery management system. In: 2019 IEEE Technology & Engineering Management Conference (TEMSCON) BIM/MR-Lean, pp. 1–6 (2019)
6. Li, X., Yi, W., Chi, H.L., Wang, X., Chan, A.P.C.: A critical review of virtual and augmented reality (VR/AR) applications in construction safety. Autom. Construct. **86**, 150–162 (2018)
7. Naycı, H.: Bir Toplu Konut Projesinde Uygulanan İş Güvenliği Yönetim Süreçlerinin OHSAS 18001 Uygulamalarıyla Karşılaştırılması, vol. 9. İstanbul Teknik Üniversitesi (2010)
8. Huang, X., Hinze, J.: The Owner's Role in Construction Safety. University of Florida (2003)
9. Melzner, J., Zhang, S., Teizer, J., Bargstädt, H.J.: A case study on automated safety compliance checking to assist fall protection design and planning in building information models. Constr. Manag. Econ. **31**(6), 661–674 (2013)
10. Gök, N.: Burdur Karaçal Mermer Ocağındaki İş Güvenliği Uygulaması Ve Risk Değerlendirmesi. Konya Teknik Üniversitesi Lisansüstü Eğitim Enstitüsü (2018)
11. Müngen, U.: İnşaat Sektörümüzdeki Başlıca İş Kazası Tipleri. İstanbul Teknik Üniversitesi (2011)
12. Kazaz, A., Acıkara, T., Ulubeyli, S.: Türk İnşaat Sektöründe İş Kazaları ve Nedenleri Üzerine Bir Araştırma, Konferans, 4. Proje ve Yapım Yönetimi Kongresi (2016)
13. Saurin, T.A., Formoso, C.T., Guimaraes, L.B.M.: Safety and production: an integrated planning and control model. Constr. Manag. Econ. **22**(2), 159–169 (2004)
14. Rozenfeld, O., Sacks, R., Rosenfeld, Y., Baum, H.: Construction job safety analysis. Saf. Sci. **48**(4), 491–498 (2010)
15. Sevim, M., Gürcanli, G.E.: İşçi Sağlığı Ve İş Güvenliği (İSİG) Sisteminin İnşaat Uygulama İş Programına Entegrasyonu. Beykent Üniversitesi Fen Bilimleri Dergisi **11**(2), 19–33 (2018)
16. Nnaji, C., Gambatese, J., Lee, H.W.: Work zone intrusion: technology to reduce injuries and fatalities. Prof. Saf. **63**(4), 36–41 (2018)
17. Riaz, Z., Arslan, M., Azhar, S.: CoSMoS: a BIM and wireless sensor-based integrated solution for worker safety in confined spaces. Autom. Constr. **45**(8), 96–106 (2014)
18. Taiebat, M.: Tuning up BIM for safety analysis proposing modeling logics for application of BIM in DfS, Doctor of Philosophy Dissertation, Virginia Polytechnic Institute and State University (2011). http://hdl.handle.net/10919/30255
19. Lopez del Puerto, C., Clevenger, C.: Enhancing safety throughout construction using BIM/VDC, EcoBuild (2010)
20. Ofluoğlu, S.: Multidisciplinary work and BIM usage. In: 10th Computational Design in Architecture National Symposium, pp. 104–117. Istanbul Bilgi University (2016)
21. Kamardeen, I.: 8D BIM modeling tool for accident prevention through design. In: 26th Annual ARCOM Conference, Leeds, Association of Researchers in Construction Management, vol. 1, pp. 281–289 (2010)
22. Zhang, S., Lee, J., Venugopal, M., Teizer, J., Eastman, C.: Integrating BIM and safety: an automated rule-based checking system for safety planning and simulation. In: Proceedings of CIB W99 Conference, pp. 1–13 (2011)

23. Hongling, G., Yantao, Y., Weisheng, Z., Yan, L.: BIM and safety rules-based automated identification of unsafe design factors in construction. Procedia Eng. **164**(June), 467–472 (2016)

24. Tekbas, G., Guven, G.: BIM-based Automated Safety Review for Fall Prevention. Ozyegin University, Department of Civil Engineering (2020)

25. Behzadi, A.: American journal of engineering research (AJER) open access using augmented and virtual reality technology in the construction industry Ajang Behzadi. Am. J. Eng. Res. **5**(12), 350–353 (2017)

26. Ratajczak, J., Marcher, C., Schimanski, C.P., Schweikopfler, A., Riedl, M., Matt, D.T.: BIM-based augmented reality tool for the monitoring of construction performance and progress. In: Proceedings of the 2019 European Conference for Computing in Construction, vol. 1, pp. 467–476 (2019)

27. Chu, M., Matthews, J., Love, P.E.D.: Integrating mobile building information modelling and augmented reality systems: an experimental study. Autom. Construct. **85**, 305–316 (2018)

28. Gheisari, M., Chen, P., Sabzevar, M.F., Irizarry, J.: An augmented panoramic environment to access building information on a construction site. In: 52nd ASC Annual International Conference Proceedings, pp. 1–8 (2016)

29. Mani, G.F., Feniosky, P.M., Savarese, S.: D4AR-A 4-dimensional augmented reality model for automating construction progress monitoring data collection, processing and communication. Electron. J. Inform. Technol. Construct. **14**(June), 129–153 (2009)

30. Zaher, M., Greenwood, D., Marzouk, M.: Mobile augmented reality applications for construction projects. Constr. Innov. **18**(2), 152–166 (2018)

31. Lin, T.J., Duh, H.B.L., Li, N., Wang, H.Y., Tsai, C.C.: An investigation of learners' collaborative knowledge construction performances and behavior patterns in an augmented reality simulation system. Comput. Educ. **68**, 314–321 (2013)

32. Le, Q.T., Pedro, A., Lim, C.R., Park, H.T., Park, C.S., Kim, H.K.: A framework for using mobile based virtual reality and augmented reality for experiential construction safety education. Int. J. Eng. Educ. **31**(No. 3), 713–725 (2015)

33. Ahmed, S.: A review on using opportunities of augmented reality and virtual reality in construction project management. Organ. Technol. Manage. Construct. Int. J. **11**(1), 1839–1852 (2019)

34. Wang, X., Dunston, P.S.: Design, strategies, and issues towards an augmented reality-based construction training platform. Electron. J. Inform. Technol. Construct. **12**(March), 363–380 (2007)

35. Sculpteo Homepage. https://www.sculpteo.com/en/3d-learning-hub/create-3d-file/fix-non-manifold-geometry. Accessed 30 Mar 2020

36. Azuma, R.: A survey of augmented reality. Presence Teleoper. Virtual Environ. **6**(4), 355–385 (1997)

37. Behm, M., Gambatese, J., Toole, M.: Construction safety and health through design. Construct. Manage. Eng. 501–502 (2014)

38. Lian, Z., et al.: SHREC'15 track: non-rigid 3D shape retrieval. Eurographics Workshop on 3D Object Retrieval, EG 3DOR, pp. 107–120 (2015)

39. Milgram, P., Kishino, F.: A taxonomy of mixed reality visual displays. IEICE Trans. Inform. Syst. **77**(12), 1321–1329 (1994)

40. Natephra, W., Motamedi, A.: Live data visualization of IoT sensors using augmented reality (AR) and BIM. In: Proceedings of the 36th International Symposium on Automation and Robotics in Construction (ISARC) (2019)

41. Seichter, H.: Augmented Reality Sketching for Architectural Design sketchand+. http://technotecture.com/projects/sketchandplus. Accessed 25 Feb 2020

42. Sidani, A., Duarte, J., Baptista, J.S., Martins, J.P., Soeiro, A.: Improving construction safety using BIM-Based sensor technologies. 2° Congresso Português de Building Information Modelling vol. 1, pp. 161–169 (2018)
43. Sofuğlu, T.: İnşaat Sektöründe İş Güvenliği Eğitimi, Yüksek Lisans Tezi, Anadolu Üniversitesi, Fen Bilimleri Enstitüsü, İnşaat Mühendisliği Anabilim Dalı, vol. 14 (2012)
44. Tümerden, İ.: Bina Yapiminda Tasarim Yoluyla İş Güvenliği Kavramının İncelenmesi, Uludağ Üniversitesi, Fen Bilimleri Enstitüsü (2015)
45. TMMOB: TMMOB Makina Mühendisleri Odası İşçi Sağlığı ve İş Güvenliği (2018). http://www.mmo.org.tr
46. Williams, G., Gheisari, M., Chen, P.J., Irizarry, J.: BIM2MAR: an efficient BIM translation to mobile augmented reality applications. J. Manage. Eng. (2015)

BIM Education

BIM Integration in Architectural Education: Where Do We Stand?

Onur Özkoç[1](✉) ⓘ, Heves Beşeli Özkoç[2](✉) ⓘ, and Duygu Tüntaş[2](✉) ⓘ

[1] Ankara Medipol University, Ankara, Turkey
onur.ozkoc@ankaramedipol.edu.tr
[2] TED University, Ankara, Turkey
{heves.beseli,duygu.tuntas}@tedu.edu.tr

Abstract. Considering the redefinition of the roles of AEC professions -and reflectively education- through Building Information Modeling (BIM), this research is interested in the integration of BIM tools and technologies into formal architectural education at the higher education level. Starting with the first attempts as a transition from teaching AutoCAD to BIM in stand-alone computer courses, the recent studies show that BIM integration in education has expanded towards adapting the architectural curriculum to prepare students for a BIM-oriented practice. Acknowledging the trends and positing possible shifts in the field, this study uses a systematic review method to map the actual experiences of researchers and academics for the integration of BIM tools and technologies into architectural education. In the Scopus database, publications that focus on BIM integration into architectural education are scanned for a period between 2005 to 2021. After the bibliometric analysis, 42 studies are selected to evaluate based on their reflection of an actual case experience in a higher education setting that engages in the integration of BIM in architectural education. Evaluating various approaches addressing the design studios and complementary courses and the challenges faced in architectural education as part of the efforts to integrate BIM is examined concerning the emerging themes. As the most frequently encountered theme in the selected studies, a particular emphasis is put on the concept of collaboration.

Keywords: Architectural design · Architectural education · Curriculum · BIM integration · Collaboration

1 Introduction

Building Information Modeling (BIM) has been transforming modes of project delivery and construction management at an increasing pace owing to its widespread adoption starting from the early 2000s. As practice via BIM redefines the roles of Architecture, Engineering, and Construction (AEC) professions, several architecture schools seek ways of implementing these tools into their curriculum for professional education and practice transitions. Although BIM is not intended as an educational tool in the first place and to date remains focused on practice, it is evident that graduates of the profession of architecture are increasingly required to understand BIM better, have a good command of its parametric ontology, and perform efficiently through its collaborative workflows.

The benefits of BIM for AEC professionals are comprehensively examined and well documented. Developing consistently from predecessors such as Charles Eastman's Building Description System (BDS) in the 1970s, the motive of increasing efficiency in the fields of design and construction is consistent throughout the development and evolution of BIM, and the primary beneficiaries remain as practitioners [1]. The impact of BIM on education, on the other hand, is not as straightforward as its impact on professional practice and can be considered as an ongoing research and adaptation process of multiple dimensions. Many studies are reporting the positive effects of BIM integration in architectural education in terms of providing the professional knowledge and skills required by the 21st century [2, 3]. Yet, critical stances which consider BIM as a barrier to the development of creativity, especially at the early stages of design also exist [4, 5]. Some educators consider BIM merely as a technology or tool while some consider it as a new form of a professional organization or design practice [6, 7]. Besides, there is no consensus among educators about at which level and in what way BIM should be implemented in the educational setting [6].

Scholars have elaborated on various strategies for the integration of BIM into architectural education, distributed over a variety of subjects [8]. In many cases, efforts to integrate BIM are focused on the organization of the design studio or single courses, rather than an integrated curriculum [9]. Usage of BIM in courses addressing complementary fields such as construction technologies, materials, detailing, structural design, and visualization have also been investigated and evaluated in terms of BIM adoption. Compilation of these efforts and the dominant themes may prove beneficial for the evaluation of the current situation as well as providing implications for further research.

2   Methodology

The design of the research method employed in this paper is based on the systematic review criteria defined by David Gough (2007) [10] and elaborated by Bearman et al. (2012) [11], and proceeds as follows: (1) defining the research questions, (2) defining the search strategy, (3) setting the criteria for inclusion and exclusion, (4) review and analyses of the articles, (5) reporting the results, (6) analysis and synthesis of findings, (7) discussing the findings and drawing conclusions relevant to the research questions.

2.1   Research Questions

This paper aims to review the reported experiences on BIM integration in architectural education. To this end, the following research questions are proposed:

(1) What are the trends in the integration of BIM into architectural education?
(2) Are there any significant shifts in focus regarding strategies for BIM integration in education?
(3) In what ways do higher education institutions approach BIM concerning architectural education?

The first question aims to reveal an overview of the efforts on BIM integration in education to provide a framework for analysis and synthesis of the various approaches. The second question focuses on the scopes of BIM integration in architectural education efforts from 2005 onwards, inquiring whether there are any significant changes in the approach and scale of interventions. The third question is targeted at the analysis and synthesis of the various methods and strategies for BIM integration to identify the variety of approaches.

2.2 Search Strategy

The systematic review performs a bibliometric analysis of BIM publications based on the Scopus database starting from 2005 to 2021. Document type was restricted to articles and conference papers to confine the research to studies with a particular effort on reporting educational experience rather than reviews and editorial texts. The language of papers was limited to English.

To access a wider range of literature referring to the research questions, an inclusive search phrase was designed to map papers containing "BIM" together with an educational keyword and a subject area keyword in the text; and containing "BIM" with an educational keyword in its title, abstract or keywords (Table 1).

Table 1. Scopus database search phrase

SCOPUS database	(ALL (("building information modeling") AND (education OR teaching OR curriculum OR pedagogy) AND (architecture OR construction OR engineering)) AND TITLE-ABS-KEY ((bim OR "building information modeling") AND (education OR teaching OR curriculum OR pedagogy)))

2.3 Inclusion and Exclusion Criteria

This study concentrates on the actual experience of integrating BIM into architectural education, which narrowed the focus to formal architectural education at the higher education level. To align the selection of papers with respect to the research questions, a set of inclusion/exclusion criteria were utilized. In this respect papers that (1) did not refer to higher education as their context, (2) did not have BIM in their foci, or (3) did not refer to architectural education were excluded. In the final step, studies that were based on an experience of an educational setting (a case study) in a formal higher education course or curriculum were selected.

2.4 Review and Analyses of Articles

The specific selection of research parameters, as reported in the previous sections, initially returned 598 results, which was considerably high for evaluation of full papers and expectedly covered duplicate and/or irrelevant articles that approached the search parameters from an unrelated perspective. In this respect, the initial review was directed on the examination of the titles and keywords of the articles, and irrelevant papers were eliminated along with the papers that focused on industrial integration or professional practice but not education. Then, the abstracts were evaluated based on the inclusion/exclusion criteria, which returned 128 papers for further review. Finally, full papers were checked concerning the inclusion/exclusion criteria, refining the list to a total of 42 studies (Table 2).

Table 2. The review process (papers marked "partial" were re-reviewed at the next round)

	Scope of review	Papers	Included	Partial*	Excluded
Initial Inquiry		597			
Round 1 Reviews	Title and keywords	597	**378**	52	167
Round 2 Reviews	Abstracts	430	**122**	6	302
Round 3 Reviews	Full text	128	**42**	–	86

The final selection of papers reflects on the experience of an actual case study in a higher education setting that focuses on the integration of BIM in architectural education. Papers that included architectural students among various disciplines were included, however, any research that excluded architecture students was eliminated from the scope of this study. The main body of research examined in this study consists of papers from 2015 onwards, with a notable increase in 2019 and 2020 (Fig. 1).

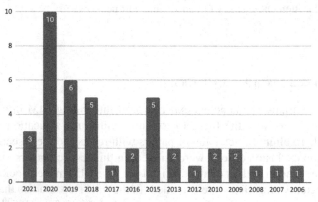

Fig. 1. Graph showing the distribution of the selected studies with respect to years

3   BIM Integration Efforts

The literature studied in the scope of this paper can be contextualized under two main stages. Earlier studies mostly focus on the transition from computer-aided drafting

(CAD) to BIM [12, 13], or the use of software suites [14–16]. These interests may at least be partially related to the rising demand for BIM-informed graduates and higher education institutions' efforts to understand the methods and outcomes of BIM practice.

Researchers investigated potentials for basic collaboration in BIM and elaborated on BIM as a process rather than a software suite [3, 17]. However, the focus on multidisciplinary workgroups and interdisciplinary design processes gain momentum in a later stage [18–24], indicating a pedagogical shift in the integration of BIM in architectural education. The collaborative potential of BIM in architectural education constitutes an important part even in articles with other concerns such as sustainable design [13, 24] and stands out as a research area that is highly referred to. The collaboration potentials of BIM for architectural education still promise novel developments for educators and researchers. The individual approaches to collaboration potentials provided by BIM processes are discussed more in detail in the discussion section of this paper.

It is observed that research from the last five years also centers around new ways of incorporating BIM in architectural education, such as the use of virtual reality (VR) or augmented reality (AR) and integration with game engines [23, 25–27], parametric design and form-finding [28], or the use of BIM for information-driven sustainable design - green BIM [29, 30]. Although these topics are not as frequently debated as collaboration potentials, they indicate important advantages for exploiting the potentials of BIM for architectural education.

In terms of course types, single-course experiences (reported in 31 papers) outweigh papers focusing on curricula with multiple courses. This data reveals that current efforts on BIM integration proceed mostly in a piecemeal fashion and is an expected outcome considering the difficulties in managing educational curricula according to accreditation criteria. BIM integration experiences are reported in compulsory or elective course settings to undergraduate, graduate, or combined student profiles. Almost half of the investigated studies do not indicate whether the setting is compulsory or elective, which renders it hard to elaborate on whether the educational institution is on a path to BIM integration or prefers only to raise awareness in students.

It is detected that more than half of the selected studies report experiences in a design studio setting as predicted. In addition to design studio experiences, courses on construction [31, 32], technology [33, 34], building systems [35], and visualization/representation [36] also contribute as important research settings.

The investigated studies' approaches to BIM in the case of architectural education can be conceptualized under two main titles: (1) teaching BIM, and (2) BIM as a learning tool. Of the 42 papers investigated, 21 approach BIM as a learning tool, while 16 papers focus on the teaching of BIM, and 5 papers report experiences on both aspects. As the title suggests, studies that focus on teaching BIM elaborate on the development of students' skills for working in BIM processes. The second title, BIM as a learning tool, indicates the utilization of the potentials of BIM to teach various components of architectural design. Studies in this approach cover a range of subjects such as the use of VR/AR in education [23, 26, 27], detailing [15, 26, 37, 38], sustainability [13, 29, 30, 39, 40], fire and life safety [41], visualization [36] and project management [20].

Collaboration appears to be one of the key aspects regarding BIM integration to architectural education with 19 papers out of 42 describing either teamwork or a multi-disciplinary learning environment. It is evident that BIM integration holds an important potential to facilitate an efficient collaborative learning environment for students. The following section of the paper elaborates on the modes and dynamics of collaboration in BIM-integrated teaching experiences, which constitutes the most common area of interest in the reviewed literature.

4   Collaboration Dynamics

Collaboration lies at the heart of contemporary design and realization of buildings and renders BIM invaluable for professionals in the AEC industry. Concordantly, research on the integration of BIM in architectural education frequently elaborates on collaboration from various points of view. Overall, the literature reviewed for this study indicates three approaches for elaborating on the collaboration dynamics of BIM-integration in architectural education: (1) collaboration among architecture students (single-discipline), (2) collaboration among students from different disciplines (multidisciplinary), and (3) teaching experiences focusing on multidisciplinary real-world scenarios with additional BIM roles.

4.1   Collaboration Among Architecture Students

The first approach involves collaboration between students of architecture who work on the analyses and/or solutions for a design problem. These experiences are especially relevant for contexts where a basic understanding of BIM concepts is sought after, often to further develop collaboration potentials as curricula are re-organized. A significant experience in this regard is elaborated by Ambrose (2012) [3], where the studio begins with a complete building information model so that students will have the opportunity to redesign the existing building in coordination and collaboration, rather than a conventional design problem that starts from scratch and does not leave time for a thorough investigation of issues such as coordination, collaboration, and constructability [3]. In this case, the architectural design studio is based on a continuous modification of an original model, which helps students to change their perspectives from a drawing-centric view to a three-dimensional one where the design task is collaborative rather than individualistic. It is important to note that students are continuously provided with knowledge from other disciplines via workshops and lectures for them to better understand the initial models they were provided with. Organizing the studio as such eliminates the problem of students' knowledge levels being inadequate for preparing proper BIM models. In this respect, learning by analyzing, dismantling, and reorganizing models present an important opportunity to work on collaborative design problems via information-driven models.

Isanović and Çolakoğlu follow a similar approach in proposing a BIM learning scenario, a new framework, and content for an existing curriculum, to attain "a student-centered flexible framework for organizing the learning activities to provide guidelines for learning to learn." [42]. In this case, architecture students are provided a complete

BIM model of a realized building, and involved in the processes of "disassembling, analyzing the structure, function, and operation." [42]. Students' post-evaluation of the course indicates that while they find working on a real project informative, they still emphasize the necessity of having a practice mentor and that software skills play an important role to fully utilize the courses' learning potentials.

Integration of BIM in the design studio also presents opportunities for more conventional project development trajectories that begin with a debrief and proceed by working on design solutions. A significant offering of a BIM-driven design studio is the ability to expand students' conception of a building beyond 2D and 3D representations towards a more complete conceptualization with various analyses, documentation, reports on building performance, feasibility, and life-cycle assessment. An example of such introduction of BIM into the design studio is reported by Jung et al., where undergraduate architecture students undertake real-world roles in the BIM process within the context of a capstone project. The studio covers a wide range of real-world scenarios beginning with pre-project planning and proceeding to design, construction documentation, feasibility and cost analyses, preparing specifications for requests for proposals (RFPs), and life-cycle assessment. The deliverables of the studio are presented as the group work capstone project [43]. While the authors note that the capstone project studio provides students with a comprehensive BIM workflow experience, they underline that there is room for improvement by inviting students from other disciplines to the collaborative experience.

Another instance of BIM integration is elaborated by Cascante and Martinez [36]. They describe an Educational Innovation Project (EIP) that integrates four third-year courses (architectural graphic expression, construction, measurement-budgeting, and technical documentation) that are compulsory in the current curriculum. The four lectures share a cyclic BIM process but focus on their very own learning outcomes. They report that students achieve a higher level of success as more students pass the lectures compared to previous methods of conduct. Yet, due to a range of lectures being combined in a collaborative method, arranging the curriculum and credits in line with accreditation requirements poses a challenge, and it is suggested to establish a BIM implementation committee for planning the integration of BIM into curricula in various universities.

As argued earlier, the collaborative BIM environment in architectural education can be significantly enhanced by involving students from other disciplines in the process. Yet, it should be noted that BIM workflows require a certain level of skills with software suites as well as knowledge of design. For this reason, single-discipline collaboration may provide an efficient method to prepare students for more complex collaborative experiences in the following years. One such case is reported by Deniz (2018), who elaborates on the perception of students in CAD and BIM-based software, based on the experience and feedback from two undergraduate courses: (1) an introductory CAD and BIM course provided in the freshmen year as a key element of the AEC curriculum, and (2) a junior year upper-level BIM Course as a collaborative studio with multidisciplinary modules [19]. While the introductory course focuses on developing software skills and modeling habits, the second makes use of these skills to foster a collaborative learning experience. In this respect, offering stand-alone BIM specialty courses may still prove beneficial for the integration of BIM in architectural education, as these courses provide the students with the necessary skills to remove "software" barriers and pave the way for more efficient BIM-driven collaboration among students.

4.2 Multidisciplinary Collaboration

Collaboration skills are considered essential in the AEC industry, therefore equipping students with collaboration and communication competencies in a multidisciplinary environment is indispensable for the integration of BIM into the educational setting. As in the case of single discipline collaboration, modes of multidisciplinary collaboration also vary in their methods and objectives.

To create an education model for exploring the collaboration potentials of BIM, Poerschke et al. develop a course as a project-based learning experience, in which architecture, landscape architecture, construction, structural, mechanical, and lighting/electrical engineering students are given the task to revise the prototype design of an elementary school by using BIM [21]. The collaborative BIM course is proposed as a one-semester vertical studio with undergraduate students of 3rd to 5th year standing and graduate students. The underlying agenda of the studio mainly dwells upon integrated design, collaboration, and sustainability.

Through this study, the students are provided with tangible experience in team organization and workflow, yet, instead of involving more with the design task, critically evaluating the model, simulation outcomes, and design alternatives; it is observed that students were more occupied and concerned in managing the model and simulation. The authors relate this unexpected outcome with the complexity of design and suggest an "urgent shift toward intensified academic collaboration of the disciplines involved in the design and construction process" [21].

The second mode of collaboration is explained by Chiuini et al., who describe a collaboration between architecture and engineering students from two different universities to design a project for the Solar Decathlon Challenge in 2013 via BIM. The experience includes assigning students to disciplinary task groups. Then, these disciplinary task groups are expected to collaborate and arrive at a design solution mutually [44].

As a result of the experiment, the authors report that there are two major challenges for the students to overcome for interdisciplinary education. Firstly, the BIM process necessitates a visual-creative thinking practice that proved to be harder for engineering students compared to architecture students. Secondly, the conventional mode of education (and mode of practice) based on a sequential order of work had to be reformatted in a collaborative BIM environment, where participants were required to be active during all of the design processes.

In a similar setting, Jin et al. elaborate on a collaborative Solar Decathlon Challenge with 72 final year undergraduate students from the disciplines of architecture, civil engineering, and architectural environmental engineering [18]. Formed into multidisciplinary groups, the students worked on the design of a residential building from scratch including architectural design, structural design, and MEP design, as well as prefabrication design and cost estimation in a BIM-driven interdisciplinary collaboration. As a result, the authors underline that the process had positive effects in terms of inter-team communication, sustainable design strategies, improved design quality in terms of clashes and technical errors, and improvement of visualization. It is also pointed out that the interdisciplinary collaboration experience for the students is the most important outcome of the process.

In "Bim in academia: Shifting our attention from product to process", Sanguinetti (2009) offers a revision to the educational curriculum for a flexible structure enabling architects with expertise in the professional roles available to them. A case study is conducted to "compare the interactions of two interdisciplinary teams participating in Stanford University's AEC web-based course" in which students from architecture, structural engineering, construction management, and building technology disciplines are required "to work together and solve a design problem in a distributed setting" [13]. While the collaborative design process is similar to the previously discussed cases, Sanguinetti also proposes a flexible curriculum inspired by the education of medical and computer science students at the Georgia Institute of Technology. Shifting the focus away from the debate on whether BIM should be taught in standalone courses or the studio environment, Sanguinetti suggests a curriculum in which the students can customize their education by combining courses according to their preferences. This approach not only fosters multidisciplinary collaboration but also lets future architects undertake new specialist roles in practice.

4.3 Additional Roles in Multidisciplinary Collaboration

In addition to the conventional disciplinary roles undertaken by students in collaborative education experiences, some of the reviewed cases introduce additional BIM roles and procedures that are akin to their real-world counterparts. In one case, Zhao et al. reflect on their experience of an "Integrated Construction Studio," which simulates real-world working conditions for students from different backgrounds in a collaborative BIM environment. The course aims to bridge the gap with AEC Industry's expectations by introducing a real-world scenario with project owners, constructors, project managers, and design disciplines' conventional roles [45]. In a similar experience, Rahhal et al. present a methodology for the development of educational content for the course entitled "Collaborative Digital Studio BIM" (SDC BIM), in which students are assigned different BIM roles regarding real-world BIM requirements (such as BIM manager, BIM coordinator, BIM modeler, etc.). In addition, students are asked to design a BIM protocol, coordinate design tasks and provide information for "client requests" such as building costs, scheduling, and running costs of the completed structure. In the end, the authors report that the students have gained "operational mastery of instrumented interdisciplinary cooperation: management of distributed work, management of meetings, document sharing-and-nomenclature, collective decision-making, conflict management, and principles of project review" as a result of the undertaken tasks [22]. In other cases, the authors explain that students report a better understanding of the whole design-to-construction process after taking Integrated Project Delivery studios [46–49].

It must be underlined that the examined cases are conducted either with senior students or a vertical composition of students that includes seniors. As discussed earlier, the complexity of a BIM process similar to professional practice requires the students to possess certain skills that are less likely to be covered in the early years of higher education.

4.4 Potentials and Challenges

Forgues and Becerik-Gerber identify two core issues that need to be addressed to accomplish a paradigm shift to BIM-integrated research and education: "(1) that research and education are built on a rigid and fragmented structure that often resists change; and (2) as opposed to industry, educational institutions are not pressured by the market to make these changes" [17]. While it can be argued that the first issue is still valid in the present day, educational institutions appear to be more interested in the novel technologies adopted in the "market," and BIM is at the forefront of focus in this respect. Consequently, many of the challenges on the way to BIM-integrated collaboration dynamics mirror those of the AEC Industry.

Defining professional roles in BIM-driven collaborative design processes has been an ongoing debate since the widespread adoption of BIM at the turn of the century [50]. It is observed that a similar concern is valid for the case of architectural education. Jin et al. explain that architecture students are resistant to BIM because of "their potential loss of leadership in the design process as their architectural decisions might be disapproved by other disciplines" [18]. They relate this projection with Thomsen's argument that BIM reduces the space for design decisions and charges architects with "extra requirements" [51]. A collaborative design paradigm requires the students to act as a team from the start, which requires a new understanding of professional roles not only for students but also for educators. Professional roles within educational settings require further investigation in terms of BIM integration.

An equally important challenge rises from the body of professional knowledge required to carry out BIM processes. As BIM practice requires more thought-out solutions and a better familiarity with other disciplines compared to conventional design methodologies, even senior students may experience difficulties in working via BIM. Consequently, some of the examined cases introduced additional workshops and lectures to provide students with the required knowledge, while others introduced collaborative BIM processes in capstone projects [43, 52]. It may be fruitful in this respect to speculate on a course that introduces the students with a BIM mindset without involving complex designs, but rather conveying the methods and importance of a data-driven decision-making process.

Students' skills with BIM software constitute another important challenge to be considered. As Isanović and Çolakoğlu point out, "if students are not skillful with the tools, design exploration can be hindered by switching the focus from the task and content to learning the tools. Consequently, this can lead to reduced quality of design solutions and loss of creativity until the new media becomes an integral part of the designer's mindset" [42]. Potential interventions to this challenge include the introduction of software courses to support design studios [53] or introducing workshops and lectures according to students' requirements. Yet there is also the challenge of the educators' knowledge becoming outdated, as the software suites are continuously evolving.

There are also frequently reflected challenges related to BIM tools and software, such as interoperability issues between various software, insufficient BIM library databases, or difficulty of the management of data in an educational environment. While a set of online software tools on the cloud are becoming commonplace for professional practice, common data environments are still posing challenges for students due to their complexity [54].

Finally, one of the most important challenges connects to the two issues Forgues and Becerik-Gerber pointed out: the rigid structure of education and research, and the limited pressure from the industry both fail to motivate enough educators to develop skills in BIM processes. This in turn results in limited and/or piecemeal efforts for integrating BIM into architectural education due to an insufficient number of educators with the required skills. In this regard, the motivation and education of educators present a potential area to investigate.

5 Conclusion

With a particular focus on collaboration dynamics, the paper has presented the attempts to integrate BIM into architectural education. The sampling area of the study has been limited to the reported experiences on BIM integration in architectural education to detect the institutional approaches, emerging themes, and any significant shifts in the integration strategies. The change in the professional practice from conventional disciplinary roles to additional BIM roles necessitates a transformation in the individual learning processes toward more integrated and collaborative learning models to prepare students for more complex experiences in higher education. Adaptation of the architectural curriculum for shared experience has been implemented in the forms of a single discipline approach, multidisciplinary collaboration, and real-world simulations. The observed shifts in professional practice –and reflectively in education models and their applications– reinforce this condition with the increase in complexity that outlines the assigned roles in the collaborative works from single-disciplinary to multidisciplinary co-operational settings. Mirroring the industrial recognition of professional practice and bringing in the empiric assets of educational implementations, the efforts to integrate BIM in education seem to grow into a platform, an interdisciplinary laboratory, where collaborative workflow becomes possible in a virtual-physical-interactive environment.

References

1. Eastman, C.M.: The use of computers instead of drawings in building design. AIA J. **63**(3), 46–50 (1975)
2. Clayton, M.J., Ozener, O., et al.: Towards studio 21: experiments in design education using BIM. In: Goosens, K., Agudelo, L. (eds.) SIGraDi 2010 Proceedings of the 14th Congress of the Iberoamerican Society of Digital Graphics, pp. 43–46. SIGraDi, Bogota, Columbia (2010)
3. Ambrose, M.A.: Agent provocateur – BIM in the academic design studio. Int. J. Archit. Comput. **10**(1), 53–66 (2012)
4. Denzer, A., Hedges, K.: From CAD to BIM: educational strategies for the coming paradigm shift. In: Proceedings of the AEI 2008 Conference - AEI 2008: Building Integration Solutions 328, pp. 59–59. American Society of Civil Engineers, Denver, Colorado, United States (2008)
5. Michalatos, P.: Design signals: the role of software architecture and paradigms in design thinking and practice. Archit. Des. **86**, 108–115 (2016)

6. Deamer, P.: BIM in academia. In: Deamer, P., Bernstein, P. (eds.), BIM in Academia, pp. 9–12. US Yale School of Architecture (2011)
7. Becerik-Gerber, B., Gerber, D.J., Ku, K.: The pace of technological innovation in architecture, engineering, and construction education: integrating recent trends into the curricula. J. Inform. Technol. Construct. **16**, 411–432 (2011)
8. Abdirad, H., Dossick, C.S.: BIM curriculum design in architecture, engineering, and construction education: a systematic review. J. Inform. Technol. Construct. **21**(17), 250–271 (2016)
9. Kocaturk, T., Kiviniemi, A.: Challenges of integrating BIM in architectural education. In: Proceedings of the 31st eCAADe Conference – Volume 2, Faculty of Architecture, Delft University of Technology, Delft, The Netherlands (2013)
10. Gough, D.: Weight of evidence: a framework for the appraisal of the quality and relevance of evidence. Appl. Pract. Based Res. **22**(2), 213–228 (2007)
11. Bearman, M., et al.: Systematic review methodology in higher education. High. Educ. Res. Dev. **31**(5), 625–640 (2012)
12. Livingston, C.: From CAD to BIM: constructing opportunities in architectural education. In: Proceedings of the AEI 2008 Conference - AEI 2008: Building Integration Solutions 328, pp. 40–48. American Society of Civil Engineers, Denver, Colorado, United States (2008)
13. Sanguinetti, P.: Bim in academia: shifting our attention from product to process. In: Tidafi, T., Dorta, T. (eds.) Joining Languages, Cultures and Visions - CAADFutures 2009, Proceedings of the 13th International CAAD Futures Conference, pp. 395–409. PUM (2009)
14. Guidera, S.G.: BIM applications in design studio: an integrative approach developing student skills with computer modeling. In: Synthetic Landscapes - Proceedings of the 25th Annual Conference of the Association for Computer-Aided Design in Architecture, pp. 213–227. ACADIA (2006)
15. Mokhtar, A.: Bim as learning media for building construction. In: CAADRIA 2007 - The Association for Computer-Aided Architectural Design Research in Asia: Digitization and Globalization, pp. 119–126. The Association for Computer-Aided Architectural Design Research in Asia (CAADRIA), Ninjing (2007)
16. Sharag-Eldin, A., Nawari, N.O.: BIM in AEC education. In: Structures Congress 2010, pp.1676–1688. American Society of Civil Engineers (2010)
17. Forgues, D., Becerik-Gerber, B.: Integrated project delivery and building information modeling: redefining the relationship between education and practice. Int. J. Des. Educ. **6**(2), 47–56 (2013)
18. Jin, R., et al.: Project-based pedagogy in interdisciplinary building design adopting BIM. Eng. Constr. Archit. Manag. **25**(10), 1376–1397 (2018)
19. Deniz, G.O.: Emerging cad and bim trends in the AEC education: an analysis from students' perspective. J. Inform. Technol. Construct. **23**, 138–156 (2018)
20. Agostinelli, S., Cumo, F., Ruperto, F.: Strategies and outcomes of bim education: Italian experiences. WIT Trans. Built Environ. **192**, 217–227 (2019)
21. Poerschke, U., Holland, R.J., Messner, J.I., Pihlak, M.: BIM collaboration across six disciplines. In: EG-ICE 2010 - 17th International Workshop on Intelligent Computing in Engineering. Nottingham University Press, United Kingdom (2019)
22. Rahhal, A., Rajeb, S.B., Leclercq, P.: Educational approach for a BIM collaboration. In: Proceedings - 2020 International Conference on Computational Science and Computational Intelligence, CSCI 2020, pp. 879–884. Institute of Electrical and Electronics Engineers Inc., Las Vegas (2020)
23. Alizadehsalehi, S., Hadavi, A., Huang, J.C.: Assessment of AEC students' performance using BIM-into-VR. Appl. Sci. (Switzerland) **11**(7), art.no. 3225 (2021)

24. Mlinkauskienė, A., Jankauskaitė-Jurevičienė, L., Christensen, P., Finocchiaro, L., Lobaccaro, G.: BIM integration possibilities in different study cycles of architecture study programme. J. Sustain. Architect. Civil Eng. **26**(1), 5–17 (2020)

25. Wu, W., Kaushik, I.: A BIM-based educational gaming prototype for undergraduate research and education in design for sustainable aging. In: Proceedings - Winter Simulation Conference 2016 February, pp. 1091–1102. Institute of Electrical and Electronics Engineers Inc., Huntington Beach, CA, USA (2016)

26. Elgewely, M.H., Nadim, W., ElKassed, A., Yehiah, M., Talaat, M.A., Abdennadher, S.: Immersive construction detailing education: building information modeling (BIM)–based virtual reality (VR). Open House Int. **46**(3), 359–375 (2021)

27. Agirachman, F.A., Shinozaki, M.: VRDR: An attempt to evaluate bim-based design studio outcome through virtual reality. In: Projections - Proceedings of the 26th International Conference of the Association for Computer-Aided Architectural Design Research in Asia, pp. 223–232. CAADRIA, Hong Kong (2021)

28. İyican, A.B., Dinçer, A.E., Bektaş, I.: A studio experience on parametric modelling approaches. Turkish Online J. Educ. Technol. **2015**, 51–60 (2015)

29. Sanchez, B., Ballinas-Gonzalez, R., Rodriguez-Paz, M.X., Nolazco-Flores, J.A.: Usage of building information modeling for sustainable development education. In: ASEE Annual Conference and Exposition, Conference Proceedings, art. no.1483. American Society for Engineering Education (2020)

30. Zakharova, G.B., Krivonogov, A.I., Kruglikov, S.V., Petunin, A.A.: Energy-efficient technologies in the educational programs of the architectural higher education schools. Acta Polytech. Hungarica **17**(8), 121–136 (2020)

31. Markiewicz-Zahorski, P.: Teaching building construction design using BIM: The benefits and difficulties. World Trans. Eng. Technol. Educ. **17**(1), 54–59 (2019)

32. Hana, M.A., Al-Hagla, K.S., Elcherif, I.: Probing potentials of digital and physical modelling in construction courses. WIT Trans. Built Environ. **195**, 43–55 (2020)

33. Dong, K., Doerfler, J., Montoya, M.: Collaborative teaching to create integrated building envelopes: In: 39th IEEE Frontiers in Education Conference, pp. 1–5. IEEE, San Antonio, Texas, USA (2009)

34. Hu, M.: BIM-enabled pedagogy approach: Using BIM as an instructional tool in technology courses. J. Profession. Issues Eng. Educ. Pract. **145**(1), art. no. 05018017 (2019)

35. Mokhtar, A.H.M.: BIM as a pedagogical tool for teaching HVAC systems to architecture students. In: AEI 2019: Integrated Building Solutions - The National Agenda - Proceedings of the Architectural Engineering National Conference 2019, pp. 123–133. American Society of Civil Engineers (ASCE), Tysons, Virginia, USA (2019)

36. Cascante, I.L., Martínez, J.J.P.: Collaborative bim teaching. per tradition and directed by architectural graphic expression [Docencia colaborativa en bim. desde la tradición y dirigida por la expresión gráfica arquitectónica] EGA Revista de Expresion Grafica Arquitectonica **23**(32), 76–86 (2018)

37. Nakapan, W.: Challenge of teaching BIM in the first year of university: problems encountered and typical misconceptions to avoid when integrating BIM into an architectural design curriculum. In: CAADRIA 2015 - 20th International Conference on Computer-Aided Architectural Design Research in Asia: Emerging Experiences in the Past, Present and Future of Digital Architecture, pp. 509–519. The Association for Computer-Aided Architectural Design Research in Asia (CAADRIA), Hong Kong (2015)

38. Agirbas, A.: Teaching construction sciences with the integration of BIM to undergraduate architecture students. Front. Architect. Res. **9**(4), 940–950 (2020)

39. Abdelhameed, W.: BIM in architecture curriculum: a case study. Archit. Sci. Rev. **61**(6), 480–491 (2018)

40. Benner J., McArthur J.J.: Data-driven design as a vehicle for BIM and sustainability education. Buildings **9**(5), art. no.103 (2019)
41. Hong, S.W., Lee, Y.G.: The effects of human behavior simulation on architecture major students' fire egress planning. J. Asian Architect. Build. Eng. **17**(1), 125–132 (2018)
42. Isanović, H., Çolakoğlu, B.: Students' perceptions of bim learning scenario in architectural education A/Z ITU. J. Faculty Architect. **17**(3), 195–209 (2020)
43. Jung, Y., Kim, H., Kim, N.: Virtual plan-design-build for capstone projects in the school of architecture: CM & B0049M studios in five-year B.Arch. Program. J. Asian Architect. Build. Eng. **15**(2), 279–286 (2016)
44. Chiuini, M., Grondzik, W., King, K., McGinley, M., Owens, J.: Architect and engineer collaboration: The solar decathlon as a pedagogical opportunity. In: AEI 2013: Building 36. Solutions for Architectural Engineering - Proceedings of the 2013 Architectural Engineering National Conference, pp. 215–224 (2013)
45. Zhao, D., McCoy, A.P., Bulbul, T., Fiori, C., Nikkhoo, P.: Building collaborative construction skills through BIM-integrated learning environment. Int. J. Constr. Educ. Res. **11**(2), 97–120 (2015)
46. Sotelino, E.D., Natividade, V., Travassos Do Carmo, C.S.: Teaching BIM and its impact on young professionals. J. Civil Eng. Educ. **146**(4), art. no. 05020005 (2020)
47. Jin, J., Hwang, K.-E., Kim, I.: A study on the constructivism learning method for BIM/IPD collaboration education. Appl. Sci. (Switzerland) **10**(15), art. no. 5169 (2020)
48. Tomasowa, R.: BIM design collaboration report: In student's perspective. In: CAADRIA 2015 - 20th International Conference on Computer-Aided Architectural Design Research in Asia: Emerging Experiences in the Past, Present and Future of Digital Architecture, pp. 387–395. The Association for Computer-Aided Architectural Design Research in Asia (CAADRIA), Hong Kong (2015)
49. Snyder, G.: MESH: Integrating BIM, engineering, and fabrication into the architectural design studio. In: AEI 2015: Birth and Life of the Integrated Building - Proceedings of the AEI Conference 2015, pp. 37–42. American Society of Civil Engineers (ASCE), Milwaukee, Wisconsin (2015)
50. Özkoç, O.: Changing Role(s) of the Profession of Architecture: Building Information Modeling in Practice. Doctoral dissertation, Middle East Technical University, Turkey (2015)
51. Thomsen, A.: The role and influence of the Architect in industrialized building. In: Second cycle, A2E. Alnarp: SLU, Landscape Management, Design, and Construction, (2010)
52. Setterfield, C., Dunn, E., Marcks, R.: Simulating the collaborative design process through a multidisciplinary capstone project. In: ASEE Annual Conference and Exposition, Conference Proceedings, art. no. 151066. American Society for Engineering Education, Louisville, Kentucky (2010)
53. Zieliński, R.: New technologies to support students in a BIM design course. World Trans. Eng. Technol. Educ. **18**(3), 313–317 (2020)
54. Comiskey, D., McKane, M., Jaffrey, A., Wilson, P., Mordue, S.: An analysis of data sharing platforms in multidisciplinary education. Architect. Eng. Des. Manage. **13**(4), 244–261 (2017)

Collaborative BIM for Construction Engineering Students

Rita Sassine[1,2(✉)] (ID), Mojtaba Eslahi[1,2(✉)] (ID), and Rani El Meouche[1,2(✉)] (ID)

[1] IRC - Institut de Recherche en Constructibilité, 28 Président Wilson Avenue, 94230 Cachan, France
{rsassine,meslahi,relmeouche}@estp-paris.eu
[2] ESTP Paris - École Spéciale des Travaux Publics, du Bâtiment et de l'Industrie, 94230 Cachan, France

Abstract. Over the past several years, the French construction industry has been using Building Information Modeling (BIM) to design, construct and manage projects. BIM provides project actors with the right information at the right time [1] and clearly identifies their responsibilities/roles, the workflow, and the information needed to make decisions effectively. ESTP Paris as an engineering school takes an initiative to teach this new technology to future engineers. This paper aims to present three different project approaches used to teach BIM at different maturity levels at ESTP Paris. The first project is geared towards familiarizing students with the modeling process, BIM theoretical approach and software learning. The second project is based on a real-time collaborative approach to implementing a digital BIM model. The third project is aimed at combining geographic information and BIM to meet various multidisciplinary challenges in building modeling and urban simulations through the IFC format. This article presents the content, the maturity level, the prerequisites, the workgroup method, and the digital environment needed in each course. The list of deliverables and the rating criteria are detailed as well as the advantages and difficulties faced by students and professors. As a result of these projects, students are able to work efficiently in BIM projects. They can collaborate and solve problems quickly to model a coherent construction project.

Keywords: BIM · Construction engineering · Collaborative engineering · Information management · GIS

1 Introduction

BIM is a process for creating and managing information in a construction project during the project lifecycle [2]. BIM is used to define the process of generating, storing, managing, exchanging, and sharing information in the building process in an interoperable way using a 3D model to simulate the planning, design, construction, and operational phases of a project [3]. Different maturity levels ranging from 0 to 3 are used in order to represent the process of information exchange within the project [4]. Choosing each of these levels depends on the BIM project and the goals of the team. The more information added to the digital model, the higher Level of Development (LOD) is achieved. LOD

© Springer Nature Switzerland AG 2022
O. Ö. Özener et al. (Eds.): EBF 2021, CCIS 1627, pp. 115–131, 2022.
https://doi.org/10.1007/978-3-031-16895-6_8

is a reference that enables project members to specify the content and the representation volume of Building Information Models at various stages with a high level of clarity. Depending on the requirements of the project stage and its complexity, specific parameters are added to the existing information. Each BIM dimension, i.e. 3D, 4D, 5D, 6D, and 7D, has its own purpose and it can be useful to know how much a project would cost, what its schedule is, when it would be completed, and how sustainable it could be [2]. In a BIM project, BIM Manager and BIM Coordinator act as the intermediaries between designers, clients and architects in order to keep the projects efficient and effective.

Building Information Modeling is a new collaborative method [4] that is adopted in many construction projects in France, and it requires a high level of organization and software skills. In this regard, several issues are critical, including interoperability, information management, intellectual property, roles and responsibilities of stakeholders. Students, nowadays, are familiar with new technologies and software, however, there is a lack of practical methodology in the use of digital tools. It is a challenge to prepare future engineers to work on BIM projects and integrate this collaborative method into construction engineering courses.

The rest of this paper is set out as follows: In Sect. 2, we review the contribution of BIM to education. In Sect. 3, we describe the use of BIM in education at ESTP. We discuss the advantages and difficulties of integrating BIM courses into the engineering program in Sect. 4, and finally, conclusions and perspectives are presented in Sect. 5.

2   BIM and Education

Many studies explored the relationship between educational institutions and industry in the context of BIM. They showed that collaboration between the engineering and architecture industry from one side and universities and schools from the other side is very important to provide students with the necessary skills. For example, Wu and Issa [5] conducted a survey-based analysis to compare the needs of the construction industry in terms of BIM knowledge with the students' competence. The findings show that there is a gap between the rapid growth of the BIM-related labor market and the integration of BIM into education. Therefore, cooperation between the construction industry and universities is suggested. Sacks and Pikas [6] also found that the content of undergraduate and graduate engineering courses is needed to be modified to meet the needs of the construction industry. Course organizers need to develop the necessary skills to incorporate BIM more in their projects, and they should set targets and learning objectives for each level of education in different areas using BIM. Arroteia et al. [7] studied the lack of integration of the BIM's collaborative approach in universities. It appears that newly graduated engineers do not meet the needs of the industry in terms of BIM knowledge. Their study focused on the importance of educating students to work with collaborative and multidisciplinary solutions. The survey in the study found that more than 70% of the participants believed that the universities play an important role in learning BIM and that their level of BIM knowledge at the end of their studies is not sufficient at the beginning of their career in the BIM industry.

Kocaturk and Kiviniemi [8] showed that there is a lack in the integration of BIM in architecture courses. The pedagogical agenda is not clear and there is no defined strategy for collaborative work in such courses. They focused on the differences between the student levels and their different backgrounds. In order to make homogenous groups, they proposed adding two major courses to the existing architecture curricula: 1) modeling and representation, and 2) collaborative working.

Bosch-Sijtsema et al. [9] studied the impact of implementing BIM in a project on the role of BIM and non-BIM actors. The study showed that working methods, roles and responsibilities related to the new technology have changed. Three role figures in BIM projects are BIM manager, BIM coordinator, and BIM modeler. Several skills are needed for a successful BIM project implementation. BIM actors should be able to use technical software and have management skills. This study underlines the importance of academic training to introduce skills, practices, and theoretical knowledge required to develop BIM competency and overcome difficulties when working on BIM projects [10].

Wang et al. [11] reviewed the BIM adoption in higher education of AEC-related disciplines including architecture, engineering and construction. The study shows that using BIM learning strategies enhances collaboration among different disciplines. New technologies such as laser scanning can be associated with BIM for data analysis. The author recommends the integration of BIM in AEC courses to reduce the gap between higher education and industrial needs in technical and management terms.

A comparative study of the use of BIM in teaching Engineering projects [12] showed that three types of learning approaches are commonly used: 1) Project-based learning method using teams to improve BIM training [13], 2) Problem-solving learning approach [14], 3) A multidisciplinary approach in which students from different backgrounds work collaboratively on a common digital BIM project [15].

Adamu and Thrope [14] stated that six keys for university BIM learning should be considered: 1) Plan, phase and prioritize which consists of identifying the courses where BIM should be integrated, the year of study and the modification that should be done, 2) Create an ecosystem of BIM technologies by identifying the necessary software and collaborative BIM environment adapted to the course objectives, 3) Identify learning outcomes and industry needs by using the national BIM standards and involve guest lecturers from the industry, 4) Receive teaching and administrative support by organizing BIM workshops for students, professors and industry representatives, 5) Develop student-centered learning methods by creating distance learning courses for postgraduate level for several semesters, 6) Form university coalitions for multi-disciplinary learning to enhance collaboration between students from different backgrounds using a cloud-based platform.

A literature review done by Barison and Santos [16] illustrated that there are three BIM experience approaches accepted by the American universities for online collaboration and 3D visualization using BIM software including single, interdisciplinary and distance collaboration courses. The single-course approach, mostly used by universities, consists of teaching BIM concepts and collaboration for students from one discipline. The interdisciplinary approach aims to teach BIM strategies to students from different disciplines in the same school; while, remote collaboration is done between students from different schools and programs. This study [16] listed eight categories of BIM courses taught by different AEC schools such as workshops, training tools, or research studies online or in person.

In the design process, the real world is often ignored or less looked at, however, all constructions take place in a real place. Allowing Geographic Information System (GIS) exposure for students can help them combine their designs with real-time textual information. Enhancing civil engineering education with GIS helps students create enriched conceptual designs that extend spatial context to BIM and engineering conceptions [17].

3 BIM at ESTP Paris

Given the importance of the construction sector in Europe, the European Commission has supported, promoted and developed several initiatives to promote its digitalization. The European Construction Sector Observatory (ECSO) [18] has published a report entitled "Building Information Modelling in the EU construction sector" to study the evolution of BIM in Europe. The ECSO examines the importance of BIM in construction and the level of adoption for some European Countries.

In France, the adoption of BIM has made significant progress, notably with the introduction of the Digital Transition Plan for Buildings (PTNB) in 2015, a strategic plan intended to stimulate the application of BIM. The industry hoped that this could be implemented across the country by 2022 but some difficulties are faced. BIM standards concerning the law and regulation are not defined yet [19]. In addition, there is no agreement between the French construction companies, which are still facing problems concerning interoperability issues.

MINnD [20] (Modélisation des INformations INteropérables pour les INfrastructures Durables), is a French national collaborative research project, implemented in 2014, to develop BIM for infrastructures. The project aims to organize, use and exchange information during the project life cycle, i.e. design, construction, operation and maintenance. As a result, the BIM implementation guide and the BIM application guide are two self-supporting deliverables that are produced to support decision-makers and project stakeholders in the execution of BIM. MINnD also provides feedback and recommendations on practical topics such as project reviews in a digital environment, digital surveys and the management of the convergence of BIM/GIS tools.

In order to emphasize the integration of BIM into education, EduBIM was created, as a part of MINnD, to gather researchers, students, construction companies, architects and software leaders around new BIM technologies. EduBIM Scientific Workshop has an objective to reunite a community of researchers and industrials from MINnd project. The objective is to integrate the latest finding of BIM into the academic courses. In this context, ESTP has joined EduBIM in order to integrate the most recent technologies into its programs (see Fig. 1).

ESTP Paris is an international gold-standard school of sustainable construction. It trains and develops highly-skilled professionals equipped to design and implement innovative and operational solutions to the challenges of building the world of the future [21]. ESTP Paris offers students the possibility of integrating different majors during the last three years of the engineering curriculum including Topography, Buildings construction engineering, Public works and Mechanical/Electrical/Energy Efficiency engineering. As a driving force in research and innovation, and a leading construction company

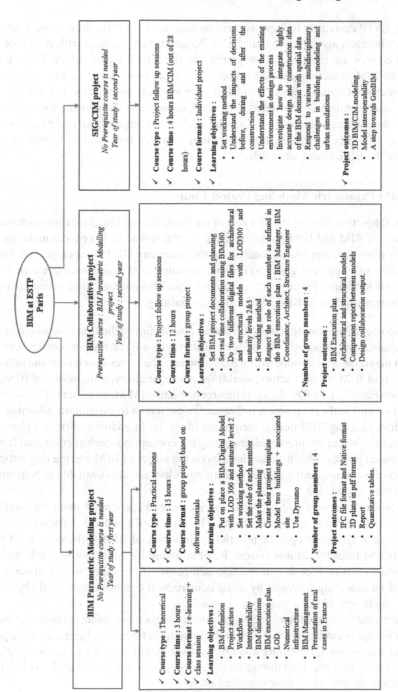

Fig. 1. BIM at ESTP workflow

partner, ESTP Paris aims to improve continuously academic programs to meet new technologies in urban and building scales [21]. To familiarize students with BIM processes, several courses are created and integrated into the school's curriculum. These courses deal with BIM modeling and collaborative processes using real case project examples. The objective of these projects is to familiarize students with the skills needed by each BIM project member, i.e. architects, engineers, consultants and constructors (see Fig. 1).

All engineering students in the second year of the engineering cycle have a course called GIS/CIM (City Information Modeling) in which they launch a small project to integrate the BIM model into GIS.

3.1 BIM Parametric Modeling Project Course

Course Objective. During the first year of engineering, our objective is to teach students the basics of BIM and BIM modeling using several software. In order to make sure that students from different backgrounds have the necessary BIM competencies during the three years of engineering at ESTP Paris, we integrated a new course entitled "BIM Parametric Modeling Project" during the first year. This course is divided into two parts: 1) theoretical content of BIM and 2) software training.

Methodology. Integrating the BIM learning course during the first year of engineering was a challenging approach. We decided to start with a three-hour-theoretical course to present the collaborative work within BIM projects. The topics covered are the following: definition of BIM, project actors, workflow, interoperability, dimensions of BIM, BIM execution plan [22], LODs, digital infrastructure and BIM Management. To enhance the content several real case projects in France are presented to explain the advantages and difficulties of using BIM during the project lifecycle. In addition, different phases of a construction project are presented, including the conception, construction, and lifecycle management phases. This first part focuses on the basics of BIM and the major topics to be covered in the upcoming weeks. E-learning videos are also available to help students deepen their knowledge.

Once the theoretical part is completed, six tutorial sessions of two hours and a half each are held to build a Digital Model. The choice of the BIM software to be used was not easy. Different open or proprietary/commercial BIM software is used by the Construction industry. In this course, Revit software by Autodesk was selected since it is used by many French construction companies. Like other BIM software, Revit is based on modeling a project by using construction components, called objects, e.g. beams, doors, etc. [23].

During the first three tutorial sessions, course instructors explain the basics of the software. The digital environment as well as different tools for using objects, creating parameters, extracting data, importing and linking files, producing plans, etc., are explained. Practical examples are done during these sessions. Once the necessary knowledge base is obtained, students start their modeling project.

The project consists of creating an architecture model for three types of buildings: 1) a school, 2) a shopping center, and 3) a residential building and its corresponding site. Students use two different approaches to set the models. For the residential building, they should do their digital model based on AutoCAD 2D files that are given by their professor. The objective is to allow students to pass information from a 2D to a 3D model. In this way, they would understand the advantages of using intelligent models. For example, once they modify a component in a BIM project, all sections will be updated, which is not the case with 2D modeling applications. The other constructions should respect criteria that professors set at the beginning of the project. The decision for the type of the building and the number of floors is left up to students. The objective of this part is to verify that each member has acquired the necessary knowledge for BIM modeling. The site is expected to respect the location of the two buildings and take into account their geo-referencing (see Fig. 2).

Fig. 2. Example of digital BIM model based on the link file method

Students work in a group of four persons. LOD 300 and maturity level 2 are required for this project. Before starting the modeling phase, each group is expected to set its working method, the role of each member, and the planning process. They should decide what information is necessary to present, and how they will organize their project. Students will be able to model construction elements and assign/create data such as color, material, product manufacturer, etc. They are also supposed to create their project template, define levels/elevations, and naming standards.

Once the work method is identified, each group creates different buildings and the associated site using different Revit files. These files are linked together to make the project. Objects and families, which are the libraries of fully functional templates and 3D models of various objects in Revit, can be used to model projects. If students don't find the element needed for their project, they can create objects or import them from different open source libraries. Dynamo is also used to export and import Excel data to Revit. Groups will be able to extract quantities and model elements using Dynamo's plugin (see Fig. 3).

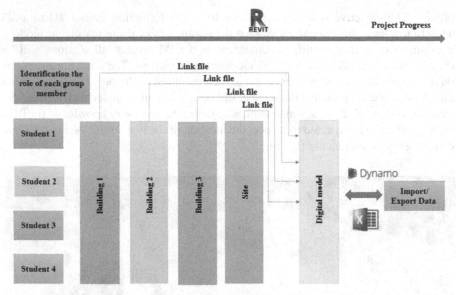

Fig. 3. BIM parametric project

Course Outcomes. The purpose of this project is to teach students the ability to work simultaneously on BIM Model using the link files method. Digital skills are needed to model architectural plans using different approaches. To make sure that students reach these objectives, a list of the documents is required for evaluation. Students submit three digital models in both IFC and native formats, 2D plans for floors, elevations, and sections in PDF format, a written report to explain their methodology, and schedules in a delivery folder.

3.2 BIM Collaborative Project Course

Course Objective. Working simultaneously on the same BIM project is a sensitive topic. The construction industry shows resistance to adopting BIM with a maturity level 3 because of the responsibilities involved for each project member. Maturity level 3 requires specific contracts that govern the new type of partnership between all actors. Multi-party agreements, risk and benefit sharing, and specific insurance should also be considered in level 3. Studies showed that adopting a collaborative method across different disciplines seemed to be productive for optimizing the design. Adjusting the protocols of BIM is beneficial to minimize the conflicts between the digital models [24].

During the second year of the engineering curriculum, ESTP Paris offers a real-time collaborative BIM project. Students work on the same BIM model hosted on a cloud-based platform. Having already acquired the necessary skills for BIM modeling, students are ready at this stage to work on digital models with a high maturity level. BIM360, a synchronous virtual collaborative workspace, is used to ensure project members' interactions during the project sessions. Architectural and structural models for a residential building are done and uploaded continuously on the BIM360 platform. Students are able to check conflicts between these two digital models and do the necessary corrections.

Methodology. The course is composed of five follow-up project sessions of two hours and a half each. The purpose of each session is to present a topic related to BIM collaboration and to answer students' questions. The project is done in groups of four. It is based on a case example where each member has a specific role as in a real BIM project such as BIM Manager, BIM Coordinator, Architect and Structure Engineer. During the first session, instructors present the project specifications and required deliverables with their deadlines. In addition to the project follow-up, different subjects are covered during the following sessions, e.g. uploading models on BIM360, publishing new versions, problems and issues and design collaboration. Instructors check frequently if all students are collaborating using the platform.

When the project is launched, the BIM Manager should establish the BIM execution plan [25], based on the French standards, to control the BIM goals and uses, the processes, the roles of project members, the planning, the workflow, and information exchanges, etc. This should be done at the beginning of the project before starting the modeling phase. The BIM Manager should verify the group member's compliance with the BIM execution plan throughout the project. All documents are updated on BIM360 and are accessible by group members. Notifications should be sent if modifications are done. The BIM Manager should prepare the digital environment on a collaborative platform and set the naming standards and templates for each model.

Once the BIM execution plan is completed, the architect start modeling using BIM software that allows the export of the model into the IFC format. In this course, Revit was chosen by students as the BIM software. The architect member submits the model based on the schedule and rules defined by the BIM Manager in the BIM execution plan. The architectural model should respect the standards related to naming, submittal dates, versioning, objects, and project specifications. The occupancy of each room should be defined as well as the furnishings used. Students are free to select their choice of materials. An example of an architectural model is presented in Fig. 4.

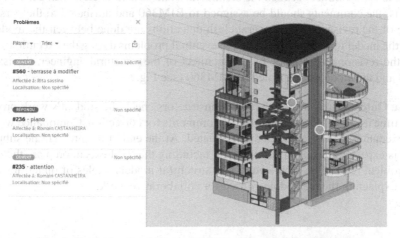

Fig. 4. Example of architectural BIM model with indicated issues.

Based on the planning, Structural Engineer can start his model using the architectural model (see Fig. 5). The groups can decide if they want to start structural analysis before completing the architectural model. The structural engineer member is in charge of designing structural vertical and horizontal elements of the project, e.g. walls, beams, columns, and foundation. Dimensioning of these components is mandatory. Each group is free to decide the type of construction that will be modeled. They can use steel, wood, or reinforced concrete structures.

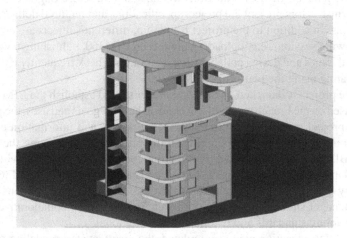

Fig. 5. Example of digital structural BIM model

After the architectural and structural models are completed in two different files, the BIM Coordinator should verify the consistency between them by using different options in BIM360, like the issues and problem tasks (see Fig. 4). To ensure the visibility of his comments on the Revit model, students should install Revit Issues Add-In. BIM coordinator can also use the Design collaboration option for clash detection, ensuring that there is no conflict between the architecture and structural elements. Based on this analysis, the comments should be assigned to BIM360 and attributed to the person in charge of the revised model. Several clash detections are done between the models to check the model feasibility and avoid the eventual problems during the execution phase. Once the revisions were made by the architect or the structural engineer, the issue is closed and the models are updated on BIM360 (see Fig. 6).

Course Outcomes. During this project, instructors check the student's work progress at any time using BIM360 and post their comments for correction. Compliance with the BIM execution plan is reviewed and evaluated. At the end of the project, the submittal folder is expected to contain various files, including the BIM execution plan, the issues and problem report, the architecture and structural models, tables of quantities and a report explaining the methodology used for collaborative work.

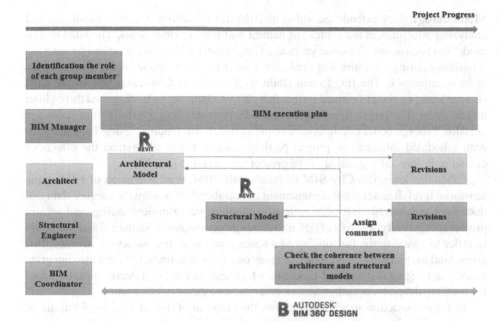

Fig. 6. The BIM collaborative project

3.3 GIS/CIM Project Course

Course Objective. The future of the construction industry lies in the use of technology. The entry of technology into design and construction work has resulted in new responsibilities and tasks for the construction manager. As a result, construction managers' knowledge must be updated to take advantage of advanced information technology such as GIS, BIM, photogrammetry, UAVs, and 3D laser scanners. These technologies provide new career opportunities for engineers, maximize managerial productivity, improve overall project performance, and efficiently perform accurate construction analysis to plan the sequence of operations on the job site. The digital advancement of the building sector, the arrival of BIM and its proliferation, GIS, CIM (City Information Modeling), etc., all have made possible the production and integration of large amounts of heterogeneous data from different disciplines throughout the life cycle of a building.

During the second year of engineering, GIS, CIM and various other software are taught in the curriculum. Part of the GIS/CIM course involves integrating a BIM model into GIS. This course is divided into three parts, including 1) The theoretical part for presenting SIG/BIM/CIM concepts, 2) The practical part for software learning and modeling, and 3) The open and distance learning part in which students discover resources provided for them. The total theoretical and distance learning parts are 12 h and the practical part is 16 h where around three hours of theoretical course consist of BIM/CIM and one hour of practical work for BIM model integration.

Methodology. GIS extends the value of BIM digital design data by visualizing and analyzing structures in the context of natural and built environments. The BIM digital model has been around for some years as an important tool for designing and monitoring a building during its entire life cycle from the first drafts made in the design phase to its maintenance. The IFC format (Industry Foundation Classes) is one of the BIM standards and an object-oriented format that allows a building to be described throughout its life cycle. The integration of BIM and GIS provides deeper information for better decision making, better communication and better understanding. Using BIM and GIS with scheduled information, project participants can better understand the effects of decisions before, during and after the project construction [26, 27].

CIM, also known as City-BIM or multi-scale BIM, is an extension of BIM at the territorial level. It enables the management of collaborative work with a secure data and document monitoring system, as well as exchanges, better understanding, and greater project acceptability. The role of GIS is to combine geographical, statistical and databases in order to visualize the functioning of a space such as an infrastructure, accessibility, areas, land use planning, flood zones, or many other constructions. CIM can also integrate model data aggregated and real-time data which can be used as a decision-making tool for municipalities, local authorities, or other organizations or companies.

In the construction sector, BIM allows the creation of digital models of buildings, including all technical information related to the building. By combining the two technologies, it is possible to model environments that extend much more than just the building and thus provide meaningful connecting networks, accessible infrastructures, or even consider simulations at the city level.

Here, the project is based on the CIM concept which combines GIS with BIM including the physical, technical, and functional characteristics of a model. In fact, the core of this course is GIS, which teaches the use of ArcGIS software, and part of it is also related to setting up BIM/CIM integration.

The ArcGIS Data Interoperability extension is a toolkit that allows integrating data from multiple sources and formats for use with geo-processing tools and publication with ArcGIS for Server. The goal of this exercise is to transform an.ifc file for viewing in ArcGIS Pro. Figure 7 illustrates an example of a simple BIM model developed in Revit which is then integrated into a 3D GIS city model.

Course Outcomes. During this project, students discover the interoperability of data from different models. Finally, students submit their GIS model containing the BIM model in the geodatabase of the GIS model as well as a process description report.

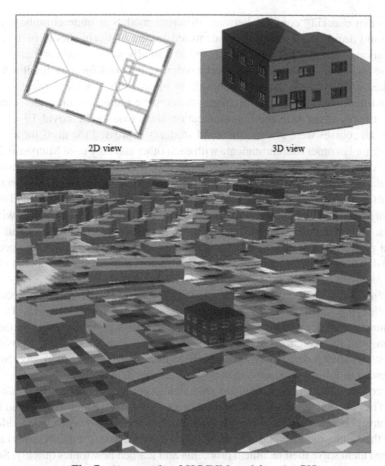

Fig. 7. An example of SIG/BIM model on ArcGIS

4   Advantages and Difficulties

Integrating BIM courses into engineering programs for students having different backgrounds is an interesting challenge. Students showed motivation to work in groups since instructors used the Team/Group based learning approach. They learned how to be organized and collaborative, given that these two characteristics are very important to engineers. They were able to share their projects and work together at any time using two different methods: 1) digital model based on linking Revit files, 2) digital model based on Design collaboration on BIM360. Both methods help to avoid conflicts between different digital models.

However, instructors faced some difficulties in order to create a collaborative environment on BIM360. The procedure to create the folder for each group, to assign members, and to attribute licenses to users has been too long. Updating models on the collaborative platform also has been time-consuming and required high-performance computers. It turns out that checking conflicts between different models is quite complicated. Students should decide if clash detection identified by the platform should be taken into consideration or not, since some conflicts found digitally are not real conflicts on site.

At the end of the collaborative project, students are asked for their feedback. They were asked for their wish list and proposals to improve the course content. Students mentioned that they faced some problems concerning online learning and stated the need for improvement with the communication tool. Due to the covid-19 pandemic situation, all courses were given online and students expressed the need for an instant messaging tool in order to communicate with each other and they used Microsoft Teams. They noticed that comments and issues via BIM360 can be misunderstood sometimes and should be clearly described by the author. Students also expressed the complexity when starting the project. It was difficult for them to write the BIM execution plan. This document is confidential for each project and tutors couldn't provide them with real examples. Only templates were given to help them write an adequate document. Some technical problems were also faced. Some students couldn't have immediate access to BIM360 due to software or hardware issues. Instructors did several attempts in order to fix such problems.

Students mentioned that introducing the BIM-based team learning approach was very challenging for them. They worked together in teams for this project. They had to communicate with each other to define tasks and work methods, to write the BIM execution plan, to create the building plans, to develop their models and to overcome problems, etc. They learned more about the BIM uses and standards in France. Some of them decided to follow an internship in companies that deploy BIM.

The collaboration approach helped students to get a general perspective of their project. They noticed that clash detection was very beneficial for their project and helped them to have coherent models. Some groups used Camtasia Studio to produce a video clip showing their entire model process. Students also benefited from the use of video tutorials that helped them solve their technical problems and learned new topics quickly. Submitting a project through a collaborative platform was helpful for the students because the final model files are so large and time-consuming to upload to our school websites.

Through GIS/CIM project, students obtained a better perspective on city information modeling and urban planning, and this helped them to imagine, design and create a more sustainable and resilient model by considering concepts of BIM and CIM. Therefore, now, they can better understand infrastructure assets in terms of geolocalisation and the interaction with the surrounding ecosystem through the project.

5   Evaluation Criteria

Various criteria were used to for evaluating student work and deliverables. Table 1 shows the list of parameters considered for each of the student groups. These are included in the evaluation form to correct the project.

Table 1. BIM courses evaluation criteria

BIM parametric modeling project	BIM collaborative project
-Georeferencing the site and the buildings -Quality of the architectural models -List of quantities -Final model using the link method approach -Group work -Respect for the graphic chart and plans naming -List of deliverables -Respect the deadlines	-BIM Execution plan -Respect for the role of each group member -Comparison report between different models -Problems follow up report -Quality of the architectural model -Quality of the structural model -Final model with both architectural and structural parts -Work methodology -List of deliverables -Respect the deadlines

6   Conclusion and Future Direction

This paper presents different approaches that are used for BIM learning at ESTP Paris with different levels and multiple educational objectives. The first course is used to introduce the modeling tools that will be used for collaboration during the second course. Project learning approaches are used to motivate students and prepare them for future engineering projects. Different digital tools are used to design digital models and to allow collaboration between group members. Both native and IFC formats are used for information exchange between structural and architectural models. For future courses, it will be interesting to study the collaboration using a new file format such as BIM Collaboration Format (BCF) used in BIM collaborative platforms.

In the third course, a BIM model is integrated into a GIS model. This data integration is beneficial in both domains of geographic information and building information modeling, and it is a critical step in addressing multidisciplinary environmental challenges. GIS and BIM integration can be used for several queries regarding pollution estimation, road safety design improvements, solar radiation estimation, traffic management and many more applications in both 2D and 3D simulations.

As a future teaching and research direction, we at ESTP Paris would like to focus more on GeoBIM which deals with the integration of GIS data into BIM and the georeferencing of BIM models. In this regard, a translation from CityGML to IFC can be developed to further integrate BIM and GIS as future work which requires an agreement between multiple stakeholders from both Geo and BIM sides.

References

1. What is BIM (Building Information Modeling)?. https://esub.com/blog/building-information-modeling-bim. Accessed 7 July 2021
2. dos Santos, S.D., Vendrametto, O., González, M.L., Correia, C.F.: Profile of building information modeling – BIM - tools maturity in brazilian civil construction scenery. In: Umeda, S., Nakano, M., Mizuyama, H., Hibino, H., Kiritsis, D., von Cieminski, G. (eds.) APMS 2015.

IAICT, vol. 459, pp. 291–298. Springer, Cham (2015). https://doi.org/10.1007/978-3-319-22756-6_36

3. Azhar, S.: Building information modeling (BIM): trends, benefits, risks, and challenges for the AEC industry. Leadersh. Manag. Eng. **11**(3), 241–252 (2011)
4. Bolshakova, V., Halin, G., Humbert, P., Boton, C.: Digital synchronous collaboration workspace and 3d interactions for an AEC project. decision-making scenario evaluation. In: Luo, Y. (ed.) CDVE 2017. LNCS, vol. 10451, pp. 168–176. Springer, Cham (2017). https://doi.org/10.1007/978-3-319-66805-5_21
5. Wu, W., Issa, R.R.A.: BIM education and recruiting: survey-based comparative analysis of issues, perceptions, and collaboration opportunities. J. Profess. Issues Eng. Educ. Pract. **140**(2) (2014)
6. Sacks, R., Pikas, E.: Building information modeling education for construction engineering and management. I: industry requirements, state of the art, and gap analysis. J. Construct. Eng. Manage. **139**(11) (2013)
7. Arroteia, A.V., Do Amaral, G.G., Kikuti, S.Z., Melhado, S.B.: BIM knowledge assessment: an overview among professionals. Build. Inform. Model. **2**(2), 315–324 (2020)
8. Kocaturk, T., Kiviniemi, V.: Challenges of integrating BIM in architectural education. Comput. Perform. **2**(2), 465–474 (2013)
9. Bosch-Sijtsema, P.M., Gluch, P., Sezer, A.A.: Professional development of the BIM actor role. Autom. Constr. **97**, 44–51 (2019)
10. Sudha Venkatesh, A. A. A., Status of BIM adoption and the BIM experience of cost consultants in Australia. J. Profession. Issues Eng. Educ. Pract. **140**(3) (2014)
11. Wang, L., Huang, M., Zhang, X., Jin, R., Yang, T.: Review of BIM adoption in the higher education of AEC Disciplines. J. Profession. Issues Eng. Educ. Pract. **146**(3) (2020)
12. Sanchez-Lite, A., Gonzalez, C., Zulueta, P., Sampaio, Z., A comparative study of the use of building information modeling in teaching engineering projects. IEEE Access **8** (2020)
13. Udomdech, P., Papadonikolaki, E., Davies, A.: An alternative project-based learning model for building information modeling using teams. In: Proceeding of the 34th Annual ARCOM Conference, pp. 57–66. Belfast, UK (2018)
14. Adamu, Z.A., Thorpe, T.: How universities are teaching bim: a review and case study from the UK. J. Inform. Technol. Construct. **21**, 19–139 (2016)
15. Abdalla, S.B.: Re-Exploring the potentiality of bim: incorporating bim into the multi-disciplinary educational setup. In: Proceedings of the Joint 8th IFEE2017 and 3rd TSDIC2017, pp. 1–13. Sharjah, United Arab Emirates (2017)
16. Barison, M.B., Santos, E.T.: BIM teaching strategies: an overview of the current approaches. Gestão & Tecnologia de Projetos **6**(2) (2012)
17. GIS in Civil Engineering: Resources for teaching and research in higher education. https://www.esri.com/en-us/industries/higher-education/gis-in-engineering. Accessed 15 Aug 2021
18. European construction sector observatory. https://ec.europa.eu/growth/sectors/construction/observatory_en. Accessed 15 Aug 2021
19. BIM adoption in Europe: 7 countries compared. https://www.planradar.com/gb/bim-adoption-in-europe. Accessed 15 Aug 2021
20. MINnD National Project. https://www.minnd.fr/en/. Accessed 15 Aug 2021
21. École spéciale des travaux publics, du bâtiment et de l'industrie (ESTP Paris). https://www.estp.fr/en/school. Accessed 15 Aug 2021
22. Building Information Modeling Execution Planning Guide. https://vdcscorecard.stanford.edu/sites/g/files/sbiybj8856/f/bim_project_execution_planning_guide-v2.0.pdf?msclkid=3c6476a6bc0a11ec85169dddbe058563. Accessed 10 July 2021
23. Woo, J.H.: BIM (Building information modeling) and pedagogical challenges. In: Proceedings of the 43rd ASC Annual International Conference. Flagstaff (2007)

24. Pihlak, M., Deamer, P., Holland, R., Poerschke, U., Messner, J., Parfitt, K.: Building information modeling (BIM) and the impact on design quality. J. Architect. Eng. Technol. **1**(1) (2011)
25. BuildingSMART France, Mediaconstruct, and MINnD, Comment rédiger une convention BIM ?. https://buildingsmartfrance-mediaconstruct.fr/wp-content/uploads/2021/05/Guide-Convention-BIM.pdf?msclkid=0cadc2b2bc0e11ec82bf1aa81242594d. Accessed 15 July 2021
26. Sani, M.J., Rahman, A.A.: GIS and BIM integration at data level: a review. In: International Conference on Geomatics and Geospatial Technology (GGT 2018), vol. 42, issue 4, pp. 299–306, Kuala Lumpur, Malaysia (2018)
27. Bolshakova, V., Halin, G., Humbert, P., Boton, C.: Digital Synchronous Collaboration Workspace and 3D Interactions for an AEC Project. Decision-Making Scenario Evaluation, 14th International Conference, CDVE 2017, pp. 168–176. Mallorca, Spain (2017)

Novel Viewpoints on BIM

Kinetic Architecture and BIM: The State of Art and Future Visions

Yenal Akgün[1](✉) ⓘ and Ozan Önder Özener[2] ⓘ

[1] Faculty of Architecture, Yaşar University, Izmir, Turkey
yenal.akgun@yasar.edu.tr
[2] Faculty of Architecture, Istanbul Technical University, Istanbul, Turkey

Abstract. Kinetic architecture is the design of buildings or building systems with transformative elements using mechanical components. Recent developments in construction technology, robotics, design computing and material science have increased the interest and demand for kinetic building systems and applications. This motivation relates to the growing need for functional flexibility, adaptability, sustainability and extended capabilities of structural performance. Although the concept of kinetic architecture is not new in architectural theory and practice for a few decades, it has not been sufficiently discussed in the context of Building Information Modeling (BIM) methods. Most studies in the related literature only focus on the parametric design and modeling of kinetic façade systems in a supportive parametric design tool and synchronous or nonsynchronous integration of these models into the BIM environment as 3D objects or families. Although these applications with BIM and parametric design tools have significant potentials, a large number of recent studies ignore the essential concepts of kinetic architecture and critical aspects of the kinetic design, simulation and analysis processes. In order to meet these deficiencies, this paper provides a comprehensive investigation of BIM methods in the milieu of kinetic design applications along with a suggestive object-oriented ontological framework and holistic integrative strategies. The arguments are based on the parametric modeling and simulation of kinetic systems, subsystems and components, as they are similar to parametric product models in other manufacturing engineering disciplines. The paper includes the following: (1) a critical review of the existing approaches of BIM methods and parametric applications for kinetic architecture (2) a thorough discussion of holistic BIM integration strategies for kinetic building systems with well-reasoned arguments along with theoretical and practical perspectives.

Keywords: Building information modeling · Kinetic architecture · Parametric design

1 Introduction

Kinetic Architecture can be defined as *"creating spaces, objects, surfaces and structures that can physically re-configure themselves to meet changing needs, whereby an adaptable architecture is formed"* [1]. As a fundamental difference from conventional

O. Ö. Özener et al. (Eds.): EBF 2021, CCIS 1627, pp. 135–144, 2022.
https://doi.org/10.1007/978-3-031-16895-6_9

architectural design, architects accept the concept of motion as a design input, while designing a kinetic architectural product [2]. Although the concept is not new in the discipline of architecture, the rapid developments in construction, material and robotic technologies gave kinetic building systems a visible momentum in the construction industry. Since kinetic architecture has many applications, it is possible to classify contemporary kinetic architecture products as kinetic structures, kinetic façade systems, kinetic systems that (1) transform and augment the spatial quality of the spaces and (2) create environmentally responsive or mobile buildings [3]. These types of buildings, building subsystems or building components have the ability to change their geometries according to the functional and spatial needs of the users, or environmental conditions such as wind, sun, or dynamic loads.

As the concept of kinetic architecture has grown in architectural theory and practice for several decades, such research and development applications became a popular topic in contemporary domains like parametric design, computational architecture, and Building Information Modeling (BIM). The literature documents many studies on the integration of parametric design tools and methods with kinetic building systems, especially at the upstream level [4–6]. With the use of graph-based programming and parametric object modeling add-ons, implementation of kinetic building system concepts in BIM environments are partially possible today.

Janssen describes the synchronous workflow using BIM platforms connected with graph-based parametric modeling systems as the *"coupled approach"* for the design process and software interoperability [7]. This coupled approach has become more popular in the AEC practice since the extended project scopes –*with complex geometries, advanced structural designs and adaptive building systems* necessitate tightly integrated processes that are facilitated with adequate methods, capable software tools and cutting-edge technology.

In this regard, the literature documents a number of application examples focusing on the "coupled approach" and the synchronous use of parametric design tools and BIM. Example research studies can be listed as the bioinspired kinetic envelope of Wang and Li [8], Sync-BIM of Shen and Wu [9], and the studies of Wahbeh [10] and Brancart et al. [11]. In addition, some studies also focused on building energy modeling (BEM) applications including integrated energy performance analyses and green building regulations [12–16] integrated automation and physical models into a parametric BIM design environment; and Hu et al. [17] emphasized the importance of the interlinked "family" concept in the BIM environment, and established a methodology based on the parametric family components.

From the perspective of kinetic systems, the existing literature on the coupled approaches does not cover the essential tasks, phases and processes of design and development. Specifically, kinematic design tasks, dynamic kinetic component analysis, kinetic structural analysis and other BIM-specific nD applications are largely neglected. The majority of these studies involve responsive building envelope and kinetic façade design using parametric design tools and BIM methods. Apart from these case-based studies, holistic approaches for kinetic BIM applications and theoretical propositions with ontological arguments may bridge the existing gap in the BIM literature.

This paper addresses the aforementioned issues through a comprehensive review of kinetic architecture and BIM approaches. Fundamental design principles and workflows of kinetic building systems are reviewed in order to provide a foundation for BIM-enabled design, simulation and analysis necessities. Based on the concepts derived from this effort and the coupled approach propositions an object-oriented ontological framework is proposed for further discussion and exploration of a holistic approach for BIM-enabled kinetic architecture.

2 Design Principles of Kinetic Architecture

An adequate kinetic building, building component, or kinetic structure should (1) meet the required architectural, spatial, functional and structural performance expectations; (2) have affordable actuator(s) with acceptable location(s) and type(s); (3) transform and deploy with a designed or predefined geometry [18, 19]. Thus, the process of kinetic design necessitates an interdisciplinary approach between architecture, mechanical engineering and structural engineering [3]. Due to the demand for responsive and automated kinetic systems and the use of smart materials for kinetic systems, mechatronics and material science have also been added to this highly integrated research, development and design domain. These brought forward the digital design and manufacturing technologies, parametric design, modeling, simulation and robotic fabrication tools for the design and simulation processes of kinetic systems.

The current design flow and connected phases of kinetic building systems are presented in Fig. 1. While most of the kinetic buildings or building components can be assumed as "mechanisms", the design phases in the figure are largely adapted from the workflows of mechanism design. Here, three important design phases exist for kinetic architecture: (1) Definition of the design specifications; (2) kinematic synthesis; (3) analysis and design of parts. Since they are interconnected with byproducts and their behaviors, none of these phases can be omitted during the design, simulation and fabrication process, in order to obtain an aesthetic, functional, and durable final product.

The first phase is the definition of the design requirements as the pre-design phase. These requirements mostly cover the architectural, functional, structural, spatial and other design requirements that change according to the type and function of the kinetic building component(s).

The second phase is the kinematic synthesis, which involves the main geometric design of the kinetic system. Type synthesis is the first step of this phase. In this step, topological choices of the mechanism, such as the number and type of actuators, shape and type of the mechanism are developed. Mechanism atlas is a database including all types of mechanisms in the literature and this atlas helps to select the correct mechanism type at this phase. Dimensional synthesis and design is the second step. During this step, the basic dimensions of the kinetic system and geometry of the movement are determined based on the predefined requirements. In the current practice, kinematic synthesis tasks are mostly conducted in various parametric architectural and engineering design environments.

Analysis and design of the parts are the next interconnected phases. In the scope of this phase, all dynamic and static loads are assigned and reaction forces are calculated via finite element analysis software (FEA) packages. Parts of the kinetic building component are designed, dimensioned and simulated according to these analyses. Synchronously, component types, required force and torque of the actuators are defined according to the assigned loads and weight of the system. In the final step, the strength of the critical parts should be tested again via FEA analysis and/or prototypes. If needed, electronic controls of the system are devised in this phase.

As it is seen from these phases, mechanism design processes and transformation simulations of kinetic building system sets and components require a large set of tools, which arguably differ from current BIM software frameworks. There are many add-ons, plugins, or other design and simulation environments that necessitate holistic and integrated design models, novel interoperability schemes and related procedures. In the case of designing kinetic building envelope systems, such kinematic and dynamic design decisions should be made in mechanism design software such as Autodesk Inventor®, Dassault Systems Solidworks®, and/or a parametric design tool like McNeel Grasshopper® (with the contribution of some add-ons) which are further developed through off-the-shelf BIM software for architectural design development.

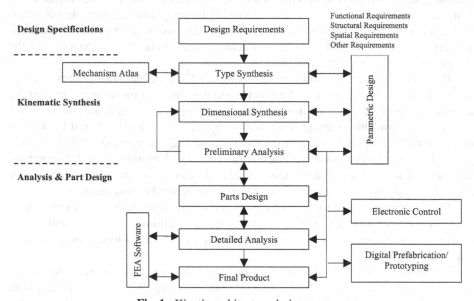

Fig. 1. Kinetic architecture design process

3   Integration of Kinetic Architecture and BIM

In recent years, many tools are available in the BIM and parametric design domain, which provided extended interoperability between BIM, parametric design platforms and other peripheral simulation software which are useful for kinetic design applications. After the development of synchronous working models between parametric modeling and conventional BIM platforms, complexity, transferability and modifiability of the model emerged as issues. In response to this, BIM platforms integrated and embed the equivalent or counterpart external tools and add-ons into their platforms such as graph-based parametric design packages like Autodesk Dynamo Studio® and Graphisoft Param-o® are integrated tools for Autodesk Revit® and Graphisoft ArchiCAD®, which aimed to extend the parametric modeling capabilities of BIM platforms with increased model and data integrity.

Conventionally, the main design stages of kinetic building systems design are conducted in complex mechanical engineering CAD/CAM software packages like Autodesk Inventor®, Dassault Systems Solidworks®, or Dassault Systems Catia®. With the aforementioned advances in graph-based tool integration in BIM platforms, it is now possible to carry out essential kinetic design tasks in the BIM environment, especially at the conceptual design and design development levels. Further operations still require complex CAM tools for manufacturing, fabrication and construction which also stresses the importance of novel project workflows with appropriate information and knowledge exchange.

The coupled approach using the aforementioned off-the-shelf BIM platforms and the supportive tools is the current design procedure in terms of software utilization. This approach benefits from the different design, simulation and analysis tools. However, it cannot cover and integrate most of the necessary tools for kinetic building design, which may be a challenging task. The discussion includes the representation of the simultaneous movements and the properties of the kinetic components as a specific part of the parametric BIM process and the conduction of necessary analyses for defining the type/force of the actuators, assigned forces and the required sections for the dynamic parts and elements.

While there is a large number of external tools available for BIM systems, common BIM platforms integrate the equivalent or counterparts' external tools/add-ons into their platforms. This is because; BIM platforms encompass all steps and disciplines of the architectural design processes synchronously through the exchange of domain-specific parametric models. Here the possibilities for kinetic design applications rely on the creation of dynamic meta-models/families with embedded object behaviors. This task necessitates a shift from conventional BIM to kinetic BIM systems, which are specifically devised for kinetic architecture applications.

Apart from these software use schemes and possibilities, design principles of kinetic building systems the whole process necessitates an interdisciplinary and integrated approach on the conceptual level. This is the core argument behind the adoption of BIM and connected delivery methods such as Integrated Project Delivery (IPD). However, the extension of the scope comes from the kinematic content of building components which resemble the design, simulation and manufacturing processes in mechanical and aerospace engineering. Since the core concepts of parametric BIM methods are similar to Product Manufacturing Information (PMI), a novel approach for kinetic building systems design should involve a synthesis of BIM, PMI and CAM methods and related data/information management schemes.

4   Extended Kinetic BIM Ontology and the KBIM Framework

In Fig. 2, a suggestive workflow model for the kinetic architecture and BIM integration is proposed. As illustrated in this workflow, kinetic design processes are still not completely integrated into the parametric BIM environment and they are conducted via a coupled approach using peripheral tools. The link between the parametric design and simulation environments is based on the common approach of object-oriented product modeling. However, these processes are domain-specific due to the distinction between the dynamic and static existence of mechanical and architectural systems and components.

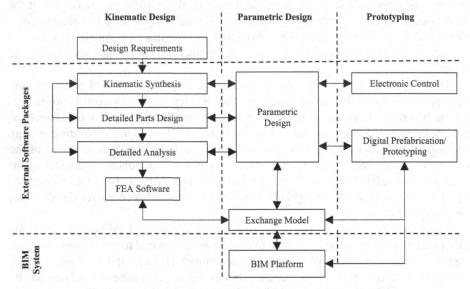

Fig. 2. Workflow for the kinetic architecture & BIM integration

This approach invites a thorough understanding of an extended kinetic BIM (KBIM) ontology-based on object-oriented abstraction. The proposed suggestive framework is similar to the current BIM with parametric data classes including geometry, dimensions, and material info along with object methods and behaviors such as building component assemblies, connections and interactions. Here, the coupled approach uses this onto-logical framework as the basis for possible BIM implementations along with layered, nested and parametric data. The profound distinction comes from the kinematic/dynamic content of the aforementioned kinetic systems characteristics. This is reflected in additional object method layers concerning motion and kinetic behaviors which are similar in mechanical and robotic applications.

The key conceptual dimension for the integration of parametric BIM and kinetic systems design is the proposed ontological KBIM framework. This framework is devised to be compatible with the dynamic/kinematic properties of kinetic building systems and components in a hierarchical object-oriented approach. The ontological framework is based on a top-down object database configured with object-oriented data structures, hierarchies, classes and connected variable types –*vector, numeric, Boolean, string etc.* which are parametrically representing a generic kinetic building system.

The framework includes the following concepts: (1) kinetic system hierarchy, construction priorities and major kinetic system and subsystems sets like structural category, kinematic system type, etc. (2) kinetic sub-systems sets including internal objects, form, size and geometry, material properties and internal object behaviors (3) relationship types like external system connections, internal system connections, object and component dependencies/interdependencies and assemblies (4) actuation variables represented as relative coordinates to a joint, angular motion in degrees and time with vector information. Such algorithmic relationships and dependencies are given as rule sets and conditional functions. Table 1 illustrates a generic object definition for a prototypical kinetic building system in the proposed KBIM framework.

Table. 1. An object definition scheme in KBIM ontology

Building (Generic)					
System: Facade (Generic)					
Component	*Form*	*Structure*	*Identifiers*	*Relationships*	*Actuation/Motion*
K-Beam (Generic)	Geometry (x) Size (x,y,z)	Core (x) Core (x). material (x)	Component ID# (x) Direction (angle)	Internal System Connections: *Substructure (x), Joint (x)*	Relative Coordinates (x,y,z) Angle (degree) Time (sec) Distance (x)
				External System Connections: *Facade (x), Roof (x)*	

The proposed object-oriented approach provides predefined and parametric semantic representations for kinetic building systems. From the implementation standpoint, the given framework and the data structure scheme are applicable using the existing graph-based programming tools or in-built API's of BIM platforms. This also supports integrated processes with essential tasks for design development among interdisciplinary project teams.

A suggestive KBIM approach is illustrated in Fig. 3. Using the portable KBIM data scheme, all kinematic synthesis and analysis tools are fully integrated into the parametric BIM platform. This approach also stresses the importance of BIM-based interoperability among tools, platforms and teams through BIM as the common design data repository during the design and development phases.

The proposed KBIM framework can be evaluated from the perspective of current BIM standards and connected tasks and procedures. As the workflow provides both definitions and content for design and implementation phases, this layout has the potential to be used for customized BIM execution plans, definitions of information requirements and the schemes of information delivery and exchange among interdisciplinary parties for KBIM applications. The operational implications also include the structure of the KBIM-specific common data environments with the shared models and modular kinetic behavior classes that are transferrable among projects.

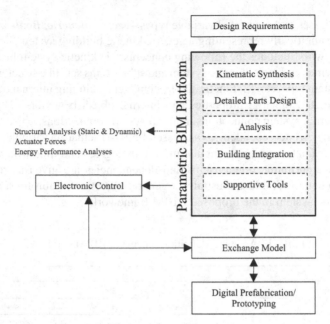

Fig. 3. Holistic approach for BIM and kinetic architecture integration

5 Conclusion

The design, evaluation, and analysis of kinetic building systems are undertaken within the context of object-oriented BIM ontology regarding improvement of the design quality through process innovation. This study has produced a suggestive framework by which the usability of the concepts of kinetic BIM models and interpretations may be explored. The suggestions presented in this paper prioritize the dynamic characteristics of kinetic buildings as the core concepts for providing a BIM-enabled approach. The proposed framework invites new discussions about BIM implementation for kinetic building systems design. As the holistic process requires true interdisciplinary tasks and evaluation schemes, a tightly integrated approach has vast potentials for comprehending kinetic systems and their physical and kinematic components. Parameterization of these properties also creates object-oriented comprehension and decision-making schemes for further design evaluation, analysis and implementation. The proposed model shows that the integration of parametric BIM models and system simulation/analysis tasks is achievable. Such implementations have the potential to evaluate different design options considered and ultimately in improving design quality and kinetic system capabilities. The BIM-enabled processes and potential integrated delivery methods are also valuable for further exploration and argumentation with experimental studies, systems design development and prototypical projects.

References

1. El Razaz, Z.: Sustainable vision of kinetic architecture. J. Build. Apprais. (2010). https://doi.org/10.1057/jba.2010.5
2. Zuk, W., Clark, R.H.: Kinetic Architecture. Van Nostrand Reinhold, New York (1970)
3. Akgün, Y.: Review of contemporary adaptive structures and future perspectives. In: Pagés Madrigal, J.M., Nikoofam, M. (eds.) Proceedings of ICCAU 2021 – 4th International Conference of Contemporary Affairs in Architecture and Urbanism. 20–21 May. Alanya, Turkey (2021). E-ISBN: 978-605-06780-8-6. https://doi.org/10.38027/ICCAUA2021165N10
4. Mahmoud, A.H.A., Elghazi, Y.: Parametric-based designs for kinetic facades to optimize daylight performance: comparing rotation and translation kinetic motion for hexagonal facade patterns. Sol. Energy (2016). https://doi.org/10.1016/j.solener.2015.12.039
5. Avellaneda, O.F.L.: Deployable structures system, hexagonal X-frame. Three case studies. ArchiDOCT **4**(2), 41–56 (2017)
6. Dragoljevic, M., Viscuso, S., Zanelli, A.: Data-driven design of deployable structures: literature review and multi-criteria optimization approach. Curv. Layer. Struct. (2021). https://doi.org/10.1515/cls-2021-0022
7. Janssen, P.: Parametric BIM workflows. In: Ikeda, Y., Herr, C.M., Holzer, D., Kaijima, S. Kim, M.J. Schnabel, M.A. (eds.) CAADRIA 2015 - 20th International Conference on Computer-Aided Architectural Design Research in Asia: Emerging Experiences in the Past, Present and Future of Digital Architecture, pp. 437–446. Hong Kong (2015)
8. Wang, J., Li, J.: Bio-inspired kinetic envelopes for building energy efficiency based on parametric design of building information modeling. In: 2010 Asia-Pacific Power and Energy Engineering Conference, pp. 1–4 (2010). https://doi.org/10.1109/APPEEC.2010.5449511
9. Shen, Y.T., Wu, T.Y.: Sync-BIM: the interactive BIM-based platform for controlling data-driven kinetic façade. In: Stephanidis, C. (ed.) HCI 2016. CCIS, vol. 618, pp. 445–450. Springer, Cham (2016). https://doi.org/10.1007/978-3-319-40542-1_72
10. Wahbeh, W.: Building skins, parametric design tools and BIM platforms. In: Advanced Building Skins. Bern (2017)
11. Brancart, S., Paduart, A., Vergauwen, A., Vandervaeren, C., de Laet, L., de Temmerman, N.: Transformable structures: Materialising design for change. Int. J. Des. Nature Ecodyn. **12**(3), 357–366 (2017). https://doi.org/10.2495/DNE-V12-N3-357-366
12. Kim, H., Asl, M., Yan, W.: Parametric BIM-based energy simulation for buildings with complex kinetic facades. In: ECAADe 33 - Real Time - Extending the Reach of Computation, pp. 657–664 (2015)
13. Shen, Y.T., Lu, P.W.: The development of kinetic façade units with BIM-based active control system for the adaptive building energy performance service. In: Chien, S., Choo, S., Schnabel, M.A., Nakapan, W., Kim, M.J., Roudavski, S. (eds.) Proceedings of the 21st International Conference of the Association for Computer-Aided Architectural Design Research in Asia CAADRIA 2016, pp. 517–526. Hong Kong (2016)
14. Chen, J.Y., Huang, S.C.: Adaptive building facade optimisation: an integrated Green-BIM approach. In: Chien, S., Choo, S., Schnabel, M.A., Nakapan, W., Kim, M.J., Roudavski, S. (eds.) Proceedings of the 21st International Conference of the Association for Computer-Aided Architectural Design Research in Asia CAADRIA 2016, pp. 259–268. Hong Kong (2016)
15. Mallasi, Z.: Integrating physical and digital prototypes using parametric BIM in the pursuit of kinetic façade parametricism vs. materialism: evolution of digital technologies for development. In: 8th ASCAAD Conference Proceedings, pp. 155–168. London (2016). http://papers.cumincad.org/cgi-bin/works/Show?ascaad2016_018

16. Mallasi, Z.: Using parametric BIM integration for prototyping future responsive façades. J. Facade Des. Eng. **6**(1), 89–100 (2018)
17. Hu, Y., Yuan, F., Li, Q., Li, H.: The BIM based responsive environmental performance design methodology. In: XVIII Conference of the Iberoamerican Society of Digital Graphics - SIGraDi: Design in Freedom, Blucher Design Proceedings, vol. 1, pp. 120–125 (2014). http://dx.doi.org/https://doi.org/10.1016/despro-sigradi2014-0020
18. Gantes, C.J.: Deployable Structures: Analysis and Design. WIT Press, Southampton (2001)
19. Akgün, Y.: A Novel Transformation Model For Deployable Scissor-Hinge Structures, PhD Thesis, Izmir Institute of Technology (2010)

Use of Integrated HBIM Methods for Historic Underground Structures: Pişirici Kastel Case Study

Fatih Uzun(✉) [ID] and Mine Özkar [ID]

Istanbul Technical University, 34367 Sisli Istanbul, Turkey
uzunfa17@itu.edu.tr

Abstract. Digital models for heritage preservation applications are generally based on non-semantic geometric information acquired through photogrammetry or laser scanning. Addressing the need for multi-faceted application information, a Heritage Building Information Model (HBIM) integrates the geometric information with other complementary and semantic data. As a comprehensive research study on HBIM, this chapter presents a case study on the digital representation of an underground historical water structure with integrated HBIM methodology. Simultaneously identifying the difficulties and obstacles encountered in the documentation process, the study proposes a system to document and examine domain-specific information obtained through digital photogrammetry and thermal imaging methods. As an application case for this, the geometric and selective semantic data of the historical structure was modeled with BIM methods and its integral visual programming language while considering the unit elements that make up the structure. A feedback mechanism was established between the parametric HBIM model and the measurement-based analyses. The model included the current and updatable data at the scale of unit elements that can be used in survey, restitution, and restoration processes, with potential implications for multidisciplinary studies in construction history, architectural conservation, and smart heritage.

Keywords: HBIM · Cultural heritage · Digital documentation · Semantic model · Photogrammetry · IR thermography

1 Introduction

Workflows for documenting and preserving cultural heritage widely involve laser scanning and photogrammetry methods as well as thermal imaging techniques to capture data that is later processed, restructured, represented, and stored in information models. These models support the holistic and accurate assessment of the multidimensional construction knowledge of historical buildings. As Heritage Building Information Modeling (HBIM) is becoming a more pervasive methodology for heritage conservation, restoration, and management, it is critical to focus on the data-capturing and representation processes to improve the workflows for allowing interactive and adaptable use.

O. Ö. Özener et al. (Eds.): EBF 2021, CCIS 1627, pp. 145–158, 2022.
https://doi.org/10.1007/978-3-031-16895-6_10

To address this need, this study proposes a systematic HBIM framework to integrate multi-layered information of a historical structure at the level of its building systems and components using BIM. The system provides extended opportunities to capture and store semantic data for dynamic use and assessment in application processes with different levels of detail. As the implementation case of the proposed HBIM system approach, the study focuses on a historic underground structure using digital photogrammetry and thermography with parametric HBIM methods.

Building Information Modeling (BIM) is frequently used for the ontological documentation of the physical and functional characteristics of a building. It serves as a source of information that provides a reliable basis for decisions made throughout the life cycle of the structure from its design onwards. During the project cycles, BIM is widely employed to produce parametric information about geometry, system behaviors, building component attributes, and energy performance. The building information is produced and shared through common data environments built on open standards for interoperability [1] whereas as-built BIM contributes to representing the properties of existing buildings through reality-based data collection and reverse engineering [2]. Increasingly, BIM platforms support 3D point clouds representing the asset surface [3] therefore they are becoming more pervasive in documenting and representing architectural heritage. As a specific application subdomain, Historic Building Information Modeling (HBIM) utilizes parametric object libraries in BIM tools for matching the point cloud and image data using a cross-software management platform.

HBIM is particularly suitable for reconstructing a historical structure from existing identification data such as those from historical documents, bibliographic references, photographs, and drawings. Using HBIM methods it is possible to deliver accurate orthographic drawings and 3D models when required [4], but it can also include (a) thorough research on the geometric and parametric aspects, (b) attributes, material and system information of the building elements at different scales; (c) possible deformations, decay, and changes over time [5]. The HBIM model is not just a geometric reconstruction but is comprised of advanced objects containing information-rich system elements and quantitative and qualitative identification of building system relationships [3]. By importing point cloud information into the BIM platforms, building components can be created using native building object definitions and data formats or BIM Industry Foundation Classes (IFC) classes for cross-platform integration. Different from generic family classes, a specific library of parametric and semantic elements such as walls, roofs, stairs, doors, and windows can be created based on field measurements, point data and legacy information for the synthesis of an as-built HBIM model [6]. While BIM is effective in planning, designing, and building new buildings and structures, it also has vast potentials for archaeological and historical preservation applications as well as smart heritage management targeting the prolongment of the present and future value of a historic site [7].

Building elements of historical buildings can be expressed with representative geometries using BIM tools. However, representative geometries are insufficient in storing specialized information on the unit materials that make up the building elements of historical buildings. In a historical building, each building material is exposed to different effects over long periods and evolves into different forms such as a unique surface texture or various forms of deterioration. In case of loss or deformation of any unit element in the structure, the data of the relevant unit is crucial and a precautionary resource. For this reason, it is desirable to examine and keep data at the scale of the unit elements that make up the structure.

This chapter dwells on an unconventional HBIM implementation for a historical building that particularly challenges straightforward documentation and modeling procedures. Regarding the study material, research on the accurate registration of underground historical structures is becoming more common. However, due to the problems with their current conditions such as insufficient lighting, humidity and difficult access, historical underground structures cannot be fully studied and included in registration inventories [8]. In addition, the occurred destructions or deteriorations, and unique features of the construction materials create critical problems that have to be addressed specifically for each case. For every unique building, it is necessary to determine the existing conditions with different surveying techniques, considering the characteristics and health status of the building. This emphasizes the potential challenges in the accurate and comprehensive documentation and modeling of building information with HBIM methods.

2 Background

Current HBIM research studies largely focus on the transfer of geometric information and the representation of existing physical features using parametric BIM methods. The current literature documents numerous cases that can be considered as precedents for this study. For the early Byzantine church of Sant'Apollinare Nuovo, Garagnani and Manferdini [9] transformed the point cloud obtained by laser scanning method into 3D objects by using Autodesk Revit software and the GreenSpider plugin they have developed for this purpose. The Green Spider plugin uses the point cloud with selectable ports. By connecting the relevant connection points to each other in the horizontal plane, it obtains sections of the model at certain intervals. In a different study, Oreni et al. [10] created an HBIM using laser scanning and photogrammetry to examine the cut stones forming a damaged column at the unit element scale. Their process speeded up the relocation of the cut stones and helped to understand the arrangement of the stones correctly. Yang et al. [11] utilized Autodesk Revit and its built-in visual programming tool Dynamo to enhance the new HBIM functionalities for the Church of St-Pierre-le-Jeune in Strasbourg, France. They transformed the HBIM framework into an ontology model in Resource Description Framework (RDF) format for data interchange and to improve the heterogeneity of the knowledge. Differently, this study incorporated semantic data to the transfer of irregular geometric forms of historical buildings into the BIM software environment and used BIM elements to create a dynamic and updatable documentation method at the scale of the unit elements that make up the whole building. In addition, the work identified the advantages and disadvantages that arise in the digital documentation process for underground structures and offered practical solutions for these specific cases.

3   Case Study: Pişirici Kastel

The case at hand was the Pişirici Kastel, an example of a historical underground waterway structure, unique in the world and included in the UNESCO World Temporary Heritage List in 2018. In Gaziantep, water was historically transported by canals known as "livas" in the local language. These canals delivered water to the users in ganes (a type of pool in the courtyard of the houses), pools, and wells, in private quarters and kastels and baths in public spaces [11]. Kastels and livas were included in the UNESCO World Temporary Heritage List in 2018 [12]. Pişirici Kastel, the oldest and the most comprehensive kastel in Gaziantep, is located at the intersection of Pişirici and Müftüoğlu Streets in Suyabatmaz District. It is thought to have been built during the Mamluk period in the late 13th century. The first restoration, carried out by the Directorate General of Foundations in 2008, included the cleaning of the adjoining livas and making the kastel operational once again [13].

The building, which is completely below the ground level, is accessed by stairs. Its main space has two shallow reservoir pools interconnected by small channels. Another pool to the south is twice as deep at approximately 65 cm. There is an additional sitting bench in this area. In the space where the pools are located, two niches with pointed arches contain a clean water system for use at the latrines. Openings in the vault above the pool area are for daylight and ventilation purposes. A mosque serving the late congregation [14] and a partially rock-cut masjid are prayer areas [11].

4   Methodology and Scope

The employed HBIM workflow from documentation to information modeling is illustrated in Fig. 1. This flow consisted of four stages in two phases. The first phase included the surveying tasks using digital photogrammetry and thermography. The modeling phase was based on the acquired field data and parametric synthesis of HBIM models through visual programming. The details are given as the following:

1. Photogrammetry: Point cloud data collection process using photogrammetry;
2. Thermography: Collection of thermographic data of the building with thermal camera measurements and analysis of thermal images;
3. HBIM: Processing of photogrammetric and thermographic data using Autodesk Revit 2020 software;
4. Output: Integration of parametric HBIM model data and thermal imaging data through data-driven visual scripts using Dynamo.

The scope of the study was limited to the main kastel space of the Pişirici complex which purposefully restrained the number of contextual parameters for the data acquisition process. Considering the data acquisition methods heavily factor in the preceding modeling stages, our report presents detailed information on the photogrammetry and thermography stages. The challenges of the site and margins of error are noted.

Close-range photogrammetry is especially a simple and convenient method in terms of accuracy, cost, speed, and accessibility for non-experts [15]. Additional data capture is possible by thermal imaging methods to assess the current material conditions of historical buildings. Thermal imaging detects in real-time the temperature changes on the surface of materials and structures and thus provides data for the evaluation of damage distribution and accumulation. It is a non-destructive, non-contact technology for assessing degradation in historical structures [16]. These technologies have made it possible to record complex structures remotely efficiently and accurately, which was not possible with previous survey methods [17]. Since data types are the determinants in the modeling phases of the workflow, data capturing processes and parameters are articulately explained.

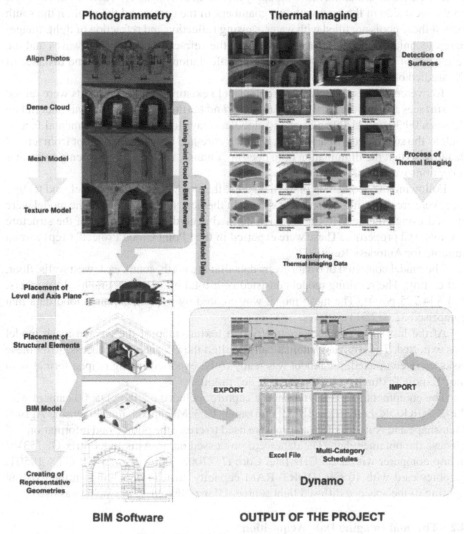

Fig. 1. The employed HBIM workflow.

4.1   Photogrammetric Data Acquisition for HBIM

Photogrammetry was the preferred survey method in the study for its low-cost and fast-documentation capabilities to capture the surface texture in a point cloud and mesh model. For the study, a total of 16 markers were placed on the appropriate parts of the studied surfaces of the kastel. The "Circular 12 bit" marker type with a center point radius of 1 cm was selected and exported from the Agisoft Metashape program in.pdf format. During the photoshoot, the underground spaces posed lighting problems. In order to collect the photogrammetric data of the Pişirici Kastel, the existing lighting elements inside were turned off and non-linear lighting elements were used to obtain more accurate information. Since the study area is an active kastel structure, the reservoir on the west side of the pool with two chambers in the center and the pool on the south side of these pools are filled with water, causing reflection and refraction of light. Image-based techniques were not successful due to the refractive effect of the waves and the refraction of water [18]. This prevented the calculation of the position and distance of the studied object.

To overcome these operational problems, (1) existing lighting elements were turned off, surfaces are illuminated with diffuse light, and (2) the photo shooting was undertaken between 09:30 and 11:00 on clear and cloudless days to stabilize environmental factors such as the sun, cloudy weather, etc., (3) such care had been taken to shoot from a fixed distance so that the illumination ratio does not change, (4) glowing segments and water reflections were masked in close-ups.

Following the acquisition of the field data, the point cloud, mesh model, and texture map were created using Agisoft Metashape. In the next step, the layers of the model were created using Autodesk ReCap Pro and defined according to the parts of the structure and material properties. These were exported in the "Point Cloud Project" (.rcp) format suitable for Autodesk Revit 2020.

The model consisted of 6 data layers data that are north, south, east, west walls, floor, and ceiling. The resulting model consisted of a total of 381 photographs, 16 markers, and 444,725 points. The mesh model was created by using this point cloud data that comprised 32,072,511 surfaces.

At the last stage of photogrammetry, the texture map of the created mesh model was exported. The software automatically applied the UV mapping process. After these tasks were completed, the model was ready to be exported in.png or.jpeg format with the "Export Texture" option from the "File" menu.

The equipment for photogrammetric capture included a Nikon D5000 camera with AF-S NIKKOR Lens (f = 18–55 mm) and 12.3 Megapixel image sensor. Agisoft Metashape and Autodesk ReCap Pro were used to create the point cloud information and process the obtained data. The data were processed on an Asus ROG Strix GL753VE laptop computer with a 2.8 GHz Intel Core i7-7700HQ processor, 4 GB GTX 1050Ti graphics card with 16 GB (DDR3) RAM capacity. Instead of relying on the existing lighting of the space, a diffused light source, Ulanzi 96 Led Video W96, was used.

4.2   Thermal Imaging Data Acquisition

The first step of setting up a thermal imaging study was to determine areas that are suitable for thermal imaging (Fig. 2). While making measurements, selections, material differences, construction technique differences, and surfaces with visible deterioration were all considered. It was observed that there are sections with the specified criteria for thermal imaging application on the eastern façade of the building. For the first section, a dividing wall with different ratios of surface deformation of the elements working similarly and made of the same material, and an arch foot working in the same plane was selected. In the second part, a suitable surface for thermal imaging was selected by carving the existing rock surface in the niche. The third section was determined as a rock surface that was intervened in later periods. Finally, thermal imaging was applied on the rock surface on the wall separating the niches from each other. Measurements were continued in the above-mentioned order. It was observed that the temperature was in equilibrium in the indoor environment because the structure was located underground. To apply the thermal imaging process, the surfaces planned to be thermally measured using an infrared heat source that was heated in 5-, 10-, and 20-min periods and their thermal images were taken at the stage when they entered the cooling state.

Fig. 2. The sequence of areas in the kastel where thermal imaging was conducted

The relative humidity and temperature values in the kastel have a significant effect on the damage to the surface and interior parts of the building. Since kastels are underground water structures, it was inevitable to have high humidity due to the contextual features of the historic structure.

The temperature value and relative humidity measurements in the kastel were taken on September 24 through September 29, 2020, between the hours of 09:00 and 11:00 am. Indoor and outdoor data were recorded with the Tzone TempU03 data logger at 30-min intervals. It was observed that the indoor and outdoor temperature values were in the appropriate temperature range. In all measurements, the surfaces were heated with an infrared heat source from 1.5 m away for 5, 10 and 20 min. When the surfaces passed to the cooling stage, thermal camera shots were taken from 2.5 m away at certain intervals. The optimum heating time was determined as 20 min. The obtained thermal images for detecting surface and internal deformations using the Testo 875 thermal camera from the inventory of the Gaziantep University Physics Engineering Department. Indoor and outdoor temperature (T) and relative humidity (RH) values were calculated using the Tzone TempU03 data logger. Analysis and classification of images were made using Testo IRSoft software.

5 Information Modeling

HBIM relies on BIM platforms, and there lies a difficulty that the point cloud obtained from the real model cannot be defined as an information model rapidly and effectively [19, 20]. For this reason, representative geometries were used to define the relevant parts of the point cloud and these parts were defined within a suitable family group. After importing the point cloud into the BIM environment, a reference grid and working plane were placed. The vertical elements were modeled using a custom-made wall family referencing the point cloud coordinates since the building has a masonry construction. Roof (roof family) and floor (floor family) were modeled after the completion of the parametric wall structures. The stone block walls were manually placed using the point cloud information with the material information. However, each block had different conditions due to environmental effects and physical deterioration. The modeling process required the extension of physical and material information embedded in parametric building components. For this reason, the structural elements were subdivided with the thermal imaging analysis into their unit elements. This process allowed the data entry for each element separately. Accordingly, the operation "divide parts" was applied to the wall and niche sections that underwent thermal imaging, over the parameterized geometric components. The elements that make up the surface (stone blocks, carved walls, etc.) were fragmented on the building basis. Each piece was given a parametric component ID within the model. Number codes were given to each module to distinguish the created modules (Table 1). This process was applied only on the eastern façade surfaces where thermal imaging was performed within the scope of the study. A total of 50-unit elements were created.

In the continuing stage of the study, the material information was parameterized and embedded in meta-building elements using Autodesk Revit 2020. The materials available in the library are selected with the "Materials" menu under the "Manage" tab. The material information for the floor, wall and roof sections are reproduced separately and labeled according to the applied family types. This information helped to extend the customized BIM database for the deriving and processing of parametric material information with Dynamo.

Table 1. Code numbering method for modules.

View	Type/Function	Type sequence number (From left to right)	Unit number
	Niche Wall - **NW**	02	
	Arch Wall - **AW**	01	
East view **EV**	Limestone Carved Wall **LCW**	03	It increases from bottom to top
	Upper Wall - **UW**	02	
	Plaster Surface - **PS**	02	

5.1 Documentation of Model Data and Thermal Imaging Data with the Visual Programming Language

To further process the modeled information and provide a customized HBIM database for the building in question Autodesk Dynamo was utilized [21]. The key objectives for using the add-on visual scripts were:

1. To filter specific analytical models or component sets from the HBIM model;
2. To establish a data link for the transfer of external data into the HBIM database;
3. To make BIM database queries for application-specific purposes;
4. To create an open HBIM model basis for parametric modification and propagation.

Adding Parameters to Models. In the next step, the mesh model obtained by photogrammetry and the reports created as a result of the thermal imaging application was defined as parameters. The parameterization scheme is given in Table 2 using the "Project Parameters" command under the "Manage" tab.

Table 2. The way the desired parameters are defined in the model.

Parameter	Type of parameter	Group of parameter	Category of the parameter
Mesh model	URL	Identity data	Parts
Ambient relative humidity RH	Integer	Other	Parts
Ambient temperature C°	Integer	Other	Parts
Thermal imaging reports	URL	Identity data	Parts
Thermal imaging history	Text	Identity data	Parts

The defined parameters are used to transfer the data obtained by external measurements as a result of the study to the model.

Selecting Parameters in the Dynamo Interface. The parametric building components included multi-layered data forming the holistic information model. These data layers helped to separate and organize geometric information into units and connected material attributes. In order to determine the required parameters, the unit materials were listed according to the code numbers created in the previous stage. These were selected using the Dynamo interface component *"Element.GetParameterValueByName"*. All parameters in the module lists created using the *"Element.Parameters"* component were called. From the parameter list, the sequence number and the necessary parameters were selected.

Converting Model Parameters into Updatable Tables. The selected parameters were viewed and changed as *"Multi-Category Schedule"* in the Autodesk Revit 2020 interface. However, data must be exported so that expert users can make instant revisions. In the initial stage, a common Excel file was created and defined in the Dynamo interface with the *"File Path"* component. The same file was linked with the *"Data.ExportExcel"* and *"Data.ImportExcel"* components. Using this procedure, a simultaneous data link was established to make updates on the field and the BIM environment.

The parameter types of *"Mesh Model"* and *"Thermal Imaging Reports"* were transferred into the created Excel file using the *"URL"* type with Dynamo.

In the previous phases, the photogrammetry mesh model was uploaded to the Google Poly website with the code numbers for each module defined in the Dynamo interface. The link address of each loaded module was placed in the relevant column of the Excel table.

Similar processes were applied for thermal imaging reports transferred to a folder in the cloud storage services of Google Drive. Thermal imaging data, ambient temperature, and ambient relative humidity data were transferred to the table in line with the information obtained by the data logger during operation.

After these processes, the *"Data.ExportExcel"* component was frozen in the Dynamo interface, and the *"Data.ImportExcel"* procedure was activated. When the created system chart was running, the data in the Excel table was transferred into the *"Multi-Category Schedule"*.

5.2   Results

The proposed HBIM approach and the devised workflow engaged the parametric synthesis of the holistic BIM model derived from the photogrammetry-based mesh model of Pişirici Kastel. The obtained field data in the point cloud and processed thermal images were used as the basis for parametric building components and system families. The geometric information was matched using the point cloud coordinates with the determined building layers such as walls, arches, and roofs. The parametric building components were further developed with material and physical condition information. The holistic HBIM model provided the material and component-based query and take-off options for further systemic evaluations.

The study approached the concept of materiality in a preservation-focused fashion. The material properties of each stone block were parametrically captured with the thermal imaging method which allowed the creation of specific material histograms to evaluate systemic and component-based deteriorations. Structural anomalies were represented in the HBIM model for further assessment and documentation. The superposition of thermal images made it possible to access critical factors like relative humidity and the average temperature on the component surfaces.

The level of detail (LoD) of the HBIM model was prepared in LOD300 detail according to the LOD Spec 2019 standards determined by BIMForum [22] (Fig. 3).

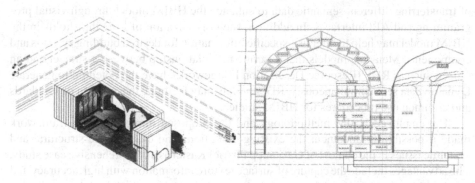

Fig. 3. Documentation of representative geometries at unit element scale (LOD 300).

The holistic HBIM model was derived from the point cloud and synthesized with IFC-based components and parametric objects. This combined the HBIM semantic model and the Kastel structure representation model. The semantic model included the data at the unit element level using the "code ID numbers" assigned to the fundamental unit elements. By using a *"double-channel data link"* method, a feedback loop was established between the surveying and HBIM documentation workgroups. Such changes made using the Revit software were exported in Excel format through the coded Dynamo interface. Likewise, the data obtained in the field was imported to the HBIM model software using the tabulated spreadsheet. One of the important advantages of the prepared model was that the surface texture could be digitally archived with any scale of units. This scale transitive approach allowed the creation of the object-based database for future interventions and restorative applications. The HBIM model also provided a time-labeled parametric library for comparative evaluations related to the surface texture of the building.

6 Conclusion

The study elaborated on HBIM as an effective documentation method for smart heritage applications along with distinct advantages and current problems for implementation. With the point cloud support in BIM software platforms, historical building point cloud data obtained through real-time measurements techniques like digital photogrammetry,

LiDAR, etc. can be utilized as the basis for application-specific HBIM models. In addition, the employed HBIM implementation approach provides the concurrent evaluation of structural and systemic properties of historic buildings. As the critical part of this approach, optimal conditions should be met in order to improve the accuracy of surveying and measurement techniques. Another issue is the time-consuming process of unit-based parameterization and hierarchical organization of IFC building components in BIM. With the future automation methods for geometric recognition, IFC-based component generation may help to overcome the problems for complex modeling tasks. From the operational perspective, the use of a Dynamo-based data interface made it possible to embed the HBIM model with thermal measurements. This also implies the possibility of transferring different semantic data to enhance the HBIM model through visual programming and API interfaces. In addition, such organization of LoD thresholds in the HBIM model may help to filter use-specific information for desired building systems and components. Metadata models that describe the relationship between a subject and an object, such as RDF (Resource Description Framework), have the potential to generate Dynamo data sets. Simultaneously, RDF models may facilitate the creation of standards and common use procedures for HBIM studies.

The employed HBIM methodology and the proposed implementation framework made it possible to document the existing conditions and evaluate the structural and systemic issues in the context of Gaziantep Pişirici Kastel as a comprehensive case study. The advantages include the capture of surface texture information with high accuracy and the determination of sub-surface components and anomalies which are also applicable to different historic buildings.

The study also provided usable parametric information at the unit element scale, obtaining texture and 3D data for any need-oriented processes or reproduction of building elements due to loss, deformation and systemic deteriorations. On the other hand, it provided the opportunity to store all kinds of information, including physical analyses and archival documents related to sociocultural memory. As an extension of this study, it is possible to incorporate various information in different formats to form a cloud-based common data environment. As the expertise levels are limited in terms of technological capabilities and application knowledge, the exchange of HBIM models and related databases are more likely to integrate distributed workgroups through the sharable BIM models and parametric components.

Acknowledgments. This chapter was produced from a Master's thesis completed at Istanbul Technical University Institute of Graduate Studies, Architectural Design Computing Program. Authors would like express their gratitude to the Department of Physics Engineering at Gaziantep University for providing the thermal camera, and the staff at Pişirici Kastel for their help during the field studies.

References

1. Barlish, K., Sullivan, K.: How to measure the benefits of BIM—a case study approach. Autom. Constr. **24**, 149–159 (2012)
2. Arayici, Y.: Towards building information modelling for existing structures. Struct. Surv. **26**, 210–222 (2008)

3. Yang, X., Lu, Y.C., Murtiyoso, A., Koehl, M., Grussenmeyer, P.: HBIM modeling from the surface mesh and its extended capability of knowledge representation. ISPRS Int. J. Geo Inf. **8**(7), 301 (2019)
4. Murphy, M., et al.: Developing historic building information modelling guidelines and procedures for architectural heritage in Ireland. Int. Arch. Photogramm. Remote. Sens. Spat. Inf. Sci. **42**(2), 539–546 (2017)
5. Yang, X., Grussenmeyer, P., Koehl, M., Macher, H., Murtiyoso, A., Landes, T.: Review of built heritage modelling: integration of HBIM and other information techniques. J. Cultural Heritage **46**, 350–360 (2020). https://doi.org/10.1016/j.culher.2020.05.008
6. Abd ElWahab, H.A., Bakr, A.F., Raslan, R.A.: Towards a parametric plug-in for conservation of built heritage. Alex. Eng. J. **58**(1), 325–331 (2019)
7. López, J.B., et al.: 3D modelling in archaeology: the application of Structure from Motion methods to the study of the megalithic necropolis of Panoria (Granada, Spain). J. Archaeol. Sci. Rep. **10**, 495–506 (2016)
8. Bieda, A., Bydłosz, J., Warchoł, A., Balawejder, M.: Historical underground structures as 3D cadastral objects. Remote Sens. **12**(10), 1547 (2020)
9. Garagnani, S., Manferdini, A.M.: Parametric accuracy: building information modeling process applied to the cultural heritage preservation. Int. Arch. Photogram. Remote Sens. Spatial Inform. Sci. **40**(5), 88–92 (2013)
10. Oreni, D., Brumana, R., Della Torre, S., Banfi, F., Previtali, M.: Survey turned into HBIM: the restoration and the work involved concerning the Basilica di Collemaggio after the earthquake (L'Aquila). ISPRS Ann. Photogram. Remote Sens. Spatial Inform. Sci. **2**(5), 267 (2014)
11. Uçar, M.: Gaziantep tarihi su sistemi ve su yapıları. METU J. Facul. Architect. **33**(2), 73–100 (2016). https://doi.org/10.4305/METU.JFA.2016.2.4
12. UNESCO World Heritage Convention. http://whc.unesco.org/en/tentativelists/6345/. Accessed 9 Aug 2021
13. Gaziantep Şahinbey Belediyesi. https://www.sahinbey.bel.tr/proje-d/6/524/pisirici-kasteli. Accessed 9 Aug 2021
14. Çam, N.: Türk Kültür Varlıkları Envanteri Gaziantep 27, Türk Tarih Kurumu Yayınları, Ankara (2006)
15. Arias, P., Ordóñez, C., Lorenzo, H., Herraez, J.: Methods for documenting historical agro-industrial buildings: a comparative study and a simple photogrammetric method. J. Cult. Herit. **7**(4), 350–354 (2006)
16. Kordatos, E.Z., Exarchos, D.A., Stavrakos, C., Moropoulou, A., Matikas, T.E.: Infrared thermographic inspection of murals and characterization of degradation in historic monuments. Constr. Build. Mater. **48**, 1261–1265 (2013)
17. Dore, C., Murphy, M., McCarthy, S., Brechin, F., Casidy, C., Dirix, E.: Structural simulations and conservation analysis-historic building information model (HBIM). Int. Arch. Photogram. Remote Sens. Spatial Inform. Sci. **40**(5), 351 (2015)
18. Skarlatos, D., Agrafiotis, P.: A novel iterative water refraction correction algorithm for use in structure from motion photogrammetric pipeline. J. Marine Sci. Eng. **6**(3), 77 (2018)
19. Borin, P., Bernardello, R.A., Grigoletto, A.: Connecting historical information with BIM ontologies. HBIM methods for the visualization of harris matrix for the torrione in carpi. In: Agustín-Hernández, L., Muniesa, A.V., Fernández-Morales, A. (eds.) Graphical Heritage: Volume 1 - History and Heritage, pp. 757–770. Springer International Publishing, Cham (2020). https://doi.org/10.1007/978-3-030-47979-4_65
20. Ewart, I.J., Zuecco, V.: Heritage Building Information Modelling (HBIM): a review of published case studies. Advances in Informatics and Computing in Civil and Construction Engineering, pp. 35–41 (2019)

21. DynamoBIM. https://dynamobim.org/wp-content/uploads/forum-assets/colin-mccroneautod esk.com/07/10/Dynamo_language_guide_version_1.pdf. Accessed 7 Oct 2020
22. BIMForum.   https://bimforum.org/resources/Documents/BIMForum_LOD_2019_reprint. pdf. Accessed 21 Sept 2021

Review of Uncertainties in Building Characterization for Urban-Scale Energy Modeling

Said Bolluk and Senem Seyis(✉)

Özyeğin University, 34794 İstanbul, Turkey
said.bolluk@ozu.edu.tr, senem.seyis@ozyegin.edu.tr

Abstract. Bottom-up modeling appears to be a suitable approach for the urban-scale building energy performance assessment with providing valuable inferences on the complicated building energy patterns and helping authorities monitor/predict the energy demand for urban planning and retrofitting. Archetype characterization is the utmost challenging process when developing bottom-up models since there is a large diversity in characteristic features of building stocks. This gap induces practitioners to seek stochastic methods even though the deterministic approaches are solid guides in archetype characterization. Hence, the research objective of this study is to provide insights into the motivation, challenges, and methods of the studies conducted to assess the buildings' energy demand at the urban scale. The original value of this research is to analyze/question different archetype characterization methods and their practicability over wide-ranging studies, identify the most crucial characterization parameters and assess the validation techniques to enhance the demand estimations of urban building energy models (UBEMs). To that end, this study performs a literature review and mainly provides the following findings: (1) The required characterization method is highly dependent on the purpose and scope of the study. (2) The Bayesian calibration makes ground in UBEM practices as it consolidates the models' estimation power through the probabilistic archetype characterization. (3) Considering the notable fluctuations in buildings' energy demand induced by occupancy patterns, detailed occupancy profiles could improve the archetype characterization. Finally, the major setback is the lack of available data to characterize energy models with building-specific information. (4) Building information models (BIMs) could soon play a pivotal role in supplying such data for UBEM practices. This study contributes to the literature by fulfilling the lack of perspective that concentrates on the archetype characterization methods in UBEM. The findings could help practitioners (e.g., policymakers and city planners) and academics to comprehend the potential of the UBEM that improves energy management strategies at the urban scale.

Keywords: Urban building energy modeling (UBEM) · Archetype characterization · Occupancy-related uncertainties

© Springer Nature Switzerland AG 2022
O. Ö. Özener et al. (Eds.): EBF 2021, CCIS 1627, pp. 159–182, 2022.
https://doi.org/10.1007/978-3-031-16895-6_11

1 Introduction

The world's energy consumption has reached a critical point with 31.5 Gt CO_2 emissions in 2020 [1]. The demand caused by growing populations urges authorities to develop energy reduction strategies. In addition to the incentives for using renewables, governments intend to decrease greenhouse gas (GHG) emissions by notable amounts. In 2020, European Commission set a 20% reduction target in GHG emissions than in 1990 [2]. The building industry accounts for 17.5% of global GHG emissions [3]. Hence, it bears a tremendous responsibility to achieve such targets and overcome sustainability problems. Previous studies show that individual models are commonly used to predict the buildings' energy demand and develop energy-efficient design concepts. However, considering large and dynamic cities with many unknowns, the building energy models (BEMs) are insufficient to reveal the actual performance of building stocks. For this reason, the crucial and urgent need is to observe the interaction between building clusters to comprehend similar energy consumption patterns and propose district-level energy management strategies.

Different approaches in mass building energy modeling at the urban scale have been introduced in the field. These are the top-down and bottom-up approaches [4]. In the top-down approach, the aim is to interpret the historical data to predict the overall energy consumption using economic assumptions for the future trend. However, the building stocks of cities reserve a large variety of building types with heterogeneous energy demand. Thus, this approach remains incapable of imitating reality [4]. On the other hand, the bottom-up approach focuses on single buildings or building clusters of the same type by making statistical inferences on the historical data or generating dynamic energy models. Additionally, this approach provides insights into refined energy consumption patterns, and it is valuable to determine the possible energy reduction measures over the models tested with retrofit actions [21].

The objective of this study is to provide generalized insights into the motivation, challenges, and methods of the studies conducted to analyze the buildings' energy demand at the urban scale by investigating model characterization techniques and identifying the vital characterization parameters. In this sense, this study presents the statistical and engineering bottom-up models, examines the model validation via the Bayesian calibration method, and investigates different techniques to create sophisticated occupancy profiles. The absence of the digitized databases at the urban scale, such as rarely seen BIMs, geographic information systems, or energy benchmarking and consumption reports, obstructs obtaining information for building energy performance assessment to characterize the models with unique features or calibrate their outputs with the measured data [6]. Since UBEMs are parametric district models in which the development and simulation depend on digital format data, BIMs could improve the interoperability of the platforms used in such practices [7]. In this sense, this study also discusses the possible contributions of BIMs to UBEM practices.

A literature review was conducted to achieve the research objective of this study. Web of Science was used as a database for identifying the publications. Different sources, including articles, conference proceedings, academic dissertations, software, web-based tools, and technical reports, were examined, and the related ones were manually selected. The reviewed sources were published between 2002 and 2022 since urban-scale building energy modeling is a nascent research area. A total of 71 publications addressing urban-scale building energy modeling were included within the scope of this research. All selected papers are in Q1. Special attention was paid to select the journals with impact factors bigger than 1.0.

2 Bottom-Up Energy Models

With the increasing energy demand of the building sector [1], cities' building stocks must be analyzed for energy efficiency. However, analytical findings on the energy performance of the buildings are not easy to be derived considering the challenge of storing the relevant data and the great variety in building typology and occupancy characteristics. In this sense, Swan and Ugursal reviewed the existing literature to describe the various energy modeling efforts at the urban scale [4]. Accordingly, the top-down approach predicts the districts' energy demand and provides generalized suggestions using historical data and economic models while missing the diversity at the individual level. On the other hand, the bottom-up approach investigates the energy performance of buildings or clusters of buildings by generating statistical/physical models [4]. These models are also great devices to implement retrofit actions properly on the building stocks because they hold valuable databases that enable altering buildings' characteristics to evaluate the energy performance [5]. The benefits and limitations of the bottom-up energy modeling studies are provided in Table 1 based on the literature review findings.

Table 1. Benefits and limitations of the studies on the bottom-up building energy models

Reference	Bottom-up model	Archetype characterization	Benefits	Limitations
[8, 10, 11, 17]	Statistical	Deterministic	Simple model development Representing the aggregated demands	Acquiring building-specific data Lack of detailed occupancy profiles Unsuitability for retrofit assessment
[9]	Statistical	Probabilistic	Accurate results/ GIS-based visualization	Acquiring building-specific data Lack of detailed occupancy profiles

(continued)

Table 1. (*continued*)

Reference	Bottom-up model	Archetype characterization	Benefits	Limitations
[20, 28]	Statistical and Engineering	Deterministic	Suitability for retrofit assessment	Oversimplified archetype characterization No detailed occupancy profiles
[29, 30]	Engineering	Deterministic	Representing the aggregated demands Suitability for retrofit assessment [30]	Oversimplified archetype characterization No detailed occupancy profiles Serious error with the small-scale analysis [29]
[35, 40, 41]	Engineering	Deterministic and Probabilistic	Representing the aggregated demands Providing value ranges for characterization parameters [40] Comparing the effectiveness of multi-scale energy models [41]	Weak archetype characterization Weak and complicated result validation [35, 41]
[39]	Engineering	Deterministic and Probabilistic	Sensitivity Analysis Testing the Bayesian Calibration Comparing the deterministic and probabilistic archetype characterizations	Acquiring building-specific data Lack of detailed occupancy profiles Complicated model development and simulation
[13, 16, 18, 38]	Engineering	Probabilistic	Sensitivity Analysis Testing the Bayesian Calibration [13, 16] Suitability for retrofit assessment [13, 16, 38]	Acquiring building-specific data Lack of detailed occupancy profiles

When conducting urban-scale building energy performance assessment, it is difficult to separately analyze each building due to the uncertainties arising from the diversified energy characteristics of building stocks. Therefore, the archetypes representing building clusters with the same physical, thermal, and functional properties are created in bottom-up models using the available building literature (e.g., surveys, regulations, census, and building audits). Some of the essential archetype characterization parameters are the building's geometry, envelope properties, the detail of the mechanical equipment installed in a building, and the occupancy profiles.

2.1 Statistical Models

The statistical models investigate the relationship between the buildings' energy-related parameters and the metered energy data via data-driven reasoning. Identifying the archetypes that represent building clusters is entirely based on the statistical interpretation of the historical data. The energy demand calculations might be inaccurate since there is no physical interaction regarded entirely in such models. However, considering the simplicity of the model development and simulation, statistical models can assess the generalized trends at the urban scale. Plus, with the recent development in machine learning and artificial intelligence, data-driven models might be handy in observing the building energy demand of cities [75, 76].

Statistical models usually feel the absence of detailed archetype characterization due to the data unavailability, and the oversimplification of the model elements may lead to discrepancies in result validation. Dall'O' et al. developed a system that simplifies the energy certification process by allowing web-based access for building databases in Northern Italy [8]. With a regression model, they analyzed the correlation between the buildings' age and compactness ratio and predicted the final energy demand with a 9.7% deviation from the metered data.

Howard et al. developed a district-based energy model of New York in [9]. The floor area alone was used in the linear regression to determine the annual energy demand. Although the model values only one input parameter to perform the regression, the authors predicted the demand within the 2.5% error range [9]. Similarly, Mata et al. created 598 archetypes to mimic the energy performance of the building stocks of four different EU cities with a simple archetype characterization and observed around 4% error in result validation [10]. Ballarini et al. created 18 archetypes and analyzed the buildings' energy performance before and after the retrofit actions [11]. The authors utilized TABULA [12], a platform integrated with the geographic information system (GIS) aiming to initiate a comprehensive database for the EU countries' building stocks. Using suggestions from TABULA, they obtained satisfactory results that enable retrofit assessment over the building stock [11].

When archetypes are obliged to be rendered with a limited amount of information, predetermination of the critical parameters (i.e., sensitivity analysis) becomes even more critical. Thus, the focus can be directed to those parameters in data collection and verification. Several studies conducting sensitivity analysis showed that parameters, such as indoor air temperature [13], construction period [15], climate [10], air change rate [13, 14], compactness ratio [15, 16], and orientation, and thermal/light transmittance [16, 17], fundamentally influenced the building energy demand.

Besides the simple linear models, some statistical models utilize more advanced machine learning algorithms. Such models could be valuable when the relationship between the building characterization parameters and the energy demands is in complicated forms, or the input data lacks a notable amount of information. Table 2 summarizes the machine learning algorithms and the processes the algorithms were used in UBEM applications below. One should be careful about the dynamics of the available dataset and the essentials of the problem in choosing the machine learning algorithm for clustering and classifying the archetypes and predicting the building energy demand.

Table 2. Machine learning algorithms used in statistical models

Process	Operation	Algorithm
Archetype Development	Clustering	K-means Clustering [77], Segmentation [78].
Archetype Characterization	Regression and Classification	Quasi-Linear Regression [78], Ran-dom Forest Classifier [80].
Energy Demand Estimation	Regression	SVM Regressor & MLP Regressor [79], Gradient Boosting Regressor [81], SVM Regressor and Random Forest Regressor [82], Multiple Linear Regression [83]

2.2 Engineering Models

The bottom-up engineering models reserve the most sophisticated and accurate technique for the energy performance assessment of building stocks as they evaluate the thermal interaction between the model elements in the dynamic calculations (Fig. 1). These models are great tools for energy reduction strategies over retrofit measures as they are regeneratable physical models [19–25].

Generating a dynamic model of building stocks might be challenging considering the required computational power over the vast number of model elements with high resolution. The existing building literature usually does not allow equipping models with detailed information. Therefore, the model development maintains its complication even with the archetype approach that relieves the simulation effort with representative buildings. In addition, the optimal number and the quality of archetypes are in doubt since the answer depends on the functional and characteristic diversity of the urban building stocks [26, 27]. Thus, the common practice indicates the deterministic characterization when dealing with archetypes. This approach assumes single values for input parameters and might be missing the variation from the structural ambiguity of the built environment while enabling concrete interpretation over the district energy patterns with the simplified approximation.

As an early attempt of UBEM, Ascione et al. developed 16 archetypes and simulated the model via EnergyPlus [28]. They considered the active/passive systems' efficiency

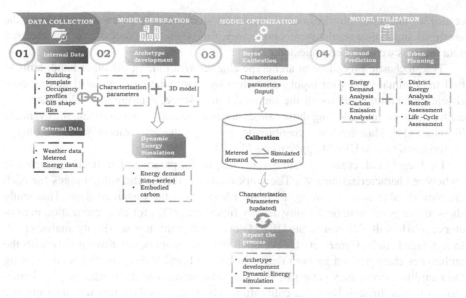

Fig. 1. UBEM workflow

and the building envelope properties to characterize archetypes. This deterministic app-roach does not comprise most of the building stock, and the result's validation reveals a 10% error [28]. Österbring et al. created an engineering model of Gothenburg in which the dynamic calculations were relied on the single zoning principle [29]. They aver-aged the input parameters from several databases and deterministically characterized the archetypes. This induced a remarkable deviation between the calculated and mea-sured data for clusters with higher resolution, whereas the aggregated results showed that the district level calculations had only a 3% error from the measurements [29].

Chen et al. introduced a fluid platform that enables automatically generating UBEMs [30]. The platform is called CityBES [31, 32]. It uses the available literature to gather and convey the building data to an existing tool, CBES [33], which sets and simulates the energy models. CBES [33] also facilitates the calibration of the simulated results, and it harbors an excellent control function over the urban stocks' energy performance by mak-ing retrofit and cost-effectiveness analyses. However, CityBES [31, 32] only covers a limited scope of commercial buildings, and the complete framework becomes paralyzed during a lack of data [30]. Moghadam et al. developed a new method that combines the statistical and engineering models to analyze the building stock's current and improved performance [20]. The statistical model detected the districts with poor energy perfor-mance using linear regression correlating the building types and the energy demands. The selected districts were then used in the engineering model to analyze the effect of the retrofit actions. This oversimplified archetype characterization led to a 10% prediction error [20]. Using a simplified methodology in dynamic building simulation through the TEASER platform [34], Schiefelbein et al. created a Python-based framework that accel-erates the UBEM development [35]. A simple deterministic characterization was applied to the model. However, the sophisticated occupancy profiles adapted from Richardson et al. [36] and some physical parameters were stochastically characterized. While the averaged simulation results were satisfactory, the validation process over the metered data remains weak and complicated [35].

The stochastic procedure in archetype characterization, on the other hand, aims to find the optimal values for input parameters by manipulating them until getting consistent simulation results with the metered data. Hence, it requires a value range for each parameter, and selecting those ranges depends on both experience and the available literature [14]. Therefore, the probabilistic archetype characterization is troublesome to perform and rare in UBEM applications [5, 37].

De Jaeger et al. created possible value ranges for parameters utilized in stochastic archetype characterization [38]. The work covers detecting the value ranges for each random variable and examining their likelihood over the historical data. This study showed that generating probability density functions (PDF) for characterization parameters could be valuable in accurate UBEM development through sensitivity analysis [38]. In a detailed study, Cerezo et al. developed the energy model of Kuwait City with the archetypes characterized by both deterministic and probabilistic methods considering the simplified occupancy patterns [39]. They also optimized the stochastically characterized model through Bayesian calibration. The result displays that the deterministic models' prediction varies significantly from the metered data, whereas the output is satisfactory for the probabilistic and calibrated cases.

The probabilistic characterization does not guarantee a certain level of agreement with the metered data, even with the sophisticated input parameters. Some studies caused hesitance on its feasibility and necessity with their scope and modeling approach. For example, Buffat et al. created a UBEM combining the deterministic and probabilistic characterization [40]. The database and the assumptions used in this partly stochastic approach fell short of imitating buildings' actual characteristics, and the calculated demand mirrors the measurements by only 60% [40]. Accordingly, Ali et al. examined a UBEM at four different scales: National, city, county, and district [41]. After processing the building-specific data to elaborate its reliability, they deployed a simple probabilistic archetype characterization. However, the simulation results were not validated with the metered data, and the demand estimations are internally consistent for only the smaller resolutions rather than the national scale [41].

3   Bayesian Calibration in UBEM

Using the available literature to classify and characterize buildings might not be enough to comprehend the actual case in the built environment with many uncertainties. This is because the building characterization parameters may differ from what was specified in the literature, the occupancy patterns affect the energy performance, or the modeling might not be wholly performed. Therefore, calibration of the demand prediction is essential to offer reliable energy models. In this section, the Bayesian calibration (Fig. 2) is explicitly observed as it facilitates the probabilistic characterization of the building archetypes and is a popular method in UBEM applications [37, 89].

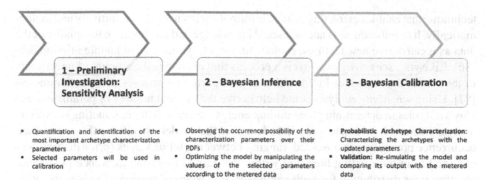

1 – Preliminary Investigation: Sensitivity Analysis

* Quantification and identification of the most important archetype characterization parameters
* Selected parameters will be used in calibration

2 – Bayesian Inference

* Observing the occurrence possibility of the characterization parameters over their PDFs
* Optimizing the model by manipulating the values of the selected parameters according to the metered data

3 – Bayesian Calibration

* **Probabilistic Archetype Characterization:** Characterizing the archetypes with the updated parameters
* **Validation:** Re-simulating the model and comparing its output with the metered data

Fig. 2. An effective workflow for the Bayesian Calibration in UBEM

Bayes' Decision Theory is based on predicting the possible outcomes of an event by observing the prior distribution of that event [84, 85]. In our case, the Bayes' estimator works to estimate the possible outcomes for different values of each characterization parameter by examining the error between the metered and simulated demand (Eq. 1):

$$P(C_i|x) = \frac{P(x|C_i)P(C_i)}{\sum_i P(x|C_i)} \qquad (1)$$

The likelihood function $P(x|C_i)$ is an error function (Eq. 2) that minimizes the error between the metered and simulated demand [39, 45]:

$$P(x|C_i) = \begin{cases} 1, & Error[y(C_i), x] < \alpha \\ 0, & otherwise \end{cases} \qquad (2)$$

The term $y(C_i)$ represents the simulated demand according to the parameters setting C_i, whereas x represents the metered demand. α is the maximum error term set by the modeler. In Bayesian Calibration, the goal is observing the prior distribution of each characterization parameter $P(C_i)$ according to the likelihood function $P(x|C_i)$, and then normalizing the numerator term with the marginal probability of the likelihood function over all parameter settings to get the posterior probability for the specific parameter setting. Here, the parameter should be considered either as discrete or continuous. For example, an archetype's thermal transmittance (U-value) can vary from 1.0 to 3.0. Then, the prior and posterior distributions of this parameter should be a discrete function (probability mass functions (PMF)) or a continuous (probability density function (PDF)) comprising the values zero to three. Bayesian Decision theory can be easily implemented and effective in UBEM cases. However, this type of naïve assumption might yield bias when there is a high correlation between the input parameters, in our case, characterization parameters [85]. Therefore, the modeler should value the number of parameters calibrated during the process, which brings us to the topics: *Feature selection* and *sensitivity analysis.*

To calibrate a UBEM based on the Bayes' theorem, one should first perform feature engineering and then sensitivity analysis to detect the most critical parameters affecting the buildings' energy performance [39]. *Feature engineering* is a data pre-processing technique that enables extracting critical information from the data intuitively and mathe-matically. It requires domain and statistical knowledge and can improve the quality of the data as it can derive new features, exclude unnecessary features, or handle missing data [86]. Likewise, *sensitivity analysis* is a process that examines the amount of uncertainty in the output that is induced by the change in a particular or a set of input parameters [87]. Using sensitivity analysis could help derive the optimal number of parameters that play vital roles in determining the building energy demand. After conducting sensitivity analysis, selected parameters are introduced in the model as initial values, and their occurrence probability is observed, ranging between a set of values (prior distribution) obtained from the existing literature within the part of Bayesian inference [42]. Once creating prior distribution for each parameter, Bayesian calibration examines this vari-ation in the parameters' values and seeks the best fit between the predicted and metered results by introducing errors about inherent uncertainties in building energy performance and climatic conditions [18].

The normative modeling in energy performance simulation is a popular approach as it employs simplistic assumptions on the buildings' envelope and surroundings [88] and thus requires less simulation effort than the dynamic simulation [43]. Such a reduced-order modeling approach enables the calibration of models, which is a labor-intensive task considering the required computational power over the massive amount of data.

Heo et al. calculated and validated a building's energy demand with a normative mod-eling process [18]. The simulation error was reduced from 24% to 3% after the Bayesian calibration. The authors also investigated the efficiency of the calibrated model by com-paring it with the dynamic energy model and concluded that the normative approach could be tailored to the UBEM practices considering its time efficiency in model cre-ation and validation [18]. Similarly, Heo et al. used normative models of two commercial buildings to analyze the possible effects of several retrofit measures after Bayesian cali-bration at the individual and aggregate levels [23]. The calibration improved the model's demand estimation by about 52% and allowed better saving predictions through the mea-sures [23]. Using the normative method, Booth et al. assessed the energy performance of a residential building in the UK and analyzed the benefits of the Bayesian calibra-tion [44]. The calibrated results demonstrate a significant improvement in the energy demand estimations. However, this enhanced model can still reserve uncertainties within its inputs. Calibrating the results based on merely the selected parameters neglects the disregarded parameters' impact on the overall energy demand, and thus it interrupts the model's estimation power [44]. Therefore, one should carefully consider the quantity of the energy-sensitive parameters used in calibration.

Sokol et al. developed a calibration framework over the UBEM of Cambridge City [45]. They performed the Bayesian calibration on a small stock with homoge-nous features and propagated the procedure to the urban stock. The authors observed that introducing a stochastic approach to archetype development resulted in accurate demand prediction in the district-scale simulation after calibrating the results over the monthly/annual data. When the model was trained with the small-scale samples, they applied the same methodology to the urban residential stock. The results show that the deterministic scenarios lead to severe errors, whereas the probabilistic characterization still provides compatible values with the metered data [45]. Wang et al. created a UBEM to predict the heating energy demand of Amsterdam's residential stock [13]. Using the six years of metered data, the authors updated the archetypes' features according to their occurrence probability within a specified range and validated the simulation results over the Bayesian calibration. The proposed method improved the model's accuracy by around 60% in predicting the heating demand [13]. Chong et al. touched on the challenge of validating model results with metered data due to their storage form; monthly and daily/hourly [46]. They analyzed the chiller systems' performance of two buildings in different climates through Transient System Simulation Tool (TRNSYS) and EnergyPlus platforms, habilitated those models' output for the calibration, and kept the deviation between the results and metered data under the 15% error limit (stated in the ASHRAE Guideline 14 [47]) [46]. With a simplified physical model, Risch et al. validated the results of multiple BEMs to enhance their functionality in UBEM applications [48]. The archetypes representing those models were identified with different levels of detail regarding the building characteristics via the TEASER platform [34]. The Bayesian calibration enhanced the model's estimation capacity, and the results showed that the calibration could be optimized with the further-detailed archetypes as the prior distribution of the uncertainty parameters is better known [48].

The Bayesian calibration offers a reliable solution to overcome the inherent uncertainties that can arise from the diversified occupancy patterns or occur when installing the energy-related parameters in the construction phase or developing the energy models [50]. The Bayesian calibration allows detecting the most probable values for the input parameters through a stochastic approach and creating highly representative archetypes for building clusters. According to the PDFs, Sokol et al. observed that some of the characterization parameters, such as the occupancy comfort level and the occupancy rate, displayed slightly less ambiguity than the others [45]. Therefore, they might be deterministically assigned to the archetypes. This indicates that introducing a comprehensive sensitivity analysis before the calibration to assess the parameters' impact on the final energy demand forms a massive part of the UBEM calibration [39]. Furthermore, the metered consumption data at the individual-building level are essential to empower the model consistency and dynamize the calibration process [45, 49]. The benefits and limitations of the Bayesian calibration studies are presented in Table 3 by providing a relevant data source.

Table 3. Benefits and limitations of the studies on the Bayesian Calibration

Reference	Model	Calibration level	Benefits	Limitations
[18, 44]	Normative	Building	Huge error reduction via calibration Retrofit Assessment [18] Referring to the importance of the number of the parameters used in calibration [44]	Adapting the process to UBEMs Lack of the metered data with high resolution

(*continued*)

Table 3. (*continued*)

Reference	Model	Calibration level	Benefits	Limitations
[23]	Normative	Building and District	Huge error reduction via calibration Including uncertainty analysis	Only comprising the commercial buildings Adapting the process to UBEMs
[45]	Dynamic	District and City	Huge error reduction via calibration Comparing the deterministic and probabilistic archetype characterizations Calibrating the results based on both monthly and annual metered data	Lack of the metered data for each building with end-use-specific information Unsatisfactory results for the large-scale analysis
[13]	Dynamic	District	Huge error reduction via calibration	Lack of the metered data for each building with end-use-specific information
[46]	Dynamic	Building	Huge error reduction via calibration Including uncertainty analysis Calibrating the results based on both monthly and annual metered data	Adapting the process to UBEMs
[48]	Reduced order model	Building	Providing archetype characterizations with different levels of detail Huge error reduction with the most detailed archetypes	Adapting the process to UBEMs Lack of the metered data with high resolution

4 Uncertainties in Occupancy-Related Parameters

Buildings reserve many uncertainties that obstruct the calculation of the accurate energy demand. The occupant preferences with complex and multifarious patterns are an excellent example of the uncertainty parameters affecting the building energy consumption (Fig. 3). These preferences bring instant heat exchanges in the entire envelope and alter the buildings' energy demand frequently. This is because the residents manipulating the thermal, ventilation, and illumination conditions over the active/passive systems to obtain quality indoor air profoundly impact the building energy performance [51–56]. For example, Santin et al. showed that the occupancy parameters evidenced 4.2% of the variation in the final energy demand using a statistical bottom-up model [57].

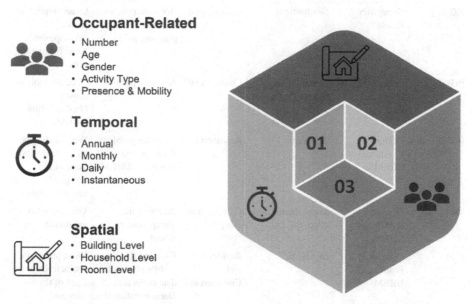

Occupant-Related

- Number
- Age
- Gender
- Activity Type
- Presence & Mobility

Temporal

- Annual
- Monthly
- Daily
- Instantaneous

Spatial

- Building Level
- Household Level
- Room Level

Fig. 3. Occupancy-related uncertainties. Adapted from Yan et al. [70]

There is a large diversity in occupancy patterns that makes the archetype characterization very complicated. This diversity is either caused by spatial parameters (e.g., the total number of occupants with seasonal variation) or individual use (e.g., change of location, use of appliances with different rates and settings) [58]. All these uncertainties have been a concern in the field, and practitioners developed various deterministic/probabilistic methods to predict the cyclic behavior of occupancy patterns using statistical data from the energy-use schedules and surveys (Table 4).

Widén and Wäckelgård developed a simple but reliable framework for the occupancy profile estimation [59]. This method analyzes the statistical patterns and assumes the probability of the following activity. The individual and shared activities, as well as their stable and cyclic natures, were regarded in the model. However, the model achieved only the linear occupancy profiles over the large-scale sample sets [59]. Page et al. predicted the presence/absence of the individuals and groups at a random moment [60]. The model

Table 4. Benefits and Limitations of the studies on the occupancy-related uncertainties

Reference	Target/Output	Approach	Building use type	Benefits	Limitations
[36, 59, 62]	Occupancy Profile	Stochastic	Residential	Accurate profiles for the aggregated patterns Easily generatable profiles [36] Considering the occupancy-related uncertainties [59]	Lack of the adequate reference data Not effective with small-scale datasets [59] Overcomplicated profile development [62]
[60, 67]	Occupancy Profile	Stochastic	Commercial	Accurate profiles Valuable in urban planning [67]	Overcomplicated profile development Need for motion sensor
[63]	Occupancy and Plug Load Profiles	Deterministic and Stochastic	Commercial	Accurate profiles	Need for motion sensor Hard to follow in UBEMs
[64]	Occupancy Profile and UBEM	Stochastic	Residential	Accurate profiles Adapting the process to UBEMs	Weak archetype characterization Lack of the adequate reference data
[66]	Occupancy Profile and UBEM	Population-Based (PopAp)	Campus and Hospital	Imitating the transportation models	Unclear result validation
[25]	Occupancy Profile and UBEM	Stochastic	Residential and Commercial	Utilizing the mobile phones in data collection Demonstrating the importance of detailed occupancy profiles	Weak archetype characterization Lack of the adequate reference data
[69]	Occupancy Profile and UBEM	Deterministic	Residential	Simple profile development Accurate profiles for the aggregated patterns Adapting the process to UBEMs	Weak archetype characterization Not revealing real-time energy demand

successfully predicted the aggregated and peak loads that could be utilized to manage the demand at a specific time. However, the complex structure of this probabilistic model and its calibration through the sophisticated data from a motion sensor complicates the model's applicability in future studies [60]. Analyzing the participants' usage intensity and mobility from a survey, Richardson et al. generated a stochastic model predicting the number of active/passive occupants and their mobility and activity patterns [36]. The resulting error was drastic due to the poorly made survey. However, this model could be optimized by averaging the most probable occupancy profiles, derivable from a tool [61], and utilized in the studies where occupant preferences have a moderate impact on the building energy performance [36]. Using a survey on French households, Wilke et al. proposed a model predicting the generalized occupancy patterns and used the validated framework for analyzing the individual patterns in more detail [62]. However, this complex model required extreme computational power and failed to reflect the induvial patterns, although the aggregated results were consistent with the recorded data [62]. Mahdavi et al. examined an office building with eight residents to generate plug load schedules based on several occupancy profiles [63]. These profiles were obtained using both deterministic and probabilistic (adapted from Page et al. [60]) approaches, and the outputs were validated with the metered data from the sensors detecting the power consumption of devices and the human movement. The results showed that the deterministic model performed well to mimic the aggregated results, whereas the peak loads matched the stochastic models' predictions [63]. Nevertheless, the study is hard to implement for mass modeling as it contains only a small-scale examination, and the proposed method requires motion data from smart monitoring devices [63].

Even though the sophisticated occupant profiles fall short of reducing the uncertainties in building performance assessment, they might help derive reasonable interpretations of general trends or extreme seasonal demands for building stocks. Thus, well-designed occupancy profiles could benefit UBEM practices by enhancing the archetype quality and simulation's reliability. An et al. analyzed the cooling energy demand of a district in China [64]. They generated detailed occupancy profiles adapted from Wang et al. [65] and energy consumption patterns concerning active/passive ventilation, lighting, and indoor comfort. The approach neglected to detail the archetype characterization, and cooling demand was the only factor influencing the occupant preferences. However, the model could be utilized in UBEM applications as it successfully reflects the aggregated and peak energy demand [64]. Gaining inspiration from the transportation models that focus on the individual activity patterns, Mosteiro-Romero et al. developed a stochastic occupancy model integrated within a basic district energy model covering campus and hospital buildings [66]. The authors compared the proposed model with the conventional deterministic and probabilistic models to analyze their variation in the prediction of occupancy profiles. Dismissing that the result validation was unclear, this study demonstrated that detailed occupancy profiles could be valuable for managing the peak energy demand [66]. Wang et al. created dynamic occupancy density profiles for the multiple commercial buildings within a UBEM and predicted the occupancy profiles with a slight variation from the field measurements [67]. To improve an existing framework called TimeGeo [68], Barbour et al. analyzed the occupancy patterns with the data gathered from mobile devices [25]. The model investigated the occupancy rate and the occupant mobility to derive stochastic occupancy profiles for a UBEM. The model was characterized using the standard and proposed profiles, and an 18% variation on average was observed for the final energy demand [25]. Considering the electricity usage rate and indoor temperature levels based on the hourly and seasonal user preferences, Fernandez et al. created simplified occupancy profiles and validated them with the census and metered data [69]. The best-suited schedule was used to characterize the selected archetypes of the UBEM. Although the proposed method could not reveal the real-time energy demand, it could be adjusted to district-level analysis with satisfactory aggregated results [69].

5 Discussion

The bottom-up models are great tools to assess the building stocks' energy performance through the archetype approach, imitating the buildings' energy-related features over representative models. The literature review results indicate that the direct comparison of the statistical and engineering bottom-up models is impossible considering the advantages and disadvantages of both models. Given that, the scope of the study and the available sources should be the determinants of the model selected in district-level analysis. For example, the statistical models could be favorable regarding the simplicity of the model development even though they are out of function without historical data and unqualified to assess the retrofit actions' impact. Likewise, the engineering models require high computational power and a labor-intensive process to make reliable demand estimations.

This unpractical comparison applies to the methods used in archetype characterization. In deterministic characterization, the characterization parameters are assigned as single values to the archetypes. This method is deficient in capturing the natural diversity of the built environment as it employs the characterization parameters without any validation/calibration. On the other hand, the probabilistic approach identifies the characterization parameters by correlating them with the metered data until getting the best fit. However, this procedure might be challenging considering the complexity of conducting detailed characterization for each parameter. Thus, the prior studies suggested performing sensitivity analysis to select the essential parameters and calibrate the model [5, 37, 39].

Allocating the utmost effort to archetype characterization with non-occupancy-related parameters prevails among the current practices since the simplified occupancy schedules usually provide the models with reliable predictions on the aggregated energy demand. However, sophisticated occupancy schedules display significant advantages in revealing the demand of the peak hours and thus presenting more precise consumption patterns. According to the literature review findings, only a few UBEMs were integrated with detailed occupancy schedules due to the exhausting model development and simulation. Hence, archetypes with elaborative occupancy profiles in UBEMs stand as a heavy target since the data composing/validating those profiles misses detailed information about the occupants' mobility and energy consumption patterns. Similarly, these sophisticated profiles require advanced monitoring systems to gather the motion and consumption data [70] and are often based on residential buildings, complicating their adaption in district-level practices with diverse building types [58].

The findings confirm that the most significant problem in evaluating building performance at the urban level is attaining the data to characterize and validate the model.

The existing building literature lacks such comprehensive data for tens or even hundreds of building clusters. Significantly, the data for the buildings that experienced several renovations are not often updated, or the metered data for validation are usually stored in aggregated forms without end-use and household-specific information. This prominently obstructs understanding the buildings' real-time demand and improving the reliability of building performance simulations. Hence, the absence of high-quality data constitutes the urgent need of the UBEM studies. To that end, BIMs play a key role in providing the archetypes with detailed characterization parameters since they reserve building-specific information within a framework that enables data update and sharing (i.e., Common Data Environment (CDE)) [90]. File formats for BIM conform with the tools used in UBEM development [91], and archetype generation by the collaboration of BIM and GIS platforms could be possible for district-level analysis [71, 72, 92], where the level of archetype detail is crucial [73, 93]. Similarly, BIMs are sophisticated models equipped with the information necessary in all project phases. Utilizing the data from those living models in UBEM could enable life cycle assessment (LCA) of building stocks [74, 94, 95].

Even though some studies integrated the statistical and engineering models, they usually provided a comparative analysis to depict the best approach [21, 96]. Only a few studies utilized the power of these two modeling approaches [82, 97–99]. According to this hybrid modeling approach, the engineering models can be utilized in establishing the base model to estimate aggregated demand. In contrast, the statistical model can be employed in more complex situations that require substantial computational cost and time, such as tuning the characterization parameters or utilizing the model in the retrofit actions. Owing to the recent development in machine learning, data-driven models may yield overachievements with valid data preprocessing and proper algorithm selection. Again, such achievements are highly dependent on the modeler's inference capacity on data, a combination of the domain and statistical knowledge.

In conclusion, one could benefit from each modeling/characterization technique by setting the target correctly and determining the parameters calibrated to enhance the models' reliability through sensitivity analysis. As the need for advanced models with higher resolution arises, it is evident that the broadly characterized UBEMs and the advanced data-driven models will soon be the key actors in energy management strategies at the urban level.

6 Conclusion

This study examines the dynamics, benefits, limitations, and future trends of the building energy performance assessment at the urban scale. The original value of this research is to analyze/question different archetype characterization methods and their practicability over wide-ranging studies, identify the most crucial characterization parameters and assess the validation techniques to enhance the demand estimations of UBEMs. Accordingly, this study contributes to the literature by fulfilling the lack of perspective that concentrates on the archetype characterization methods in UBEM practices. Therefore, the findings of this research could help practitioners (e.g., policymakers and city planners) and academics to comprehend the potential of the UBEM that improves energy management strategies at the urban scale.

The findings suggest that the Bayesian calibration enables the probabilistic archetype characterization and thus improves the models' estimation capacity. Different methods were introduced to understand the importance of the occupancy profiles with many unknowns in the occupants' mobility and energy consumption patterns. In this regard, the occupancy profiles were affirmed to be essential archetype characterization parameters since they materially impact the building's energy demand. Finally, the literature shows that the absence of data constitutes a vital problem for UBEMs. BIMs could resolve this problem as they are high-resolution databases on building-specific information.

This study attached particular importance to the archetype characterization of UBEMs. Advanced computational methods could enhance the probabilistic archetype characterization where mainly the prior distribution of the characterization parameters suffer from unreliable data sources. For example, machine learning algorithms could bridge this gap as it facilitates the recovery of such databases. Considering the findings of this review paper, curating the occupancy profiles might be the next step in the manner that enables the manipulation of those profiles in probabilistic archetype characterization. Above all, hybrid models integrating engineering and statistical models might be the next popular UBEM approach as they benefit from the advantages of each model. One question is whether the complexity of the statistical models to get more accurate results might aggravate the result interpretation since most machine learning models are black-box models performing an enormous number of calculations without revealing many insights to the users. Therefore, using explainable artificial intelligence (XAI) techniques could enhance the interpretability of such models, ease observing the interaction between the characterization parameters and the energy demand, and thus increase the capabilities of hybrid models.

References

1. IEA: Global Energy Review: CO_2 Emissions in 2020, IEA, Paris (2021). https://www.iea.org/articles/global-energy-review-co2-emissions-in-2020
2. 2020 climate & energy package: Retrieved from European Commission website (n.d.). https://ec.europa.eu/clima/policies/strategies/2020_en
3. Ritchie, H.: Sector by sector: where do global greenhouse gas emissions come from? (2020). Retrieved from Our World in Data. https://ourworldindata.org/ghg-emissions-by-sector
4. Swan, L.G., Ugursal, V.I.: Modeling of end-use energy consumption in the residential sector: a review of modeling techniques. Renew. Sustain. Energy Rev. 13(8), 1819–1835 (2009). https://doi.org/10.1016/j.rser.2008.09.033
5. Reinhart, C.F., Cerezo Davila, C.: Urban building energy modeling – a review of a nascent field. Build. Environ. 97, 196–202 (2016). https://doi.org/10.1016/j.buildenv.2015.12.001
6. Issermann, M., Chang, F.J., Kow, P.Y.: Interactive urban building energy modelling with functional mockup interface of a local residential building stock. J. Clean. Prod. 289, 125683 (2021). https://doi.org/10.1016/j.jclepro.2020.125683
7. Agugiaro, G., Benner, J., Cipriano, P., Nouvel, R.: The Energy application domain extension for CityGML: enhancing interoperability for urban energy simulations. Open Geosp. Data Software Stand. 3(1), 1–30 (2018). https://doi.org/10.1186/s40965-018-0042-y
8. Dall'O', G., Galante, A., Torri, M.: A methodology for the energy performance classification of residential building stock on an urban scale. Energy Build. 48, 211–219 (2012). https://doi.org/10.1016/j.enbuild.2012.01.034

9. Howard, B., Parshall, L., Thompson, J., Hammer, S., Dickinson, J., Modi, V.: Spatial distribution of urban building energy consumption by end use. Energy Build. **45**, 141–151 (2012). https://doi.org/10.1016/j.enbuild.2011.10.061

10. Kalagasidis, A.M.S., Johnsson, F.: Building-stock aggregation through archetype buildings: France, Germany, Spain and the UK. Build. Environ. **81**, 270–282 (2014).https://doi.org/10.1016/j.buildenv.2014.06.013

11. Ballarini, I., Corgnati, S.P., Corrado, V.: Use of reference buildings to assess the energy saving potentials of the residential building stock: the experience of TABULA project. Energy Policy **68**, 273–284 (2014). https://doi.org/10.1016/j.enpol.2014.01.027

12. IEE Project TABULA: Institut Wohnen Und Umwelt (n.d.). https://episcope.eu/iee-project/tabula/

13. Wang, C.K., Tindemans, S., Miller, C., Agugiaro, G., Stoter, J.: Bayesian calibration at the urban scale: a case study on a large residential heating demand application in Amsterdam. J. Build. Perform. Simul. **13**(3), 347–361 (2020). https://doi.org/10.1080/19401493.2020.1729862

14. Famuyibo, A.A., Duffy, A., Strachan, P.: Developing archetypes for domestic dwellings—an Irish case study. Energy Build. **50**, 150–157 (2012). https://doi.org/10.1016/j.enbuild.2012.03.033

15. Aksoezen, M., Daniel, M., Hassler, U., Kohler, N.: Building age as an indicator for energy consumption. Energy Build. **87**, 74–86 (2015). https://doi.org/10.1016/j.enbuild.2014.10.074

16. Braulio-Gonzalo, M., Juan, P., Bovea, M.D., Ruá, M.J.: Modelling energy efficiency performance of residential building stocks based on Bayesian statistical inference. Environ. Model. Softw. **83**, 198–211 (2016). https://doi.org/10.1016/j.envsoft.2016.05.018

17. Kazanasmaz, T., Uygun, L.E., Akkurt, G.G., Turhan, C., Ekmen, K.E.: On the relation between architectural considerations and heating energy performance of Turkish residential buildings in Izmir. Energy Build. **72**, 38–50 (2014). https://doi.org/10.1016/j.enbuild.2013.12.036

18. Heo, Y., Choudhary, R., Augenbroe, G.: Calibration of building energy models for retrofit analysis under uncertainty. Energy Build. **47**, 550–560 (2012). https://doi.org/10.1016/j.enbuild.2011.12.029

19. Caputo, P., Costa, G., Ferrari, S.: A supporting method for defining energy strategies in the building sector at urban scale. Energy Policy **55**, 261–270 (2013). https://doi.org/10.1016/j.enpol.2012.12.006

20. Torabi Moghadam, S., Coccolo, S., Mutani, G., Lombardi, P., Scartezzini, J.L., Mauree, D.: A new clustering and visualization method to evaluate urban heat energy planning scenarios. Cities **88**, 19–36 (2019). https://doi.org/10.1016/j.cities.2018.12.007

21. Nagpal, S., Reinhart, C.F.: A comparison of two modeling approaches for establishing and implementing energy use reduction targets for a university campus. Energy Build. **173**, 103–116 (2018). https://doi.org/10.1016/j.enbuild.2018.05.035

22. Buckley, N., Mills, G., Reinhart, C., Berzolla, Z.M.: Using urban building energy modelling (UBEM) to support the new European Union's Green Deal: case study of Dublin Ireland. Energy Build. **247**, 111115 (2021). https://doi.org/10.1016/j.enbuild.2021.111115

23. Heo, Y., Augenbroe, G., Graziano, D., Muehleisen, R.T., Guzowski, L.: Scalable methodology for large scale building energy improvement: relevance of calibration in model-based retrofit analysis. Build. Environ. **87**, 342–350 (2015). https://doi.org/10.1016/j.buildenv.2014.12.016

24. Cerezo Davila, C., Reinhart, C.F., Bemis, J.L.: Modeling Boston: a workflow for the efficient generation and maintenance of urban building energy models from existing geospatial datasets. Energy **117**, 237–250 (2016). https://doi.org/10.1016/j.energy.2016.10.057

25. Barbour, E., Davila, C.C., Gupta, S., Reinhart, C., Kaur, J., González, M.C.: Planning for sustainable cities by estimating building occupancy with mobile phones. Nature Commun. **10**(1) (2019). https://doi.org/10.1038/s41467-019-11685-w

26. Monteiro, C.S., Pina, A., Cerezo, C., Reinhart, C., Ferrão, P.: The use of multi-detail building archetypes in urban energy modelling. Energy Procedia **111**, 817–825 (2017). https://doi.org/10.1016/j.egypro.2017.03.244

27. Claudia, M., Carlos, C., André, P., Paulo, F.: A method for the generation of multi-detail building archetype definitions: application to the city of Lisbon (2015)

28. Ascione, F., De Masi, R.F., de Rossi, F., Fistola, R., Sasso, M., Vanoli, G.P.: Analysis and diagnosis of the energy performance of buildings and districts: methodology, validation and development of Urban Energy Maps. Cities **35**, 270–283 (2013). https://doi.org/10.1016/j.cities.2013.04.012

29. ÖSterbring, M., Mata, R., Thuvander, L., Mangold, M., Johnsson, F., Wallbaum, H.: A differentiated description of building-stocks for a georeferenced urban bottom-up building-stock model. Energy Build. **120**, 78–84 (2016). https://doi.org/10.1016/j.enbuild.2016.03.060

30. Chen, Y., Hong, T., Piette, M.A.: Automatic generation and simulation of urban building energy models based on city datasets for city-scale building retrofit analysis. Appl. Energy **205**, 323–335 (2017). https://doi.org/10.1016/j.apenergy.2017.07.128

31. Hong, T., Chen, Y., Lee, S.H., Piette, M.A.: CityBES: a web-based platform to support cityscale building energy efficiency. Urban Comput 2016., San Francisco, California USA (2016)

32. Chen, Y., Hong, T., Piette, M.A.: City-scale building retrofit analysis: a case study using CityBES. Building Simulator 2017., San Francisco, CA, USA (2017)

33. Hong, T., et al.: Commercial Building Energy Saver: an energy retrofit analysis toolkit. Appl. Energy **159**, 298–309 (2015). https://doi.org/10.1016/j.apenergy.2015.09.002

34. Remmen, P., Lauster, M., Mans, M., Fuchs, M., Osterhage, T., Müller, D.: TEASER: an open tool for urban energy modelling of building stocks. J. Build. Perform. Simul. **11**(1), 84–98 (2017). https://doi.org/10.1080/19401493.2017.1283539

35. Schiefelbein, J., Rudnick, J., Scholl, A., Remmen, P., Fuchs, M., Müller, D.: Automated urban energy system modeling and thermal building simulation based on OpenStreetMap data sets. Build. Environ. **149**, 630–639 (2019). https://doi.org/10.1016/j.buildenv.2018.12.025

36. Richardson, I., Thomson, M., Infield, D.: A high-resolution domestic building occupancy model for energy demand simulations. Energy Build. **40**(8), 1560–1566 (2008). https://doi.org/10.1016/j.enbuild.2008.02.006

37. Johari, F., Peronato, G., Sadeghian, P., Zhao, X., Widén, J.: Urban building energy modeling: state of the art and future prospects. Renew. Sustain. Energy Rev. **128**, 109902 (2020). https://doi.org/10.1016/j.rser.2020.109902

38. de Jaeger, I., Lago, J., Saelens, D.: A probabilistic building characterization method for district energy simulations. Energy Build. **230**, 110566 (2021). https://doi.org/10.1016/j.enbuild.2020.110566

39. Cerezo, C., Sokol, J., AlKhaled, S., Reinhart, C., Al-Mumin, A., Hajiah, A.: Comparison of four building archetype characterization methods in urban building energy modeling (UBEM): a residential case study in Kuwait City. Energy Build. **154**, 321–334 (2017). https://doi.org/10.1016/j.enbuild.2017.08.029

40. Buffat, R., Froemelt, A., Heeren, N., Raubal, M., Hellweg, S.: Big data GIS analysis for novel approaches in building stock modelling. Appl. Energy **208**, 277–290 (2017). https://doi.org/10.1016/j.apenergy.2017.10.041

41. Ali, U., Shamsi, M.H., Hoare, C., Mangina, E., O'Donnell, J.: A data-driven approach for multi-scale building archetypes development. Energy Build. **202**, 109364 (2019). https://doi.org/10.1016/j.enbuild.2019.109364

42. Kennedy, M.C., O'Hagan, A.: Bayesian calibration of computer models. J. Roy. Statist. Soc. Ser. B (Statist. Methodol.) **63**(3), 425–464 (2001). https://doi.org/10.1111/1467-9868.00294

43. Lee, S.H., Hong, T., Piette, M.A.: Review of existing energy retrofit tools. Lawrence Berkeley National Laboratory. LBNL-xxxxx (2014)

44. Booth, A., Choudhary, R., Spiegelhalter, D.: Handling uncertainty in housing stock models. Build. Environ. **48**, 35–47 (2012). https://doi.org/10.1016/j.buildenv.2011.08.016
45. Sokol, J., Cerezo Davila, C., Reinhart, C.F.: Validation of a Bayesian-based method for defining residential archetypes in urban building energy models. Energy Build. **134**, 11–24 (2017). https://doi.org/10.1016/j.enbuild.2016.10.050
46. Chong, A., Lam, K.P., Pozzi, M., Yang, J.: Bayesian calibration of building energy models with large datasets. Energy Build. **154**, 343–355 (2017). https://doi.org/10.1016/j.enbuild. 2017.08.069
47. ASHRAE Guideline 14: ASHRAE Guideline 14-2014, Measurement of Energy, Demand, and Water Savings. ASHRAE Atlanta (2014)
48. Risch, S., Remmen, P., Müller, D.: Influence of data acquisition on the Bayesian calibration of urban building energy models. Energy Build. **230**, 110512 (2021). https://doi.org/10.1016/ j.enbuild.2020.110512
49. Coakley, D., Raftery, P., Keane, M.: A review of methods to match building energy simulation models to measured data. Renew. Sustain. Energy Rev. **37**, 123–141 (2014). https://doi.org/ 10.1016/j.rser.2014.05.007
50. Macdonald, I.: Quantifying the effects of uncertainty in building simulation, PhD thesis, University of Strathclyde (2002)
51. Sağlam, N.G., Yılmaz, A.Z., Becchio, C., Corgnati, S.P.: A comprehensive cost-optimal approach for energy retrofit of existing multi-family buildings: application to apartment blocks in Turkey. Energy Build. **150**, 224–238 (2017). https://doi.org/10.1016/j.enbuild.2017.06.026
52. Reinhart, C.F.: Lightswitch-2002: a model for manual and automated control of electric lighting and blinds. Sol. Energy **77**(1), 15–28 (2004). https://doi.org/10.1016/j.solener.2004. 04.003
53. Andersen, R., Fabi, V., Toftum, J., Corgnati, S.P., Olesen, B.W.: Window opening behaviour modelled from measurements in Danish dwellings. Build. Environ. **69**, 101–113 (2013). https://doi.org/10.1016/j.buildenv.2013.07.005
54. Schiavon, S., Lee, K.H.: Dynamic predictive clothing insulation models based on outdoor air and indoor operative temperatures. Build. Environ. **59**, 250–260 (2013). https://doi.org/10. 1016/j.buildenv.2012.08.024
55. Lee, Y.S., Malkawi, A.M.: Simulating multiple occupant behaviors in buildings: an agent-based modeling approach. Energy Build. **69**, 407–416 (2014). https://doi.org/10.1016/j.enb uild.2013.11.020
56. Ren, X., Yan, D., Wang, C.: Air-conditioning usage conditional probability model for residential buildings. Build. Environ. **81**, 172–182 (2014). https://doi.org/10.1016/j.buildenv.2014. 06.022
57. Guerra Santin, O., Itard, L., Visscher, H.: The effect of occupancy and building characteristics on energy use for space and water heating in Dutch residential stock. Energy Build. **41**(11), 1223–1232 (2009). https://doi.org/10.1016/j.enbuild.2009.07.002
58. Happle, G., Fonseca, J.A., Schlueter, A.: A review on occupant behavior in urban building energy models. Energy Build. **174**, 276–292 (2018). https://doi.org/10.1016/j.enbuild.2018. 06.030
59. Widén, J., Wäckelgård, E.: A high-resolution stochastic model of domestic activity patterns and electricity demand. Appl. Energy **87**(6), 1880–1892 (2010). https://doi.org/10.1016/j.ape nergy.2009.11.006
60. Page, J., Robinson, D., Morel, N., Scartezzini, J.L.: A generalised stochastic model for the simulation of occupant presence. Energy Build. **40**(2), 83–98 (2008). https://doi.org/10.1016/ j.enbuild.2007.01.018
61. Richardson, I., Thomson, M.: Domestic active Occupancy Model - Simulation Example. Loughborough University Institutional Repository (2008). http://hdl.handle.net/2134/3112

62. Wilke, U., Haldi, F., Scartezzini, J.L., Robinson, D.: A bottom-up stochastic model to predict building occupants' time-dependent activities. Build. Environ. **60**, 254–264 (2013). https://doi.org/10.1016/j.buildenv.2012.10.021

63. Mahdavi, A., Tahmasebi, F., Kayalar, M.: Prediction of plug loads in office buildings: simplified and probabilistic methods. Energy Build. **129**, 322–329 (2016). https://doi.org/10.1016/j.enbuild.2016.08.022

64. An, J., Yan, D., Hong, T., Sun, K.: A novel stochastic modeling method to simulate cooling loads in residential districts. Appl. Energy **206**, 134–149 (2017). https://doi.org/10.1016/j.apenergy.2017.08.038

65. Wang, C., Yan, D., Jiang, Y.: A novel approach for building occupancy simulation. Build. Simul. **4**(2), 149–167 (2011). https://doi.org/10.1007/s12273-011-0044-5

66. Mosteiro-Romero, M., Hischier, I., Fonseca, J.A., Schlueter, A.: A novel population-based occupancy modeling approach for district-scale simulations compared to standard-based methods. Build. Environ. **181**, 107084 (2020). https://doi.org/10.1016/j.buildenv.2020.107084

67. Wang, C., et al.: Dynamic occupant density models of commercial buildings for urban energy simulation. Build. Environ. **169**, 106549 (2020). https://doi.org/10.1016/j.buildenv.2019.106549

68. Jiang, S., et al.: The timegeo modeling framework for urban mobility without travel surveys. Proc. Natl Acad. Sci. USA **113**, E5370–E5378 (2016)

69. Fernandez, J., del Portillo, L., Flores, I.: A novel residential heating consumption characterisation approach at city level from available public data: description and case study. Energy Build. **221**, 110082 (2020). https://doi.org/10.1016/j.enbuild.2020.110082

70. Yan, D., et al.: Occupant behavior modeling for building performance simulation: current state and future challenges. Energy Build. **107**, 264–278 (2015). https://doi.org/10.1016/j.enbuild.2015.08.032

71. Sehrawat, P., Kensek, K.: Urban Energy Modeling: GIS as an Alternative to BIM (2014)

72. Bai, Y., Zadeh, P.A., Staub-French, S., Pottinger, R.: Integrating GIS and BIM for community-scale energy modeling. In: International Conference on Sustainable Infrastructure 2017. Published (2017). https://doi.org/10.1061/9780784481196.017

73. Ferrando, M., Causone, F., Hong, T., Chen, Y.: Urban building energy modeling (UBEM) tools: a state-of-the-art review of bottom-up physics-based approaches. Sustain. Cities Soc. **62**, 102408 (2020). https://doi.org/10.1016/j.scs.2020.102408

74. Santos, R., Costa, A.A., Silvestre, J.D., Pyl, L.: Integration of LCA and LCC analysis within a BIM-based environment. Autom. Constr. **103**, 127–149 (2019). https://doi.org/10.1016/j.autcon.2019.02.011

75. Zhang, L., et al.: A review of machine learning in building load prediction. Appl. Energy **285**, 116452 (2021). https://doi.org/10.1016/j.apenergy.2021.116452

76. Oraiopoulos, A., Howard, B.: On the accuracy of urban building energy modelling. Renew. Sustain. Energy Rev. **158**, 111976 (2022). https://doi.org/10.1016/j.rser.2021.111976

77. Geraldi, M.S., Ghisi, E.: Data-driven framework towards realistic bottom-up energy benchmarking using an Artificial Neural Network. Appl. Energy **306**, 117960 (2022). https://doi.org/10.1016/j.apenergy.2021.117960

78. Pasichnyi, O., Levihn, F., Shahrokni, H., Wallin, J., Kordas, O.: Data-driven strategic planning of building energy retrofitting: the case of Stockholm. J. Clean. Prod. **233**, 546–560 (2019). https://doi.org/10.1016/j.jclepro.2019.05.373

79. Koschwitz, D., Frisch, J., van Treeck, C.: Data-driven heating and cooling load predictions for non-residential buildings based on support vector machine regression and NARX Recurrent Neural Network: a comparative study on district scale. Energy **165**, 134–142 (2018). https://doi.org/10.1016/j.energy.2018.09.068

80. Miller, C., Meggers, F.: Mining electrical meter data to predict principal building use, performance class, and operations strategy for hundreds of non-residential buildings. Energy Build. **156**, 360–373 (2017). https://doi.org/10.1016/j.enbuild.2017.09.056
81. Touzani, S., Granderson, J., Fernandes, S.: Gradient boosting machine for modeling the energy consumption of commercial buildings. Energy Build. **158**, 1533–1543 (2018). https://doi.org/10.1016/j.enbuild.2017.11.039
82. Roth, J., Martin, A., Miller, C., Jain, R.K.: SynCity: using open data to create a synthetic city of hourly building energy estimates by integrating data-driven and physics-based methods. Appl. Energy **280**, 115981 (2020). https://doi.org/10.1016/j.apenergy.2020.115981
83. Torabi Moghadam, S., Toniolo, J., Mutani, G., Lombardi, P.: A GIS-statistical approach for assessing built environment energy use at urban scale. Sustain. Cities Soc. **37**, 70–84 (2018). https://doi.org/10.1016/j.scs.2017.10.002
84. Ross, S.M.: Introduction to Probability and Statistics for Engineers and Scientists, 6th edn. Academic Press (2020)
85. Alpaydin, E.: Introduction to Machine Learning. MIT Press (2014)
86. Pedregosa, F., et al.: Scikit-learn: machine learning in python. J. Mach. Learn. Res. **12**, 2825–2830 (2011)
87. Pichery, C.: Sensitivity analysis. Encyclop. Toxicol. **236–237**,(2014). https://doi.org/10.1016/b978-0-12-386454-3.00431-0
88. Lee, S.H., Zhao, F., Augenbroe, G.: The use of normative energy calculation beyond building performance rating. J. Build. Perform. Simul. **6**(4), 282–292 (2012). https://doi.org/10.1080/19401493.2012.720712
89. Hou, D., Hassan, I., Wang, L.: Review on building energy model calibration by Bayesian inference. Renew. Sustain. Energy Rev. **143**, 110930 (2021). https://doi.org/10.1016/j.rser.2021.110930
90. Pan, Y., Zhang, L.: A BIM-data mining integrated digital twin framework for advanced project management. Autom. Constr. **124**, 103564 (2021). https://doi.org/10.1016/j.autcon.2021.103564
91. Zhu, J., Wang, X., Wang, P., Wu, Z., Kim, M.J.: Integration of BIM and GIS: geometry from IFC to shapefile using open-source technology. Autom. Constr. **102**, 105–119 (2019). https://doi.org/10.1016/j.autcon.2019.02.014
92. Ali, U., Shamsi, M.H., Hoare, C., Mangina, E., O'Donnell, J.: Review of urban building energy modeling (UBEM) approaches, methods and tools using qualitative and quantitative analysis. Energy Build. **246**, 111073 (2021). https://doi.org/10.1016/j.enbuild.2021.111073
93. Mohammadiziazi, R., Copeland, S., Bilec, M.M.: Urban building energy model: database development, validation, and application for commercial building stock. Energy Build. **248**, 111175 (2021). https://doi.org/10.1016/j.enbuild.2021.111175
94. Feng, H., Liyanage, D.R., Karunathilake, H., Sadiq, R., Hewage, K.: BIM-based life cycle environmental performance assessment of single-family houses: renovation and reconstruction strategies for aging building stock in British Columbia. J. Clean. Prod. **250**, 119543 (2020). https://doi.org/10.1016/j.jclepro.2019.119543
95. García-Pérez, S., Sierra-Pérez, J., Boschmonart-Rives, J.: Environmental assessment at the urban level combining LCA-GIS methodologies: a case study of energy retrofits in the Barcelona metropolitan area. Build. Environ. **134**, 191–204 (2018). https://doi.org/10.1016/j.buildenv.2018.01.041
96. Nageler, P., et al.: Comparison of dynamic urban building energy models (UBEM): sigmoid energy signature and physical modelling approach. Energy Build. **179**, 333–343 (2018). https://doi.org/10.1016/j.enbuild.2018.09.034

97. Nutkiewicz, A., Yang, Z., Jain, R.K.: Data-driven Urban Energy Simulation (DUE-S): a framework for integrating engineering simulation and machine learning methods in a multi-scale urban energy modeling workflow. Appl. Energy **225**, 1176–1189 (2018). https://doi.org/10.1016/j.apenergy.2018.05.023

98. Kim, B., Yamaguchi, Y., Kimura, S., Ko, Y., Ikeda, K., Shimoda, Y.: Urban building energy modeling considering the heterogeneity of HVAC system stock: a case study on Japanese office building stock. Energy Build. **207**, 109590 (2020). https://doi.org/10.1016/j.enbuild.2019.109590

99. Nouvel, R., Mastrucci, A., Leopold, U., Baume, O., Coors, V., Eicker, U.: Combining GIS-based statistical and engineering urban heat consumption models: towards a new framework for multi-scale policy support. Energy Build. **107**, 204–212 (2015). https://doi.org/10.1016/j.enbuild.2015.08.021

Building Information Modelling (BIM) and Smart Cities: The Role of Governance, Regulations and Policies

Azmina Gulamhusein(✉) and Marzia Bolpagni ⓘ

UCL The Bartlett School of Sustainable Construction, London WC1E6BT, UK
{azmina.gulamhusein.20,m.bolpagni}@ucl.ac.uk

Abstract. Existing literature focuses mainly on the benefits of SCs, particularly the impact of technology, however, efforts to explore the current challenges in implementing technology in SCs have been limited. The purpose of this research is to investigate the benefits and challenges of BIM in the development of SCs and to examine the role of governance, regulations, and policies in SCs; determining if the extant initiatives are sufficient or not. A sequential explanatory mixed-methods design approach was employed. Data has been gathered from 54 questionnaires, followed by semi-structured interviews to gain additional qualitative data. The main quantitative and qualitative findings show that data privacy and security are the biggest technological challenges in SC development and that further regulation and legislation is required to protect citizens against privacy threats. The results of this work can be useful to professionals and policy makers working on SCs as well as researchers to better understand the current gaps.

Keywords: Smart city · Technology · Governance · Regulation · Policy

1 Introduction

Cities have a major responsibility in opposing climate change, and the implementation of innovative smart technologies is an important aspect in reducing pollutants and emissions and enhancing sustainability within cities [1]. A city can be defined as smart when expenditures in human and social capital and transport and technological infrastructures, drive economic development and better standard of living, by wisely managing natural resources, via collaborative governance [2]. Smart Cities (SCs) can help tackle the issues created by growing urban populations and hastened urbanisation [3], therefore championing the UN Nations 2030 Agenda Sustainable Development Goal (SDG) 11. The aim of this goal is to transform cities into safe, resilient and sustainable places, whilst protecting the environment [4]. Digital technologies are facilitators of SCs and can be used by cities to confront environmental matters, distinguish the key trends, and uncover variances of technical and policy levels [5]. The main technological drivers behind SCs include Building Information Modelling (BIM), the internet of things (IoT), blockchain, big data, artificial intelligence (AI), cloud computing and robotics [6]. While technology is beneficial to the sustainable development of SCs, certain challenges arise through

© Springer Nature Switzerland AG 2022
O. Ö. Özener et al. (Eds.): EBF 2021, CCIS 1627, pp. 183–200, 2022.
https://doi.org/10.1007/978-3-031-16895-6_12

its application. These include disruption to the labour market, maintaining social cohesion, inclusiveness and solidarity, and questions around security and privacy [6]. The government cannot solely tackle these issues; therefore, corporations and new citizen co-operatives should exercise their social and corporate responsibility by advocating policies and regulations that resolve social difficulties [7]. Current research demonstrates that technological advancement is driving SC realization, however, the obstructions and complications in implementation are indeterminate. This paper uses mixed-methods research to combine quantitative results and qualitative findings to develop a more thorough discussion around the research questions. It explores the benefits and drawbacks of the key technological drivers in the development of SC, and enquires into how regulations, policies and governance can support technology in the advance of SCs.

2 Literature Review

2.1 Benefits of the Key Technological Drivers for Smart Cities

Alongside growing environmental demands and infrastructure requirements cities are increasingly pressurised to provide an improved quality of life (QoL) for citizens. Data and digital technologies are employed in SCs with the intention of enhancing QoL [8] as more complete and instantaneous data allows authorities to observe events as they occur, comprehend how requirements are shifting and react with quicker and more economical solutions [9]. BIM offers a valuable source for SC as it can comprise several types of data including geometric data, time-related data, geographic data, resource budgets and building properties; this allows specialists to work together during the entire life cycle of assets [10] that form the SC. As BIM develops to facilitate SCs through various software applications, open standards such as Industry Foundation Classes (IFC) and CityGML are of increasing importance for the interoperability of data [11]. Moreover, as BIM is being mandated by several governments globally such as the UK, Singapore, Italy, Germany and Peru, there is greater motivation to explore BIM for cadastral reasons [12]. Building automation systems can reduce the greenhouse gases emitted by buildings [13]. Emissions from vehicular traffic can also be reduced with smart traffic lights, congestion charges and other mobility applications [14]. Moreover, communicating real-time air-quality data with citizens via smartphone applications allows them to take appropriate precautions to diminish adverse health effects [15]. SC applications that alleviate traffic jams through smart syncing of traffic lights can lessen bus journeys significantly whilst real-time navigation warns drivers of disruptions and provides them with a quicker route [16]. Additionally, digital signage and mobile applications could provide commuters with real-time updates about disruptions and allow them to modify their journeys on the spot [17]. Although technology is not an instantaneous solution for crime, authorities can use data obtained from SC applications to employ limited resources and staff more efficiently [18] and applications such as real-time crime mapping can use statistical investigation to highlight trends [19]. The installation of IoT sensors on current physical infrastructure can assist personnel in executing predictive maintenance and repairing snags before they cause failures or interruptions [20]. E-career centres and digital hiring platforms create more effective hiring procedures and attract more unemployed citizens into the labour force [21] and data-directed formal education and online retraining courses can augment collective skill-base of a city [22]. Lastly, the digitisation of government operations including business licensing, permitting and tax filing can save time spent by local businesses on bureaucratic paperwork, thereby promoting a more effective and enterprising business environment [23]. Table 1 summarises the main benefits of technological drivers in SCs.

2.2 Challenges Arising from Technology Use in Smart Cities

Although SC technology improves and benefits the lives of urban residents, there are notable risks and challenges [24]. Significant matters of concern in the smart environment are the management of the vast quantities of data and preserving and protecting the privacy of citizens [25]. If data conservation is not appropriately managed, society could face severe repercussions, including the disturbance of services and the downturn of community life [26]. The internet is the main driving force behind the functioning of a SC; however, centralisation and a city's connection are a cause for risk and vulnerability as attackers use the internet connection as a channel for their attack [27]. Such attacks essentially halt an entire organisation for many hours, causing train disruptions, bridge closures and negative impacts on citizens' lives and the economy. Cybersecurity is therefore an imperative requirement to protect and maintain the benefits of SC technologies [28]. Moreover, the implementation of technology in SC is complicated and could pose an obstacle if not executed correctly [29]. Technological understanding and proficiency vary amongst citizens, which could create social exclusivity and hierarchy if citizens are not engaged with or educated throughout SC implementation [30]. Another significant challenge is the high cost of using smart technologies to modernise and improve infrastructure, hence governments must explore all avenues for funding and financing to develop a suitable business model [31]. Lastly the various solution and device types, with different service-specific platforms creates fragmentation, resulting in interoperability challenges [32]. Table 2 summarises the main challenges of technological drivers in SCs.

Table 1. Benefits of technological drivers in SCs

Technology benefits	Source
Better traffic flow	16, 17
Improved energy efficiency	13, 14
Augmented digital equity	22
Safer cities	18, 19
Renewed infrastructure	20
Efficient public services	23
New economic development activities	21, 23
Enhanced citizens' quality of life and health for citizens	8, 15

Table 2. Challenges of technological drivers in SCs

Technology challenges	Source
Security and hackers	26, 27, 28
Privacy concerns	25
Complicated implementation of infrastructure	29
Engaging and educating citizens for social inclusivity	30
Legislation and policies	33, 34
Funding and business models	31
Interoperability	32

2.3   Role of Governance, Regulations and Policies in Smart Cities

Cities become more productive with the application of SC policies [3], and there is numerical proof that demonstrates a positive correlation between the application of SC policies and urban economic operation [33]. Another benefit of SC policy is the stimulation of innovation that grows a city's pool of knowledge, one of the key acknowledged drivers of economic growth [34]. The use of BIM for SCs can be associated with smart governance and policy development. The IFC is an open file format established by buildingSMART alliance, used for architectural, building and construction data, that is compatible with numerous BIM tools [35]. Therefore, the use of data as a source for 3D cadastre has been investigated since the classification founded on 3D models is highly significant for SCs [36]. Similarly, the best know data format for 3D City Models, that provides semantic information and detailed data for geospatial and city objects, is the CityGML [37].

For SC proposals to obtain the required investment to be realised, legal and regulatory structures need to be up to speed with latest technologies [38]. Due to the disconnection between legal frameworks, citizens' needs and technologies, SCs encounter various legal and practical issues in employment of their innovative policies [39]. Furthermore, the lack of precise or adaptable legal frameworks for SCs could defer or hinder some of their programmes [40]. SCs face many challenges that exceed the competencies, proficiencies and reaches of their conventional organisations and their established forms of governing, hence necessitate new and inventive methods of governance [41]. Under the term smart governance which includes these innovative governance methodologies, the government administers and applies policies towards the augmentation in citizens' QoL, through information communication technologies (ICTs) and by purposefully including and working together with stakeholders [42]. There are several standards published by the International Organisation for Standardisation (ISO) relating to SCs. With regards to city services and QoL, standards under ISO 37120:2018 enable the implementation of smart city policies, technologies, and practices whilst the purpose of ISO 37122 (Indicator for Smart Cities), published in 2019, is to assess the performance of SCs regarding meeting sustainability goals throughout city advancement [11]. ISO 19152 Land Administration Domain Model (LADM) supports the creation of geographic information systems (GIS) as well as spatial planning, suggesting the assimilation of spatial planning and land administration environments [11]. The standard for BIM to GIS conceptual mapping is ISO 19166. Moreover, the purpose of the ISO/TR 23262 standard is to increase interoperability between geospatial and BIM domains, particularly to align BIM and GIS standards, whilst ISO/TS 19166 outlines the theoretical basis for representing data from BIM to GIS [43]. Nonetheless, the numerous questions surrounding concerns about government leadership and collaborative models of governance call for further research [44].

3 Methodology

This section presents the research methodology for the mixed methods-based theory investigation concerning the use of disruptive and innovative technologies in SCs. This method allows for a broader and more comprehensive insight into the various benefits and drawbacks of technologies used in SC implementation and presents a way to expand on theory using the data. When the aim of research is to analyse certain situations and outcomes by depending on the observations and opinions of relevant professionals, a qualitative study is applicable [45]. On the other hand, when the aim of research is to comprehend the connections and consequences between elements, a quantitative approach is more applicable [46].

Since the intention of this study is to analyse the benefits and drawbacks of technology use in SCs and explore how governance, regulations and policies and can address the privacy and security challenges, a mixed methodology was selected.

Sequential mixed-method research describes a study where the research stages take place consecutively, with one stage either developing from or following the other. Both the research questions and methodology employed in the second stage are contingent on the previous stage [47]. In the case of this study, analysing journal articles, reports and books performed first literature review. The purpose of the literature review was to identify the benefits and challenges of technologies that informed the quantitative research in the form of a research questionnaire, developed by a qualitative follow-up interview.

Study participants were UK-based and from within the science, technology, engineering and mathematics (STEM) field, with either an expertise or interest in innovative technologies within SCs. Career examples included, but were not limited to, engineers, project managers, architects, urban planners and researchers. Before commencing the study and contacting participants, approval from Ethics Committee at the University College London was obtained. Consequently, in May 2020 the potential participants were sent a link to the online questionnaire via email and LinkedIn messaging. Upon completion of the questionnaire, participants had the option to share their email address to arrange a follow up interview in July 2020. Interviewees were selected from the questionnaire study participants who expressed their interest in discussing their answers further. Interviews took place virtually via Zoom and were recorded with the interviewees consent. Notes were taken during the interview, but the recordings were used to fill in any information gaps. The informed consent form was available for the participants to read and agree to before answering the questionnaire. Moreover, all responses obtained from the questionnaire were anonymous, minimising confidentiality risks. Additionally, data was stored on a protected server.

The quantitative study offered a good base for the successive interviews and hypotheses from the quantitative phase were carried forward to the semi-structured interviews. No challenges were encountered at the interface between the quantitative and qualitative phases. The qualitative study was used to confirm the results of the quantitative study. Therefore, the feedback from how the investigation was interpreted informed the interpretation of the final results (Fig. 1).

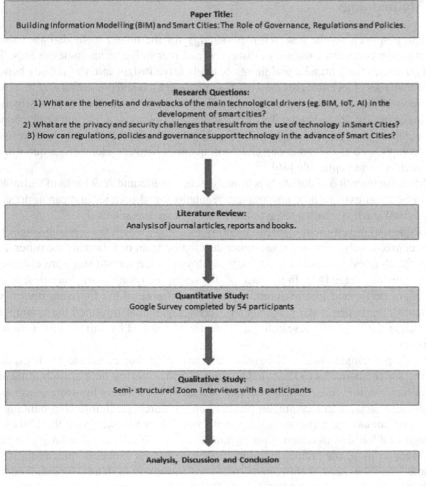

Fig. 1. Research methodology flowchart

4 Results

This section presents the quantitative study from the questionnaire followed by the results of the qualitative study from the interviews.

4.1 Quantitative Results

The online questionnaire was completed by 54 participants, whose job titles ranged from managing director and innovation lead to assistant professor and research intern. The top three represented business areas were engineering (20.4%), multidisciplinary (16.7%) and consulting (14.8%). The total years of experience in each of the sampled participant's respective field varied. Majority (44.4%) of the participants had over 10 years of experience. While 31.5% of the participants had 5–10 years of experience 24.1% of the participants had 1–5 years of experience and only 3.7% had less than one year of experience.

4.1.1 Understanding the Relevance of Smart Cities

Firstly, it was asked to rank the most relevant areas to Smart Cities. Over 50% of participants ranked the pertinent SC areas determined from the literature review, in the following order from most relevant to least relevant: people, environment, governance, economy, mobility and living (see Fig. 2). It was also asked which of the challenges ascertained from the literature review could be tackled through SC implementation. Over 90% of participants believed that air pollution and urban congestion challenges can be tackled and approximately 50% of participants also considered that water shortages could be alleviated, and safe energy access supported through SCs. In contrast, only a third of participants thought that housing shortages and crime could be reduced and less than 20% of participants deemed that SC application could confront inequality and social segregation challenges (see Fig. 3).

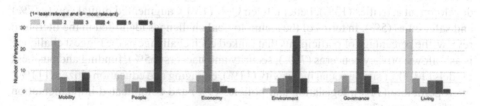

Fig. 2. Relevant areas in SCs

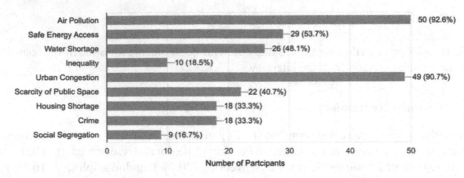

Fig. 3. Challenges that can be tackled through SC implementation

4.1.2 Technological Drivers in Smart Cities

When asked about the relevant of the numerous SC technologies discerned in the literature review, over 70% of participants considered big data, geospatial technology and IoT as being essential in SC development. Approximately 55% of participants considered robotics and augmented and virtual reality (AR and VR) to be quite significant technological drivers. A total of 28% of participants considered blockchain to be quite significant or essential, whereas the majority (55%) deemed it to be neutral on the Likert scale from not applicable at all to essential. Conversely, approximately 50% of participants regarded autonomous vehicles and drones to less applicable in SC development. It is worth nothing that the only four technologies that some participants considered to be not applicable at all were robotics, blockchain, autonomous vehicles and drones and AR and VR. Moreover, it was less than 6% of participants that considered either one of the four technologies to be not at all applicable.

With regards to the impact of technology on the eight SC benefits identified in the literature review, the percentage of participants that ranked technology as having the most influence on each benefit is as follows: better traffic flow (63%), renewed infrastructure (50%), efficient public services (30%), improved energy efficiency (22%), new economic development activities (13%), better citizen QoL (13%), augmented digital equity (7%) and safer cities (5%). In terms of the technological challenges identified in the literature review, the percentage of participants that ranked each challenge as the biggest challenge is as follows: privacy concerns (79%), security and hackers (65%), funding and business models (13%), ensuring social inclusivity (11%), engaging and education citizens (11%), interoperability (11%), legislation and policies (9%) and complicated implementation of infrastructure (7%).

4.1.3 Challenges Resulting from the Use of Technology in Smart Cities

The literature review demonstrates that there are number of challenges that arise from the use of technology in SCs. Participants were asked to rank these challenges on a Likert scale from 1 (Minor challenge) to 5 (Major challenge). Over 70% of participants, considered the need for data privacy security and portability and cyber security risk to be the most major challenges. Approximately 60% deemed the clarity of ethical approach around data sharing, assets and intellectual property (IP) and clear commercial arrangements to avoid conflict around exploitation of IP to be a major challenge. Two-thirds of participants ranked the need for internationally agreed standards and the question of insurance and liability as 4/5 on the Likert scale indicating that these challenges are slightly less significant than the four previously mentioned. On the other hand, the same proportion regarded the need for standardisation or interoperability of data (57%), regulatory compliance requirement (61%) and the need for original governance models that enable data and asset sharing (54%) to be neither a major nor a minor challenge. Moreover, an average of only 1.6% of participants rated any one of the nine challenges as a minor challenge.

Further questions focused on privacy and security challenges as they were determined to be the main challenge in the literature review. Therefore, participants were asked to rank the pertinency of the various methods used to safeguard citizens privacy and security (see Fig. 4). Over 90% of participants believed that educating citizens about the privacy and security risks involved would be beneficial. In contrast, only a third deemed consulting citizens to be a useful approach. Anonymity and privacy measures and cyber-security were also highly regarded as being valuable in confronting privacy and security issues, by over 85% of participants. Only 43% of participants deemed authentication and encryption to be a helpful approach and less than 30% of participants believed security monitory and access control as useful in safeguarding citizens' privacy and security.

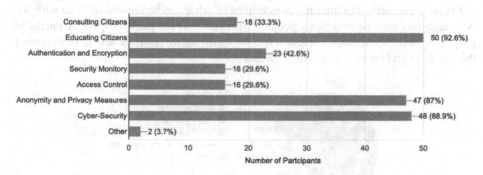

Fig. 4. Means of safeguarding the privacy and security of citizens

4.1.4 The Role of Governance, Regulations and Policies in Supporting Technological Advancement of Smart Cities

Various governance challenges that arise during the development of SCs. Participants were asked to rate ten of these challenges on a Likert scale from 1 (Not relevant) to 5 (Highly relevant). Around two thirds of participants consider lack of access to information and insufficient citizen awareness, engagement and participation to be highly relevant challenges. Moreover, no participants judge these two challenges to be not relevant at all. Likewise, no participants deem gaps between government and governed to be a completely irrelevant challenge, however a fewer percentage (56%) regard it to be highly relevant. Approximately 65% of participants believe that lack of access to technology and unbalanced geographical development are relevant challenges, whereas slightly fewer (58%) think the same of unwarranted centralisation and absence of institutional coordination and instability in governance. Over half of all participants think of shortage of social services and no equity in access to opportunities and resources to be neutral on the Likert scale. However, the percentage (40%) of participants that consider no equity in access to opportunities and resources to be relevant or highly relevant is significantly higher than the percentage (28%) for shortage of social services and no equity in access. Only one participant considers low urban institutional capacity to be a highly relevant governance challenge, but at the same time, over 70% of participants think it to be neutral on the Likert scale and roughly 10% think it to be irrelevant or not at all relevant.

There are various existing laws and regulations that support the safe use of technology in Smart Cities, however, as technology progresses and develops, these laws should be amended simultaneously (see Fig. 5). Consequently, 18.5% of participants consider improvements to privacy law and 11.1% consider built environment law to do likewise. 3.7% of participants deem that ICT law and 1.9% suppose IP rights law should be upgraded. Those participants who chose other all consider that more than one law needs to be renewed in accordance with the level of the SC. Finally, when asked if the current laws and policies in place were enough to protect citizens against threats associated with SC technologies, 82% of participants responded that they were not sufficient, and that additional laws and policies were needed. Participants were invited to explain why as open answer, and reasons included: 'Regarding AI, a lot of policies and regulations have not been implemented to limit the possibilities of what can be created or done with AI. Although this may be beneficial, people can misuse AI for personal gain or unethical purposes.' and 'Technology evolution is lighting therefore requires new laws to protect the citizenry and counter unforeseen threats'.

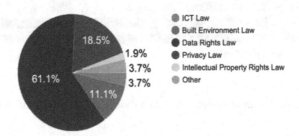

Fig. 5. Laws to be improved to support safe technology use in SCs

The literature review discerned several reasons for implementing SC policies. When asked to rank these reasons, the percentage of participants that ranked each reason to be the most important is as follows: Data protection and usage (69%), Privacy and personal rights protection (50%), Reliability and Liability (15%), Information security (13%), and Conflict of interest (13%).

The implementation of a SC and the technologies employed within it, involved several stakeholders. However, only some of these stakeholders need to be involved in the creation of policies and regulations surrounding the use of technology in SCs (Refer to Fig. 6). According to over 90% of participants, city and national governments must be involved in forming policies and regulations. Two thirds of participants deemed that research institutions should also be involved. Only 50% of participants think that energy providers, telecom providers, technology vendors and banks and insurance companies should be involved. This could be because these organisations are usually privately owned, hence might develop policies and regulations with self-bias. Similarly, even fewer (32%) participants believe that investors should be involved because they could devise policies and regulations for their own financial gain. Approximately 40% of participants consider that universities and schools, digital agencies, construction companies and public transport providers should contribute to policy and regulation development while around 30% think that start-up incubators, logistic providers, health-care providers should be involved. Participants also suggested other relevant stakeholders such as citizen (representatives), technological specialists, national standard bodies, innovation agencies, planners and consultants.

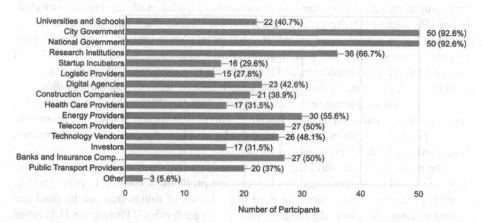

Fig. 6. Stakeholders to be involved in the creation of policies and regulations for SCs

4.2 Qualitative Results

Out of the 54 participants, 8 (hereby referred to as participant A-H) volunteered to participate in a follow-up interview.

4.2.1 Benefits and Drawbacks of the Technological Drivers in Smart Cities

Participant A believes that 'the purpose of SCs is to improve citizens QoL and technology enables cities to have a better quality of opportunities from automation to efficiency gains'. Likewise, participant E says that 'automation and efficiency gains provide a better quality of opportunities', just as participant G believes that 'technology will improve efficiency therefore improving citizen experience'. In the opinion of participant D, 'a city's services can only improve by measuring the current performance to make future improvements. This is enabled by technologies that collect data by digitally monitoring what the city is doing.' Correspondingly, participant B says that 'the purpose of technology is to augment services, provide insights and help with policies.' However, participant F mentions that 'the workforce should be reskilled as public services get automated.'

Participant C questions the technology-expense use case, 'that is whether or not a technology will reduce cost or cause improvement'. Similarly, participant G asserts that 'it is important to question if there is a good ROI for each technology'. Multiple participants mentioned the social issues that arise with the implementation of innovation technologies, for example citizen's acceptance of using individual and amalgamated data. Additionally, participant D states that 'privacy concerns are huge challenge for implementation followed by legislation and policy. Moreover, security and hackers should not be a problem if the other factors are resolved'. Participant F goes on to add 'the question of how to engage the market is another challenge'.

4.2.2 Privacy and Security Challenges

According to participant D, 'standards are extremely useful in addressing security challenges'. Participant H believes 'it is straightforward to introduce new standards, but the challenge lies in getting the standards through regulatory compliance and getting government approval'. However, participant A affirms that 'there are already a number of international agreed IT standards, and it would only be a challenge if there are many new standards to approve of'. Equally, participant B asserts that 'standards regarding data privacy and security already exist' and suggests that 'GDPR could give guidance for handling privacy and security concerns around data'. Participant H says that 'maintaining data privacy is all about permissions and who access to the data. Hence information should only be revealed on a need-to-know basis'.

'The necessity for standardisation of data and how SCs across the nation and eventually the world is interoperated, is a longer-term problem' according to participant C. Equally, participant F says that 'we need to find a set of things that can be used and re-used in future SCs to make them all uniform to each other'. Participant H believes that 'the challenge of cyber security risk lies in the managing the perception of how the population views it'. Likewise, participant G states that 'the clarity of ethical approach around data sharing, should not be a challenge with appropriate perception management'. Participant D raises 'the question of insurance and liability if the private sector is involved, and challenges how the liability would be allocated between government, private and public sector and how risk vs reward would be managed'.

Participant C considers 'new governance models to be a challenge because a new set of skills and new organisational structures are required to come up with them.' Similarly, participant A says that 'current governance models are not set up for automation'. Participant A tells that 'to escalate decision making, citizen engagement is necessary in governance structure'. Participant F deems it to 'be in the governments best interest to avoid IP problems, hence when they employ private sector capabilities, they must ensure the company to share the IP to avoid exploitation'.

4.2.3 The Role of Governance, Regulations and Policies in Smart Cities

Participant A considers 'low urban institutional capacity to be one of the biggest concerns because essentially, existing structures need to be transformed into new technologically driven structures'. Equally, participant H asserts that 'there is a lack of awareness with regards to the breadth and depth of what is best practice. Therefore, people are starting from scratch rather than looking at where there already is good practice'. Participant B adds that 'best practices have been drawn out of working with local authorities, and the best practice templates of already resolved issued can be followed'. Participant C states that 'the economic and political view is the most influential one, and the challenge lies in settling the debate between politics and technology'. Moreover, participant D affirms that 'if there is sufficient urban institutional capacity, there will not be any problems of instability in governance'. Besides, according to participant E, 'the perceived gap between government and governed can be reduced with the SC concept'. Participant F says, 'another challenge is that local authorities are often inward focused, hence don't see the world from a citizen's perspective of consider what services citizens want to consume and how they can use technologies'.

All eight participants agreed that additional laws and policies were necessary to protect citizens against the threats of innovative technologies. Though, participant F suggested that 'standards, voluntary agreed best practices are an alternative to laws and regulations'. Equally participant B says that 'it is quicker to create and approve of standards than it is to pass a new law'. Conversely, participant C states that 'standards sit hand in hand with legislation as governments sponsor or endorse standards'. Likewise, participant B reveals that 'the PAS180 range is a set of BSI (British Standards Institution) standards commissioned by the government to advice local authorities with regards to SC development'. A number of participants affirmed that most importantly, 'citizen engagement was necessary in devising new laws and policies'.

5   Discussion

SC technologies such as smart-syncing traffic lights, have the potential to alleviate traffic jams in congested cities [13]. Moreover, IoT sensors on physical infrastructure, can be employed to forewarn any problems so that reparations can be undertaken before breakdown [19]. The participants of this study would agree, as results demonstrate that the SC benefits that technology has the largest impact on are better traffic flow and renewed infrastructure. Various technologies and data from SC applications can be used to reduce the rate of crime across cities [17, 18]. Contrastingly, the study shows technology to be less influential in enabling safer cities. This potentially reflects on the fact that rather than being directly influenced by technology implementation, safer cities are result of other factors. For example, technology enables the improvement of mobility, social and economic equality, with crime rates diminishing as an after-effect.

Air quality can be improved, and energy saved by decreasing vehicular emissions through SC applications [13]. Likewise, the study reveals that the two challenges that can primarily be tackled through SC implementation are air pollution and urban congestion. By way of a positive chain reaction, some using SC technology to tackle certain challenges, could have a more extensive positive over-all effect. For example, reducing urban congestion not only reduces greenhouse gas emissions and noise pollution but also improves QoL by reducing citizens' commuting time.

SC technologies have markedly changed the concept of personal privacy [24]. The organisations who collect citizens data for SC development purposes also hold a great deal of power and responsibility and the concern lies in data misuse or disclosure [25]. Comparably, the study determines that the biggest technological challenges in SCs are security, hackers and privacy concerns. In contrast, the survey demonstrates that interoperability and funding of SC technologies are less of a challenge. This could be because as experts working in the field of SC, they have a better comprehension of how various technologies function together and witness SC projects being funded on a regular basis. Even so, interoperability plays a key role in BIM, as the data held in a model is only useful when exchangeable [48], and the IFC standard is one of the foremost ways to achieve BIM interoperability [49].

Managing the large amounts of data and maintaining the privacy of citizens are issues of significant matters in SCs [24]. BIM plays an essential part in methodically analysing and classifying the large amounts of data produced by sources including people, machines and infrastructure on a daily basis. BIM, is able to amass a building's geometric and semantic information over the course of its life-cycle and research shows that it has the potential to catalyse SC development [50]. However, BIM is not able manage the big data produced by SCs, unaided [51], therefore necessitating BIM integrated solutions with technologies including IFC, 3D point cloud, City GML, Application Programming Interface (API). The participants of this study agree that the biggest privacy and security concerns are necessity for data privacy, security and portability, cyber security risks and the issues surrounding the sharing of data, assets and IP. While the collection of citizens' data is a prerequisite of SCs, technologies such as encryption through blockchain can protect and keep the data anonymous. Contrarily, study findings show that the requirement for regulatory compliance and for governance models that facilitate data sharing and decision making to be much less significant. This perhaps insinuates that although technology operations follow correct the problem lies in the illegal undertakings that infringe on citizens' data and violate their privacy.

SC policies are key to increasing a cities productivity, cumulative knowledge and economic output [32]. On the other hand, the study indicates that the foremost reason for implementing SC policies is for the protection of data usage. While both innovative and security reasons are relevant motives for enforcing policies, the discrepancy can be explained by the fact that multiple choice options available to the participants, focused on the policy-making that provided safety and security. Standards can both enable and inhibit SC innovation [52]. An interconnected series of standard changes must evolve to allow smarter cities and policy makers to achieve their objectives. This evolution involves the creation of new standards and the maturation of those already in existence [53].

The responsibility of re-evaluating and establishing new regulations lies with city leaders and national policymakers, however they should be supported by civil society organisations, technology vendors and private companies. Although the study establishes that city and national governments should be involved in policy and regulation creation surrounding the use of technology in SCs, it conversely shows that it is not as essential for stakeholders such as investors, health care providers, start-up incubators and logistics providers, to be involved in the creation of policies and regulations. Given that many of the study participants are part of these stakeholder groups, it perhaps suggests that they either do not want the responsibility of or do not feel well enough informed to be involved in creating new regulations.

Legal and regulatory requirements should be up to date with the latest technologies, particularly for SC propositions to acquire investments [34]. The study confirms that primarily, the data rights law needs to be improved followed by privacy laws. According [39], SC agendas could be delayed or obstructed without the necessary legal frameworks. SC technologies are developing rapidly, however getting new legislation approved is a lengthier process. To overcome this obstacle, internationally agreed standards can be more easily established instead.

6 Conclusion and Future Work

The study confirmed that technologies play a significant role in the implementation of SCs bringing numerous benefits including better flow of traffic, better-quality infrastructure, more efficient public services and improved energy efficiency. These benefits contribute towards the inclusion aspect of UN 2030, SDG #11. However, there are certain challenges associated with the use of technologies in SCs, most notably maintaining the security and privacy of citizens' data. The primary solutions to safeguarding citizens' privacy and security in SCs are educating citizens, implementing anonymity and privacy measures and ensuring cyber-security. To maintain data privacy, it is suggested that the data is stored anonymously, and that information is only revealed on a need-to-know basis. Moreover, internationally agreed standards are a useful tool to address security challenges, as several ICT standards already exist. Although it is uncomplicated to initiate new standards, the consequent challenge is progressing the standards through regulatory compliance and obtaining government approval. This research also confirmed that there are not enough policies and laws in place to protect citizens against threats, making this a topic for further research. Finally, it was found that the biggest governance challenges in the development of SCs were the disparity between the government and the governed, lack of access to information and inadequate citizen awareness, engagement and participation.

It should be noted here that there are certain limitations to the research findings, stemming from the sample size. Further research can investigate a larger sample with participants from other countries too. Moreover, more work should be done to investigate how the privacy and security challenges can be faced. Further investigation could therefore determine a strategy to overcome these challenges and reap the benefits of SC technologies through new SC governance, regulations and policies.

References

1. Ahvenniemi, H., et al.: What are the differences between sustainable and smart cities? Cities **60**, 234–245 (2017)
2. Caragliu, A., et al.: Smart cities in Europe. J. Urban Technol. **18:2**, 65–82 (2011)
3. Chourabi, H., et al.: Understanding smart cities: an integrative framework. In: 45th Hawaii International Conference on System Sciences, pp. 2289–2297 (2012)
4. Diaz-Sarachaga, J., et al.: Is the Sustainable Development Goals (SDG) index an adequate framework to measure the progress of the 2030 Agenda? Sustain. Dev. **26**(6), 663–671 (2018)

5. Angelidou, M., et al.: Enhancing sustainable urban development through smart city applications. J. Sci. Technol. Policy Manage. **9**(2), 146–169 (2018)
6. Radu, L.: Disruptive technologies in smart cities: a survey on current trends and challenges. Smart Cities **3**(3), 1022–1038 (2020)
7. OECD: Smart Cities and Inclusive Growth (2020). https://www.oecd.org/cfe/ciies/OECD_P olicy_Paper_Smart_Cities_and_Inclusive_Growth.pdf. Accessed 3 Apr 2021
8. McKinsey and Company: Smart cities: Digital solutions for a more liveable future (2018). https://www.mckinsey.com/~/media/mckinsey/business%20functions/operations/our%20i nsights/smart%20cities%20digital%solutions%20for%20a%20more%20livable%future/ mgi-smart-cities-full-report.pdf. Accessed 4 Apr 2021
9. De Guimarães, J., et al.: Governance and quality of life in smart cities: towards sustainable development goals. J. Clean. Prod. **253**, 119926 (2020)
10. Eastman, C., et al.: BIM Handbook: A Guide to Building Information Modelling for Owner, Managers, Designers, Engineers, and Contractors. John Wiley and Sons, Inc., New Jersey (2008)
11. Janecka, K.: Standardization supporting future smart cities – a case of BIM/GIS and 3D cadastre. GeoScape **13**, 106–113 (2019)
12. Ayalina, L., et al.: Towards a hybrid approach to BIM implementation – a critical discourse. In: Proceedings of the CIB International Conference on Smart Built Environment, ICSBE 2021 (2021)
13. Kylili, A., Fokaides, P.: European smart cities: the role of zero energy buildings. Sustain. Cities Soc. **15**, 86–95 (2015)
14. Djahel, S., et al.: A communications-oriented perspective on traffic management systems for smart cities: challenges and innovative approaches. IEEE Commun. Surv. Tutor. **17**(1), 125–151 (2015)
15. Kök, M.U., et al.: A deep learning model for air quality prediction in smart cities. In: IEEE International Conference on Big Data (Big Data), pp. 1983–1990 (2017)
16. Goodall, W., Dovey Fishman, T., Bornstein, J., Bonthron, B.: The rise of mobility as a Service. Deloitte Review (2017). https://www2.deloitte.com/content/dam/Deloitte/nl/Documents/con sumer-business/deloitte-nl-cb-ths-rise-of-mobility-as-a-service.pdf. Accessed 10 Apr 2021
17. Yigitcanlar, T., Kamruzzaman, M.: Smart cities and mobility: does the smartness of australian cities lead to sustainable commuting patterns? J. Urban Technol. **26**(2), 21–46 (2018)
18. Hillenbrand, K.: Predicting fire risk: from New Orleans to a nationwide tool (2016). https:// datasmart.ash.harvard.edu/news/article/predicting-fire-risk-from-new-orleans-to-a-nation wide-tool-846. Accessed 3 Apr 2021
19. Schwartz, A.: Smart cities,' surveillance, and new streetlights in San Jose (2017). https://www. eff.org/deeplinks/2017/02/smart-cities-surveillance-and-new-streetlights-san-jose. Accessed 28 March 2021
20. Rehena, Z., et al.: A reference architecture for context-aware intelligent traffic management platforms. Int. J. Electron. Govern. Res. **14**(4), 65–79 (2018)
21. Jain, A., Ranjan, S.: Implications of emerging technologies on the future of work. IIMB Manag. Rev. **32**(4), 448–454 (2020)
22. Sadeh, A., Feniser, C., Ionela Dusa, S.: Technology education and learning in smart cities. In: Soares, F., Lopes, A., Brown, K., Uukkivi, A. (eds.) Developing Technology Mediation in Learning Environments. Information Science Reference (2019)
23. Gray, J., Rumpe, B.: Models for digitalization. Softw. Syst. Model. **14**(4), 1319–1320 (2015). https://doi.org/10.1007/s10270-015-0494-9
24. Curzon, J., et al.: A survey of privacy enhancing technologies for smart cities. Pervasive Mob. Comput. **55**, 76–95 (2019)
25. Kumar, H., et al.: Moving towards smart cities: solutions that lead to the smart city transformation framework. Technol. Forecast. Soc. Change **153**, 119281 (2020)

26. Sengan, S., et al.: Enhancing cyber–physical systems with hybrid smart city cyber security architecture for secure public data-smart network. Futur. Gener. Comput. Syst. **112**, 724–737 (2020)
27. Jameel, T., et al.: security in modern smart cities: an information technology perspective. In: Computer Science, 2nd International Conference on Communication, Computing and Digital systems, pp. 293–298 (2019)
28. Varfolomeev, A., et al.: Overview of five techniques used for security and privacy insurance in smart cities. J. Phys: Conf. Ser. **1897**, 012028 (2021)
29. Rachmawati, R.: Towards better city management through smart city implementation. Hum. Geograph. J. Stud. Res. Hum. Geograph. **13**(2) (2019)
30. Appio, F., et al.: Understanding Smart Cities: innovation ecosystems, technological advancements, and societal challenges. Technol. Forecast. Soc. Chang. **142**, 1–14 (2019)
31. Timeus, K., et al.: Creating business models for smart cities: a practical framework. Public Manag. Rev. **22**(5), 726–745 (2020)
32. Nalchigar, S., Fox, M.: Achieving interoperability of smart city data: an analysis of 311 data. J. Smart Cities **3**(1) (2017)
33. Caragliu, A., Del Bo, C.: The economics of smart city policies. Scienze Regionali Italian J. Region. Sci. 81–104 (2019)
34. Caragliu, A., Del Bo, C.: Smart innovative cities: The impact of Smart City policies on urban innovation. Technol. Forecast. Soc. Chang. **142**, 373–383 (2019)
35. Steel, J., et al.: Model interoperability in building information modelling. Softw Syst Model **11**, 99–109 (2012)
36. Oldfield, J., et al.: Can data from BIMs by used as input for a 3D cadastre?. 5th International FIG 3D Cadastre Workshop, Athens (2016)
37. Shutkin, V., et al.: City and building information modelling using IFC standard. In: Semenov, V., Scherer, R. (ed.) ECPPM 2021 – eWork and eBusiness in Architecture, Engineering and Construction, 1st edn. CRC Press, Moscow (2021)
38. Wadhwa, M.: Understanding the impact of Smart Cities and the need for smart regulations. SSRN Electron. J. (2015)
39. Moses, L.: How to think about law, regulation and technology: problems with 'technology' as a regulatory target. Law Innov. Technol. **5**(1), 1–20 (2013)
40. Schicklinski, J.: Socio-ecological transitions in the green spaces resource system. In: Sauer, T., Garzillo, T.C., Elsen, S. (eds.) Cities in Transition Social Innovation for Europe's Urban Sustainability. Routledge (2016)
41. Rodríguez Bolívar, M.P.: Smart cities: big cities, complex governance? In: Rodríguez-Bolívar, M.P. (ed.) Transforming city governments for successful smart cities. PAIT, vol. 8, pp. 1–7. Springer, Cham (2015). https://doi.org/10.1007/978-3-319-03167-5_1
42. Bertot, C., Jaeger, P.T., Grimes, J.M.: Promoting transparency and accountability through ICTs, social media, and collaborative e-government. Transf. Govern. People Process Policy **6**, 78–91 (2012)
43. Clemen, C.: Trends in BIM and GISStandardization – Report from the Jointiso/TC59/SC13–ISC/TC211 Wg: GIS/BIM. The International Archives of the Photogrammetry, Remote Sensing and Spatial Information Sciences, XLVI-5/W1-2022, pp. 51–58 (2022)
44. Meijer, A.J., Gil-Garcia, J.R., Bolívar, M.P.R.: Smart city research: contextual conditions, governance models, and public value assessment. Soc. Sci. Comput. Rev. **34**(6), 647–656 (2016)
45. Stake, R.: Qualitative research: Studying How Things Work. Guildford Press (2010)
46. Creswell, J.: Research Design: Qualitative, Quantitative and Mixed Methods Approaches. 4th edn. International Student. SAGE, Los Angeles; London (2014)
47. Cronholm, S., Hjalmarsson, A.: Experiences from sequential use of mixed methods. Electron. J. Bus. Res. Meth. **9**(2), 87–95 (2011)

48. Fallon, K., Palmer, M.: General Buildings Information Handover Guide: Principles, Methodology and Case Studies. National Institute of Standards and Technology, NISTIR 7417, pp. 99 (2007)
49. Santos, E.: Building information modeling and interoperability. In: SIGraDi 2009 - Proceedings of the 13th Congress of the Iberoamerican Society of Digital Graphics, Sao Paulo, Brazil (2010)
50. Pal, A., Hsieh, S.H.: A trend review on BIM applications for Smart Cities. In: Semenov, V., Scherer, R. (ed.) ECPPM 2021 – eWork and eBusiness in Architecture, Engineering and Construction, 1st edn. Moscow: CRC Press (2021)
51. Correa, F.: Is BIM Big Enough to Take Advantage of Big Data Analytics? (2015). https://doi.org/10.22260/ISARC2015/0019
52. Hawkins, R., et al.: Standards, Innovation and Competitiveness: The Politics and Economics of Standards in Natural and Technical Environments. Edward Elgar, Northampton, MA (1995)
53. Hogan, et al.: Using standards to enable the transformation to smarter cities. IBM J. Res. Develop. 55(1.2), 4:1–4:10 (2011)

Author Index

Printed in the United States
by Baker & Taylor Publisher Services